Sustainability of Public Debt

CESifo Seminar Series
Edited by Hans-Werner Sinn

A Constitution for the European Union
Charles B. Blankart and Dennis C. Mueller, editors

Labor Market Institutions and Public Regulation
Jonas Agell, Michael Keen, and Alfons J. Weichenrieder, editors

Venture Capital, Entrepreneurship, and Public Policy
Vesa Kanniainen and Christian Keuschnigg, editors

Exchange Rate Economics: Where Do We Stand?
Paul De Grauwe, editor

Prospects for Monetary Unions after the Euro
Paul De Grauwe and Jacques Mélitz, editors

Structural Unemployment in Western Europe: Reasons and Remedies
Martin Werding, editor

Institutions, Development, and Economic Growth
Theo S. Eicher and Cecilia García-Peñalosa, editors

Competitive Failures in Insurance Markets: Theory and Policy Implications
Pierre-André Chiappori and Christian Gollier, editors

Japan's Great Stagnation: Financial and Monetary Policy Lessons for Advanced Economies
Michael M. Hutchison and Frank Westermann, editors

Tax Policy and Labor Market Performance
Jonas Agell and Peter Birch Sørensen, editors

Privatization Experiences in the European Union
Marko Köthenbürger, Hans-Werner Sinn, and John Whalley, editors

Recent Developments in Antitrust: Theory and Evidence
Jay Pil Choi, editor

Schools and the Equal Opportunity Problem
Ludger Woessmann and Paul E. Peterson, editors

Economics and Psychology: A Promising New Field
Bruno S. Frey and Alois Stutzer, editors

Institutions and Norms in Economic Development
Mark Gradstein and Kai A. Konrad, editors

Pension Strategies in Europe and the United States
Robert Fenge, Georges de Ménil, and Pierre Pestieau, editors

Foreign Direct Investment and the Multinational Enterprise
Steven Brakman and Harry Garretsen, editors

Sustainability of Public Debt
Reinhard Neck and Jan-Egbert Sturm, editors

See http://mitpress.mit.edu for a complete list of titles in this series.

Sustainability of Public Debt

edited by Reinhard Neck and
Jan-Egbert Sturm

The MIT Press
Cambridge, Massachusetts
London, England

MIT Press books may be purchased at special quantity discounts for business or sales promotional use. For information, please e-mail special_sales@mitpress.mit.edu or write to Special Sales Department, The MIT Press, 55 Hayward Street, Cambridge, MA 02142.

This book was set in Palatino on 3B2 by Asco Typesetters, Hong Kong, and was printed and bound in the United States of America.

Library of Congress Cataloging-in-Publication Data

Sustainability of public debt / edited by Reinhard Neck and Jan-Egbert Sturm.
p. cm. — (CESifo seminar series)
Includes bibliographical references and index.
ISBN 978-0-262-14098-0 (hardcover : alk. paper) 1. Debts, Public. 2. Budget deficits. 3. Finance, Public. I. Neck, Reinhard. II. Sturm, Jan-Egbert, 1969–
HJ8015.S87 2008
336.3′4—dc22 2007031410

10 9 8 7 6 5 4 3 2 1

Contents

Series Foreword

This book is part of the CESifo Seminar Series. The series aims to cover topical policy issues in economics from a largely European perspective. The books in this series are the products of the papers and intensive debates that took place during the seminars hosted by CESifo, an international research network of renowned economists organized jointly by the Center for Economic Studies at Ludwig-Maximilians-Universität, Munich, and the Ifo Institute for Economic Research. All publications in this series have been carefully selected and refereed by members of the CESifo research network.

1 Sustainability of Public Debt: Introduction and Overview

Reinhard Neck and Jan-Egbert Sturm

1.1 The Policy Problem

The development of public debt and budget deficits has become a crucial policy problem in most industrialized countries.[1] Political debates about the future course of fiscal policy and the need to keep government debt under control abound, and the sustainability of public finances is one of the most widely discussed topics in economics these days. In recent decades, many countries have built up substantial amounts of public debt, often accompanied by growing public sectors and shortsighted fiscal policies. The need for a coordination of fiscal policies in the European Economic and Monetary Union (EMU), the understanding that today's overspending poses a threat for the well-being of future generations, the increasing pressure on fiscal policy in a globalized world, and future challenges to public finances owing to aging societies have brought about a lively and controversial discussion in both academia and the public.

1.2 The Concept of Sustainability

Although sustainability of public finances has been discussed for more than a century now, it is still an imprecise concept. While it is intuitively clear that a sustainable policy must be such as to eventually prevent bankruptcy, there is no generally agreed upon definition of what precisely constitutes a sustainable debt position. The literature has proposed several methods to define and assess debt sustainability, differing in both time horizons and choice of variables. Debt sustainability can be regarded as a short-, medium-, or long-term concept, with the open question of how to define these horizons, and debt and deficits can be measured gross or net, including or excluding the liabilities of social security systems and other items.

1.3 Historical Development

Early contributions to the analysis of fiscal policy sustainability date back to classical authors like Hume, Smith, and Ricardo,[2] who discussed public debt mainly in terms of its general effects on the economy. The initial analysis focused on the comparison between tax and deficit financing of public expenditure, with the latter mostly assumed to be given exogenously. Government debt neutrality (i.e., the hypothesis that deficit and tax financing of government budgets are equivalent with respect to capital accumulation) and the intergenerational distribution of the debt burden were first discussed by Ricardo. He pointed out (but did not believe in) the possibility of public debt neutrality, which was later called the "Ricardian equivalence theorem," revived and analytically derived by Barro (1974).

The issue of the generational distribution of the debt burden has also been discussed since the time of the classical economists. In the wake of the Keynesian approach, according to which markets are generally unable to ensure full employment of available resources, the "real resources view" argued that debt finance was necessary to ensure an adequate level of aggregate demand because intended savings cannot be fully absorbed by private investments. In addition, the Keynesians took up the position originally held by Ricardo that the burden of public debt is completely shouldered by the generation that issues the debt. The real resources view argues that this holds because current generations pay the opportunity cost of financing the debt, while debt service and repayment is only a transfer from taxpayers to bondholders, given that the debt is held within the respective country. In a nutshell, this view can be summarized by the phrase "we owe the public debt to ourselves." Government budget deficits and hence rising government debt do not, therefore, pose particular problems: they are not harmful, and they are desirable in times of low aggregate demand and high unemployment to restore the full-employment equilibrium.

Other contributions focused on less excessive justifications of positive debt levels in the short and medium term. The theory of tax smoothing, which is due to Barro (1979) and derives from strict neoclassical premises, shows one mechanism by which public debt and deficits can be welfare improving. Barro's model features a benevolent social planner who minimizes the welfare loss associated with distortionary taxation. In every period, the government needs to finance a given amount of spending, which is financed by a tax. The crucial finding in Barro (1979) is that the social planner should keep the tax rate constant. The level of taxes is determined by the government's intertemporal budget constraint, which says that the present value of spending, which is exogenous in the model, has to be equal to the present value of taxes. Budget deficits and surpluses are used as a buffer when spending is temporarily high or low, or revenues are temporarily low or high, respectively. The tax smoothing policy is dominant in welfare terms, as the distortion caused by taxation increases more than proportionally in the tax rate. Hence, the distortion of a large tax rate in one single period is larger than the net present value of several small distortions caused by a tax smoothing policy.

Another rationale that justifies a positive level of public debt concerns intergenerational equity. Government spending today—in the form of public investment, or as spending on structural reforms that have upfront costs—can benefit future generations. If this spending today is financed by current revenues only, the generation living today is forced to bear all the costs but will not be able to reap the full benefits of public spending. However, if policies that deliver long-term economic benefits but require significant investment in the short run are financed by issuing debt, future generations will contribute to the cost. If the issuance of new debt is severely constrained, currently living voters will favor a suboptimally low level of public investment, as income is redistributed away from current generations to future generations in the case of full tax financing of public investment.

Hence the legitimacy of debt finance for public investment was increasingly recognized; the so-called golden rule that deficits be allowed up to the level of public investments even made it into the German constitution. Today, the exclusion of public investments from the calculation of deficit levels relevant for the EMU's Stability and Growth Pact is suggested by policymakers and economists.[3]

The discussion on public debt sustainability was revived in the 1980s, when public finances came into focus owing to a growing public sector and demographic trends leading to large liabilities of welfare systems. The literature was inspired by the discussion of sustainable resource use in environmental economics. Several characteristics of public debt suggest conceptual and methodological similarities to the analysis in resource economics.[4] First, public debt has some similarities to a renewable resource. Renewable resources, like fishing grounds, can be used up to a certain threshold. Beyond that point, the reproductive capacity of the resource is harmed; the resource becomes a nonrenewable one and is finally used up. In much the same way, public debt, or its servicing, need not be a problem for an economy if it is low enough, but it can lead to default if overused. Second, deficits have the character of a pollutant. Pollutants can be released with no harm up to a certain level given by nature's absorptive capacity. Beyond that level, they may cause negative externalities for other individuals in the short run until the system eventually collapses in the long run. The parallel to public finances is straightforward here. Finally, the formal analysis of both environmental and fiscal policy sustainability involves the use of dynamic intertemporal or intergenerational models.

1.4 Sustainability of Government Debt in the EMU

In Europe, the discussion on sustainability became a public issue owing to the introduction of a common currency in the European Union. Politicians from countries with hard currencies, especially from Germany, feared that member states with lax fiscal policies could destabilize the common currency. Specifically, they feared that the European Central Bank (ECB) would have to bail out a fiscally troubled EMU member state. Following Eichengreen and Wyplosz 1998, when the government of an EMU country gets into fiscal trouble, investors might fear suspension or modification of debt service and start to sell their bonds. The prices of the bonds consequently fall. Banks, which generally hold large amounts of sovereign bonds, lose a lot of capital, possibly violating the minimum capital requirements, which causes a bank run. Bond markets in other countries are negatively affected too, as investors in EMU debt become demoralized. To prevent a collapse of the banking system, the EMU member states or the ECB would be forced to buy up the bonds of the government in distress. Alternatively, the ECB could be forced to inflate away the real value of the troubled country's debt. The cost of this bailout will eventually be borne by all EMU members. Such a bailout is formally forbidden by the Maastricht Treaty, but this is actually a time-inconsistent rule, since ex post a bailout might be the least costly response to a debt crisis.[5]

Another rationale for the introduction of a fiscal rule in the EMU was the fear that excessive spending in one or several member states could cause higher interest rates for the whole union owing to both large capital demand and imperfect financial markets, in the sense that higher risk premia are demanded not only from the members borrowing excessively but from all union members. Excessively high public deficits and debt may be the outcome of the political process for many reasons.[6] This spending bias, which is already present in a single country, can be augmented in a monetary union if the deficits of individual countries give rise not only to higher spreads on their own bonds but also to a higher rate of interest in the whole union. Hence governments do not incur the full cost of additional spending, since the cost is borne by the union as a whole. As a consequence, higher financing costs lead to lower growth rates, inefficient intertemporal resource allocation, and financial instability.[7]

Additionally, not only the outright default of a member state can put a central bank under inflationary pressure. In their seminal paper, Sargent and Wallace (1981) argue that if monetary authorities can credibly commit to a low rate of money supply growth, fiscal authorities will anticipate that fiscal imbalances will not be offset by inflation. Hence, credible inflation targets can create a hard budget constraint, as governments will have to run primary surpluses to repay debt. The fiscal theory of the price level, developed by Woodford (1995) and Sims (1994), departs from the analysis of Sargent and Wallace in a crucial way. According to this theory, the intertemporal budget constraint will be respected even if the monetary or fiscal authorities do not actively follow policies to ensure compliance with the constraint. In the case that both monetary authorities stick to targeting low money supply growth and fiscal authorities keep running excessive deficits, market forces will induce the price level to adjust in the sense that government spending, through its effect on aggregate demand, induces changes in the price level and hence inflation. In a monetary union, this reasoning gains another dimension, as one single monetary authority has to deal with several fiscal policy authorities. Given that overspending in one or several member states leads to a heterogeneous inflation pattern across the union, the determination of an adequate monetary policy will be highly complicated. This holds not only for the EMU but also for other federal countries like the United States or Switzerland.

1.5 Conditions for Sustainable Public Finances

The starting point in the formal discussion of the requirements for debt sustainability is the government's budget constraint, which requires that current spending on goods and services plus the cost of servicing current debt equals current tax revenues plus the issuance of new debt. This can be illustrated as follows. Assume that government borrowing takes the form of one-period bonds that pay an interest rate $i_t > 0$ in period t. Government spending for goods and services in period t is denoted by G_t, T_t denotes tax revenues in period t, and B_t denotes government debt issued in period t. Then the government's budget constraint in period t is[8]

$$G_t + (1 + i_t)B_{t-1} = T_t + B_t. \tag{1.1}$$

Let g_t, τ_t and b_t be the ratios of government spending for goods and services, tax revenues, and debt issuance to GDP in period t, respectively. Debt issuance in period t equals total debt at the end of period t, as government debt is assumed to be issued as one-period bonds. Then, equation (1.1) can be rewritten as

$$d_t + \frac{1 + i_t}{1 + \hat{y}_t} b_{t-1} = b_t, \tag{1.2}$$

where $d_t = g_t - \tau_t$ is the primary budget deficit ratio and $\hat{y}_t$ is the growth rate of GDP. Equation (1.2) implies that the debt ratio increases if the government runs a deficit and, at the same time, the nominal interest rate exceeds nominal GDP growth.

Governments cannot run Ponzi games in the long run; namely, governments cannot run a policy that uses the issuance of ever increasing new debt to repay old debt and to finance interest payments. Hence, the present discounted value of government debt, calculated over all future periods, must equal zero. Together with the No Ponzi Condition, equation (1.2) gives the government's intertemporal budget constraint

$$\sum_{t=1}^{\infty} \left(d_t \prod_{s=1}^{t} \frac{1 + \hat{y}_s}{1 + i_s} \right) + b_0 = 0, \tag{1.3}$$

where b_0 is the current debt ratio. For fiscal policy to be sustainable, sustainability being defined as the absence of default risk, this condition must be met. Equation (1.3) says that the present discounted value of primary deficits plus the value of current debt must be zero. This also implies that running substantial deficits over a long time is consistent with sustainability as long as these deficits can be compensated for by sufficiently high future surpluses.

A second interpretation of sustainable fiscal policy considers the evolution of debt in the medium term. Here, sustainability is interpreted as a given reduction of the debt-to-GDP ratio over a given time horizon toward a target ratio.[9] This interpretation of debt sustainability is mainly justified by the view that governments with high debt levels are less flexible to respond to adverse shocks, as high debt servicing costs leave little room for fiscal policy intervention.

Consider the budget constraint of the government, formalized in the following way:

$$\Delta b_{t+1} \equiv b_{t+1} - b_t = (r - \hat{n})b_t + d_{t+1}, \tag{1.4}$$

where r denotes the real interest rate and $\hat{n}$ the real GDP growth rate. Thus, in order to reduce the public debt ratio, the primary surplus must be larger than debt servicing, which can be expressed as

$$-d_{t+1} \geq (r - \hat{n})b_t. \tag{1.5}$$

Equation (1.5) says that that the debt ratio will increase indefinitely if the real interest rate exceeds real GDP growth unless the primary budget is in sufficient surplus. In this approach, the interest rate and the GDP growth rate are taken as exogenous.

Making the evaluation of fiscal policy sustainability dependent on the preceding conditions might be of little practical use. Bohn (1995) shows that policies that are sustainable in a certain world may no longer be so in case of uncertainty. Hence, while ex post evaluation of fiscal sustainability is rather straightforward, ex ante evaluation of current or planned fiscal policies is not trivial. The literature has thus proposed a large number of methods and indicators for the evaluation of fiscal policy.[10] This volume extends the existing literature and applies its methods to actual fiscal policies.

In the econometric evaluation of fiscal policy, two approaches are often pursued. The first examines whether the time series of public debt is nonstationary—that is, whether the debt-to-GDP ratio is increasing in real terms and exceeds future discounted surpluses. If it is not found to do so, the country's fiscal policy is regarded as sustainable. This approach requires finding an appropriate discount rate for the future surpluses, however, which is somewhat difficult. For this, and for more general, reasons, Bohn (chapter 2) calls this concept "ad hoc sustainability." His own concept and the criterion he developed circumvent this problem by showing that a fiscal policy that embodies strong enough reactions of the primary surplus to an increase in public debt is sustainable. He gives a more precise definition of these two concepts, together with a discussion of their relation and their application to a long series of U.S. data, in chapter 2.

1.6 New Results

The results reported in the contributions to this volume that give an ex post evaluation of fiscal policy for various countries (chapters 2, 3, 4, and 5) do, at least in part, depend upon the definition of sustainability therein. The interesting point in these chapters from a policymaker's point of view is hence not only that for most of the countries that are studied in this volume, fiscal policy turns out to be sustainable in the long run, but that all countries, except for perhaps Italy, did manage to bring their debt back onto a sustainable path after a period of unsustainable policy. These results provide a more optimistic picture than that of Afonso (2005), who found evidence for sustainable fiscal policies in most European countries only toward the end of the 1990s.

In Europe, the Stability and Growth Pact (SGP) and the fiscal criteria of the Maastricht Treaty for entering the EMU are considered major devices to prevent excessive debt increases. Buti, Eijffinger, and Franco (chapter 6) discuss the pros and cons of the Stability and Growth Pact and possible remedies for the latter. Against established criteria for an ideal fiscal rule, its design and compliance mechanisms show strengths and weaknesses. The latter tend to reflect trade-offs typical of supranational arrangements. In the end, only a higher degree of fiscal integration would remove the inflexibility inherent in recourse to predefined budgetary rules. In the judgment of the authors, no alternative solution put forward in the literature appears clearly superior. This does not mean that the original pact of 1997 could not be improved. The debate on the SGP has shown that any reform should aim to overcome the excessive uniformity of the rules, improving their transparency, correcting pro-cyclicality and strengthening enforcement. The reform of the pact agreed upon in 2005 moves in this direction but leaves out a number of issues, as pointed out by Buti, Eijffinger, and Franco.

As mentioned earlier, an answer to the question as to whether a particular country's fiscal development has been sustainable or will be so in the future may depend crucially upon whether public liabilities from the system of social security are included or not. While most country studies in this volume concentrate on the central government budget, Andersen, Jensen and Pedersen (chapter 7) focus on social security issues, showing that existing welfare arrangements in Denmark suffer from a lack of fiscal sustainability. This assessment is fairly robust to a number of demographic changes, with the important exception of changes in life expectancy. They also question the appropriateness of the current long-term fiscal strategy of prefunding, both with respect to its implications for intergenerational distribution and for its lack of ability to cope with the inherent economic uncertainty.

Evidence that a return to sustainable public finances can be reached not only through measures of fiscal policy—namely, by raising taxes and/or lowering government spending—is presented in the contributions by Hughes Hallett (chapter 8) and Feld and Kirchgässner (chapter 9), who study the effects of changes or differences in the institutional setup on fiscal policy performance.[11] Hughes Hallett examines the interaction of fiscal and monetary policy in the United Kingdom and finds that fiscal policy performance has greatly improved since fiscal policy Stackelberg leads an independent monetary policy, where fiscal policy concentrates on long-term objectives and monetary policy takes care of short-term stabilization.

Feld and Kirchgässner study the effects of fiscal rules and direct democracy on fiscal policy in the Swiss cantons. Fiscal rules, they find, do have a dampening effect on public deficits. This finding is supported by Galli and Padovano's study (chapter 3) of Italian fiscal policy, which shows a clear effect of the Maastricht rules.[12] Furthermore, Feld and Kirchgässner show that direct democracy is negatively correlated with public debt while it does not have a significant effect on deficits. This is a rather interesting observation, because it identifies direct democracy as a mechanism that is flexible enough to allow for short-term deficits owing to exogenous economic developments or large-scale one-off investment projects, but that ensures the sustainability of fiscal policy in the long run.

From the policymakers' view, however, the question as to whether past fiscal policy has been sustainable is only one point of interest. The question policymakers have to ask themselves is the following: given past fiscal policies, that is, given the current amount of public debt, is current fiscal policy and are future fiscal policies sustainable? That an unsustainable state of fiscal policy can be successfully changed is shown in the examples of the Netherlands (chapter 4) and possibly (though the evidence is mixed) of Austria (chapter 5). The crucial point is, however, the evaluation of fiscal policies. As noted previously, this evaluation hinges on both the definition of sustainability and, at least within the concept of ad hoc sustainability, the choice of a correct discount factor. While the main determinants of this discount factor, the growth rate, the rate of inflation, and the real interest rate, can be forecast for some periods, in the long run apparently nearly anything can be assumed about these determinants. In addition, if public spending not only has consumptive character but is used at least in part to finance investments that benefit future generations, finding a proper discount rate to evaluate the sustainability of fiscal policy becomes even more difficult. First, the policymaker would have to compute the net present value of the investment projects. Second, to find the optimal level of investment, the policymaker would have to find a way to measure the aggregate level of intergenerational altruism, which may be rather challenging if not impossible.

Nevertheless, good reasons exist for examining the sustainability of public finances. First, at least Bohn's method of checking for sustainability is fairly easy to apply, thus providing a strong tool for a first assessment of the long-run implications of current fiscal policies. Moreover, and most important, several chapters in this volume show that the time horizon is crucial for determining whether fiscal policies are sustainable or not. The entire concept of public debt sustainability shifts policymakers' and citizens' attention toward the long run, which, owing to political constraints and to the (probably "pseudo") Keynesian legacy, often tends to be neglected in the actual political process. Although it is true that in a world of fully informed rational agents with perfect foresight, there will never be unsustainable government debt development because nobody will lend money to a government that is going to repudiate, in the actual economic environment of imperfect information and other market failures and, not the least, government failures, this is no longer true. If, in such a situation, economic analysis manages to demonstrate that certain fiscal policies violate the sustainability criterion, this can serve well to bring back such a government to the virtuous path of sound public budgets. Thus, although it will be some time before economists can provide clear-cut and unambiguous policy advice on fiscal matters with respect to public debt sustainability, using the methods and analytical concepts presented in this volume may give the applied economist a tool for raising the public's awareness of misguided policies and affixing an emergency sign to such policies. Perhaps this is more than the "dismal scientist" can usually hope for.

1.7 Acknowledgments

The chapters published in this book were discussed during a conference on the sustainability of public debt jointly organized by CESifo, Munich, and the Ludwig Boltzmann (now Robert Holzmann) Institute for Economic Policy Analyses (LBI), Vienna. The editors of this volume wish to express their sincere appreciation to all presenters, discussants, authors, and other participants of this conference held in Tutzing, Germany, October 22–23, 2004. In addition, we thank Frank Somogyi (KOF Swiss Economic Institute, ETH Zurich), Helen Heaney, Christina Kopetzky and Anita Wachter (Klagenfurt University), and the CESifo staff who helped organize the conference and prepare this volume. Special thanks also go to a number of anonymous referees and to CESifo and LBI for funding both the conference and this publication.

Notes

1. It is even more true for many developing countries, which are, however, not under consideration in this volume. See, e.g., Cuddington 1999.

2. See Balassone and Franco 2000 for a survey and Rowley, Shughart, and Tollison 2002 for a collection of readings.

3. E.g., Blanchard and Giavazzi (2004).

4. See, e.g., Chichilnisky 1996, Heal 1998, and Hellwig 2005 for a general characterization of the notion of sustainability and Harris et al. 2001, Pezzey and Toman 2002, and Toman and Pezzey 2006 for surveys of the literature referring to environmental economics.

5. See, e.g., Beetsma and Bovenberg 1999, 2003.

6. See, e.g., Alesina and Perotti 1995, Persson and Tabellini 2000, and Drazen 2000 for surveys.

7. See, e.g., Fatas and Mihov 2003 and Schuknecht 2005.

8. The presentation follows Balassone and Franco 2000.

9. Blanchard et al. 1990 and Wyplosz 2005.

10. See, e.g., Balassone and Franco 2000, Chalk and Hemming 2000, and Artis and Marcellino 2000.

11. The influence of political institutions on budgetary outcomes has been investigated previously, e.g., in Poterba and von Hagen 1999.

12. Other suggestions for reforming the Stability and Growth Pact toward a "Sustainability and Growth Pact" are proposed by Coeuré and Pisani-Ferry (2005).

References

Afonso, A. 2005. Fiscal sustainability: The unpleasant European case. *FinanzArchiv* 61:19–44.

Alesina, A., and R. Perotti. 1995. The political economy of budget deficits. *IMF Staff Papers* 42:1–31.

Artis, M., and M. Marcellino. 2000. The solvency of government finances in Europe. In *Fiscal Sustainability*, ed. Banca d'Italia, 209–241. Rome: Bank of Italy.

Balassone, F., and D. Franco. 2000. Assessing fiscal sustainability: A review of methods with a view to EMU. In *Fiscal Sustainability*, ed. Banca d'Italia, 21–60. Rome: Bank of Italy.

Barro, R. J. 1974. Are government bonds net wealth? *Journal of Political Economy* 82:1095–1117.

Barro, R. J. 1979. On the determination of the public debt. *Journal of Political Economy* 87:940–971.

Beetsma, R. M. W. J., and A. L. Bovenberg. 1999. Does monetary unification lead to excessive debt accumulation? *Journal of Public Economics* 74:299–325.

Beetsma, R. M. W. J., and A. L. Bovenberg. 2003. Strategic debt accumulation in a heterogeneous monetary union. *European Journal of Political Economy* 19:1–15.

Blanchard, O. J., J.-C. Chouraqui, R. P. Hageman, and N. Sartor. 1990. The sustainability of fiscal policy: New answers to an old question. *OECD Economic Studies* 15:7–36.

Blanchard, O. J., and F. Giavazzi. 2004. Improving the SGP through a proper accounting of public investment. CEPR Discussion Paper no. 4220.

Bohn, H. 1995. The sustainability of budget deficits in a stochastic economy. *Journal of Money, Credit, and Banking* 27:257–271.

Chalk, N., and R. Hemming. 2000. Assessing fiscal sustainability in theory and practice. In *Fiscal Sustainability*, ed. Banca d'Italia, 61–93. Rome: Bank of Italy.

Chichilnisky, G. 1996. An axiomatic approach to sustainable development. *Social Choice and Welfare* 13:231–257.

Coeuré, B., and J. Pisani-Ferry. 2005. Fiscal policy in EMU: Towards a Sustainability and Growth Pact? *Oxford Review of Economic Policy* 21:598–617.

Cuddington, J. T. 1999. Analyzing the sustainability of fiscal deficits in developing countries. Policy Research Working Paper no. 1784. The World Bank, Washington, DC.

Drazen, A. 2000. *Political Economy in Macroeconomics*. Princeton: Princeton University Press.

Eichengreen, B., and C. Wyplosz. 1998. The stability pact: More than a minor nuisance? *Economic Policy* 13:65–104.

Fatas, A., and I. Mihov. 2003. The case for restricting fiscal policy discretion. *Quarterly Journal of Economics* 118:1419–1447.

Harris, J. M., T. Wise, K. Gallagher, and N. R. Goodwin, eds. 2001. *A Survey of Sustainable Development: Social and Economic Dimensions*. Washington, DC: Island Press.

Heal, G. 1998. *Valuing the Future: Economic Theory and Sustainability*. New York: Columbia University Press.

Hellwig, K. 2005. Sustainability revisited. *Economics Letters* 87:193–197.

Persson, T., and G. Tabellini. 2000. *Political Economics: Explaining Economic Policy*. Cambridge, MA: MIT Press.

Pezzey, J. C., and M. A. Toman, eds. 2002. *The Economics of Sustainability*. Aldershot, UK: Ashgate.

Poterba, J. M., and J. von Hagen, eds. 1999. *Fiscal Institutions and Fiscal Performance*. Chicago: University of Chicago Press.

Rowley, C. K., W. F. Shughart, and R. D. Tollison, eds. 2002. *The Economics of Budget Deficits*. 2 vols. Cheltenham, UK: Edward Elgar.

Sargent, T. J., and N. Wallace. 1981. Some unpleasant monetarist arithmetic. *Federal Reserve Bank of Minneapolis Quarterly Review* 5 (3): 1–17.

Schuknecht, L. 2005. Stability and Growth Pact: Issues and lessons from political economy. *International Economics and Economic Policy* 2:65–89.

Sims, C. A. 1994. A simple model for study of the determination of the price level and the interaction of monetary and fiscal policy. *Economic Theory* 4:381–399.

Toman, M., and J. C. Pezzey. 2006. The economics of sustainability: A review of journal articles. Discussion paper. Resources for the Future, Washington, DC.

Woodford, M. 1995. Price-level determinacy without control of a monetary aggregate. *Carnegie-Rochester Conference Series on Public Policy* 43:1–46.

Wyplosz, C. 2005. Fiscal policy: Institutions versus rules. *National Institute Economic Review* 191:64–78.

2 The Sustainability of Fiscal Policy in the United States

Henning Bohn

2.1 Introduction

The U.S. fiscal balance has shown tremendous variation in recent years. Large budget deficits in the 1980s and early 1990s triggered a substantial literature examining the sustainability of U.S. budget deficits. Concerns about U.S. budget deficits evaporated in the late 1990s as deficits turned into record surpluses, leaving a stack of unreconciled theoretical and empirical findings. As the U.S. fiscal balance has turned sharply negative since 2001, the sustainability of U.S. fiscal policy is again a pressing issue.

This chapter critically reviews the conceptual issues and presents new evidence, drawing on the historical record of U.S. fiscal policy from 1792 to 2003. Section 2.2 lays out a framework and summarizes U.S. data, emphasizing the role of economic growth. Sections 2.3–2.4 examine commonly used "ad hoc" versions of the government's intertemporal budget constraint (IBC) and test the implied stationarity restrictions. Sections 2.5–2.7 derive the IBC in a general equilibrium setting and examine its theoretical and empirical implications. U.S. primary surpluses are found to respond positively to fluctuations in public debt. This response satisfies a sufficient condition for sustainability. Section 2.8 concludes.

2.2 U.S. Fiscal Data and Economic Growth

The starting point for analyzing government budgets is the budget identity linking the deficit to revenues, spending, and public debt. The deficit is the difference between outlays and revenues. It also equals the change in public debt. In algebraic terms, let DEF_t denote the with-interest deficit in year t, T_t total revenues, G_t non–interest spending,

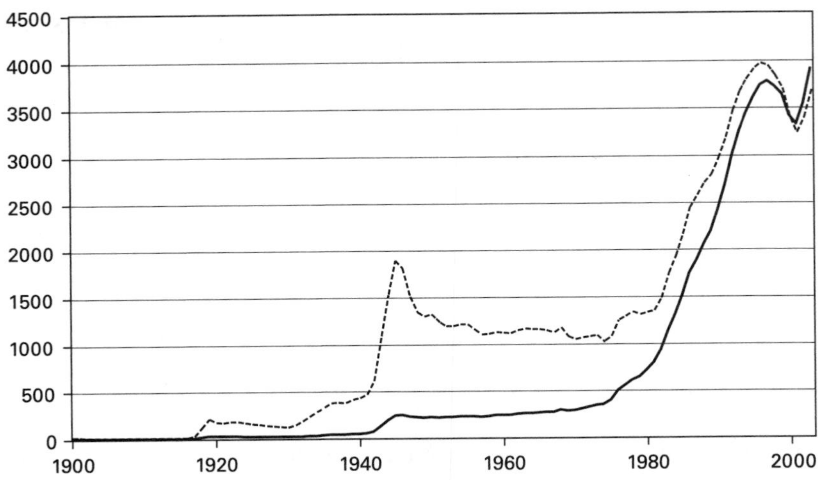

Figure 2.1
The U.S. public debt: Nominal (line) and real (dotted), 1900–2003
Note: Debt is in $bill. Real debt is at year 2000 prices.

D_{t-1} the public debt at the end of year $t-1$ (all in nominal dollars), and i_t the interest charge. Then the budget identities are

$$DEF_t = G_t - T_t + i_t \cdot D_{t-1} \tag{2.1}$$

and

$$D_t = D_{t-1} + DEF_t. \tag{2.2a}$$

Most policy debates about the U.S. budget deficit focus on the nominal with-interest deficit and on the resulting buildup of public debt. Data for revenues and outlays are commonly taken from the Unified Budget, which includes social security and other trust fund accounts as well as Federal Reserve transfers to the Treasury.[1]

Figure 2.1 displays U.S. public debt in nominal and real terms for 1900–2003. Nominal debt is barely visible until the 1940s and flat until the 1970s. The post-1970s debt growth reflects large deficits in the 1980s and in the post-2001 period. The U.S. government has run budget deficits in every single year since 1970, except for the 1998–2001 period. Adjusting for inflation magnifies historical debt values relative to recent ones. In the real series, debts from World War I become noticeable, but pre-1916 values look negligible relative to current debt. The

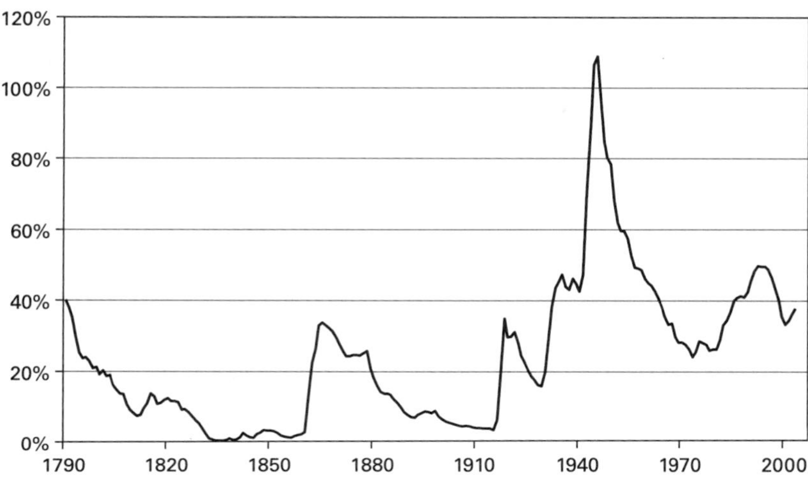

Figure 2.2
The U.S. public debt as a percent of GDP, 1791–2003

real series shows that debt growth from 1950 to 1980 was entirely nominal, whereas the post-1980 debt growth was real.

Figure 2.2 displays the ratio of U.S. public debt to the size of the economy (GDP) for 1791–2003. Scaling debt by the size of the economy further shrinks recent debt values relative to earlier ones, to such an extent that it becomes instructive to display the entire history of U.S. debt. The debt-to-GDP ratio suggests a more benign view of U.S. fiscal policy than the nominal and real series. The 36 percent debt-to-GDP ratio in 2003 is comparable to the starting value in 1791 (about 40 percent). With the exception of World War II, the U.S. time series lies below 60 percent, the value European politicians seem to view as the hallmark of responsible fiscal policy.

Figures 2.1 and 2.2 highlight the central role of wars in the build-up of debt. Five major wars—the American War of Independence, the Spanish-American War, the American Civil War, World War I, and World War II—were largely deficit-financed. This explains the high debt-to-GDP ratio in 1791 and the sharp increases in 1812–1816, 1861–1866, 1916–1919, and 1941–1946. The debt-to-GDP ratio generally declined during peacetime periods, with the exception of the Great Depression/New Deal era (1929–1939), the 1980s, and the post-2001 period. One might even interpret the 1980s as a hot phase in the cold

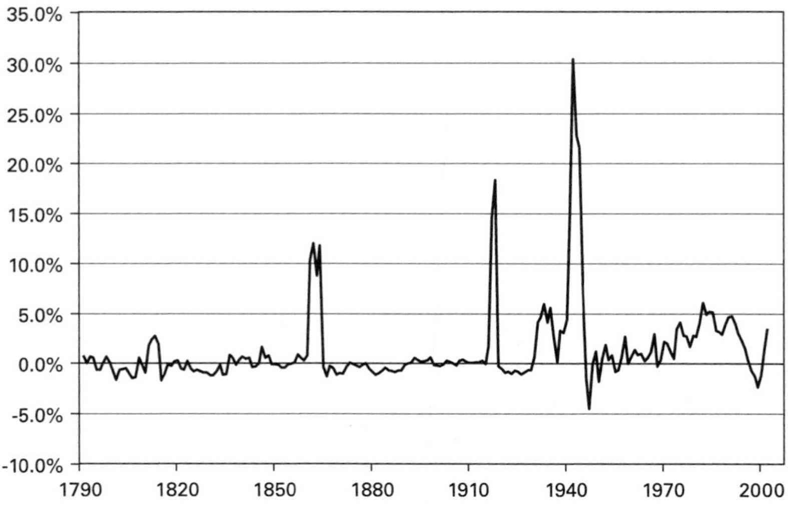

Figure 2.3
The U.S. budget deficit as a percent of GDP, 1792–2003

war and the post-2001 period as the war on terror, which would leave the Great Depression as the sole episode of peacetime increases in the debt-to-GDP ratio.

Figure 2.3 displays the deficit-to-GDP ratio, the ratio of nominal unified deficits over GDP. The deficit-to-GDP ratio illustrates the extraordinary magnitude of wartime deficits, the persistently high deficits in the post-1980 period, and the late-1990s surpluses. Note that peacetime budget surpluses are not nearly as large as the wartime deficits, neither year-by-year nor as integral over time.

The contrast between the flat path of debt in figure 2.2 and the positive deficits in figure 2.3 illustrates a key point: The common intuition equating deficits with increases in debt does not apply to real values or to GDP ratios. While $DEF = \Delta D$ holds in nominal terms as shown in (2.2a), changes in real debt differ from the real value of the deficit by an inflation term,

$$\Delta(D/P)_t = \frac{D_t}{P_t} - \frac{D_{t-1}}{P_{t-1}} = \frac{DEF_t}{P_t} - \frac{D_{t-1}}{P_{t-1}} \frac{\pi_t}{1+\pi_t}, \tag{2.2b}$$

where P_t is the price level (empirically, the GDP deflator) and $\pi_t = P_t/P_{t-1} - 1$ is the inflation rate. Similarly, changes in the debt-to-GDP ratio differ from the deficit-to-GDP ratio by a nominal growth term,

$$\Delta(D/Y)_t = \frac{D_t}{Y_t} - \frac{D_{t-1}}{Y_{t-1}} = \frac{DEF_t}{Y_t} - \frac{D_{t-1}}{Y_{t-1}} \frac{\gamma_t}{1+\gamma_t}, \tag{2.2c}$$

where Y_t is nominal GDP and $\gamma_t = Y_t/Y_{t-1} - 1$ is nominal GDP-growth. The nominal growth term—a "growth dividend"—could be decomposed into an inflation term (as in [2.2b]) plus a real growth effect. I omit the decomposition to highlight that GDP ratios are ratios of nominal dollar values and hence not subject to controversies about measuring inflation. Because of the inflation and growth effects, the interest charge $i_t \cdot D_{t-1}$ in the headline deficit systematically overstates the impact of initial debt on real debt accumulation and on the debt-to-GDP ratio. This explains the mismatch between figure 2.2 and figure 2.3.

The primary deficit, $DEF_t^0 = G_t - T_t$, is useful in this context, both to separate the stock of debt from the flows of outlays and revenues, and to obtain a scale-invariant exposition of debt dynamics. From (2.1) and (2.2a), the nominal budget equation can be written as

$$D_t = G_t - T_t + (1+i_t) \cdot D_{t-1} = DEF_t^0 + (1+i_t) \cdot D_{t-1}. \tag{2.3}$$

The corresponding real and GDP ratio versions,

$$\frac{D_t}{P_t} = \frac{DEF_t^0}{P_t} + \left(\frac{1+i_t}{1+\pi_t}\right) \cdot \frac{D_{t-1}}{P_{t-1}} \quad \text{and} \quad \frac{D_t}{Y_t} = \frac{DEF_t^0}{Y_t} + \left(\frac{1+i_t}{1+\gamma_t}\right) \cdot \frac{D_{t-1}}{Y_{t-1}},$$

are similar in that they express period-t debt as the sum of a flow variable—the primary deficit—and the previous period's debt multiplied by a propagation factor. Let d_t denote a generic, scaled version of debt (e.g., D_t or D_t/P_t or D_t/Y_t, as needed), let s_t denote the corresponding version of the primary surplus (meaning $-DEF_t^0$ or $-DEF_t^0/P_t$ or $-DEF_t^0/Y_t$), and let r_t denote the appropriate version of the "return" on debt (meaning, $r_t = i_t$ or $r_t = (1+i_t)/(1+\pi_t) - 1 \approx i_t - \pi_t$ or $r_t = (1+i_t)/(1+g_t) - 1 \approx i_t - \gamma_t$). Then the dynamics of public debt can described compactly as

$$d_t = (1+r_t) \cdot d_{t-1} - s_t. \tag{2.4}$$

Equation (2.4) demonstrates that budget accounting is scale-invariant if one uses the appropriate propagation factor. Equation (2.4) also

Table 2.1
U.S. budget deficits versus changes in the debt-to-GDP ratio

Period From	Period To	Deficit with interest (1)	Primary deficit (2)	Interest charge (3)	Nominal growth effect (4)	Real growth effect (5)	Inflation effect (6)	Change in debt/GDP (7)
1792	2003	1.2%	0.3%	0.9%	1.3%	0.8%	0.5%	0.0%
1792	1868	0.4%	−0.1%	0.5%	0.6%	0.5%	0.1%	−0.1%
1869	2003	1.7%	0.5%	1.2%	1.7%	1.0%	0.7%	0.0%
1792	1914	0.1%	−0.4%	0.5%	0.5%	0.5%	0.0%	−0.3%
1915	2003	2.8%	1.2%	1.6%	2.4%	1.2%	1.2%	0.4%

Note: The sample split in 1914 is motivated by World War I and the Sixteenth Amendment (start of income taxation). The 1868 sample split is motivated by the American Civil War. Interest charge refers to the difference between with-interest and primary deficits. Growth effects refer to the reduction in nominal/real debt/GDP owing to GDP growth.

highlights that alternative tax and spending policies have an impact on debt accumulation only to the extent that they affect s_t and r_t.

Table 2.1 documents the quantitative importance of economic growth for the dynamics of U.S. debt. Column (1) shows average with-interest deficits as percent of GDP. Columns (2)–(4) display corresponding values for the primary deficit, the nominal interest charge, and the growth dividend from (2.2c), all as percent of GDP. In columns (5)–(6), growth dividend is decomposed into real growth and the inflation effect from (2.2b). Column (7) displays the average growth rate of the debt-to-GDP ratio.

Over the full 1792–2003 sample (top row), the U.S. government has run with-interest deficits averaging about 1.2 percent of GDP (column [1]). Even excluding interest, the United States has run deficits averaging about 0.3 percent of GDP (column [2]). The debt-to-GDP ratio, in contrast, has remained essentially constant (column [7]), suggesting that $(1+i_t)/(1+\gamma_t)-1$ must have been negative on average. Column (4) confirms that the growth dividend has been enough to cover average interest changes and primary deficits. Economic growth rather than primary surpluses have held down the debt-to-GDP ratio.

The role of economic growth is robust if one splits the sample. Subsample variations arise mainly because inflation rates differ in the pre– and post–Gold Standard periods and because subsamples may include an above or below average number of war years. If one splits the sample in 1914, the 1792–1914 sample shows a lower with-interest deficit, a

Table 2.2
Interest rates on public debt versus growth rates

Period		Interest rate*	Nominal growth	Real growth	Inflation	Interest–growth
From	To	(1)	(2)	(3)	(4)	(5)
1792	2003	4.5%	5.2%	3.8%	1.4%	−0.6%
1792	1868	4.8%	4.9%	4.2%	0.6%	−0.1%
1869	2003	4.4%	5.3%	3.5%	1.8%	−1.0%
1792	1914	4.6%	4.3%	4.1%	0.2%	0.4%
1915	2003	4.4%	6.4%	3.4%	3.1%	−2.1%

*The interest rate on public debt is computed as the ratio of interest payments over the average of outstanding debt at the start and the end of each year.

declining debt-to-GDP ratio, and a primary surplus, whereas the 1915–2003 sample shows higher with-interest and primary deficits and an increasing debt-to-GDP ratio. While GDP growth for 1792–1914 was noninflationary, inflation was a major component of nominal growth for 1915–2003. The increase in the inflation component (from −0.02 percent to 1.17 percent) was matched almost one-for-one by an increased nominal interest change (from 0.49 percent to 1.57 percent). This suggests that the Fisher effect reasonably approximates the long-run data; that is, the relation between interest charge and growth dividend is not due to unexpected inflation. Similar results are obtained if one splits the sample in 1868.

Table 2.2 displays average growth rates, inflation rates, and interest rates on U.S. debt for the same sample periods as in table 2.1. Columns (1)–(4) present essentially the same information as in columns (3)–(6) in table 2.1, but as simple averages (versus averages weighted by debt-to-GDP ratios in table 2.1). Table 2.2 confirms that average economic growth has usually exceeded the average interest charge on public debt.[2]

Note that table 2.2 does not allow inferences about the dynamic efficiency of the U.S. economy. As shown by Abel et al. (1989), dynamic efficiency depends on the relationship between capital share and investment share in GDP (or approximately, the return on real capital and the growth rate). Abel et al. show that the U.S. capital share has consistently exceeded the investment share, indicating dynamic efficiency. Tables 2.1–2.2 suggest that the U.S. government has exploited the gap between the return on capital and the return on bonds to economize on its debt service.

In summary, for the last two hundred plus years the U.S. government has been able to rely on economic growth to keep its debt-to-GDP ratio from rising. Most of the time, the United States has had no need to run primary surpluses, and indeed, it did not run primary surpluses on average. Much of the sustainability literature, in contrast, starts from the premise that primary surpluses are necessary to keep public debt from growing exponentially.

2.3 Ad Hoc Sustainability

This section examines the U.S. fiscal record from an applied perspective and review, sustainability conditions commonly used in the literature. In principle, sustainability involves two questions. Which fiscal policies are sustainable? And what can we say about the sustainability of particular policies encountered in practice?

Much of the sustainability literature has skipped the first question and focused on the empirical implications of a simple ad hoc definition of sustainability:

DEFINITION (AD HOC SUSTAINABILITY): A fiscal policy satisfies ad hoc sustainability, if it is on a trajectory such that the present value of expected future primary surpluses equals the initial debt.

This is a flawed definition—as I will demonstrate—but worth examining, in part because it motivates standard empirical tests, in part to highlight the flaws.

From equation (2.4), one can readily compute the paths of public debt implied by arbitrary sequences of primary surpluses and of interest charges,

$$d_{t+n} = \left(\prod_{k=0}^{n} (1 + r_{t+k}) \right) \cdot d_{t-1} - \sum_{j=0}^{n} \left(\prod_{k=j+1}^{n} (1 + r_{t+k}) \right) \cdot s_{t+j}. \tag{2.5}$$

Conditions for ad hoc sustainability are obtained from (2.5) in three steps, all of which are valid in nominal terms, in real terms, and for GDP ratios. First, replace the returns in (2.5) by a fixed value r and take conditional expectations,

$$E_t[d_{t+n}] = (1 + r)^n \cdot d_t^* - \sum_{j=0}^{n} (1 + r)^{n-j} \cdot E_t[s_{t+j}],$$

where $d_t^* = (1 + r_t) \cdot d_{t-1}$ denotes debt at the *start* of period t and where $E_t[\cdot]$ denotes conditional expectations. Second, divide by $(1 + r)^n$ and rearrange to obtain

$$d_t^* = \sum_{j=0}^{n} \frac{1}{(1+r)^j} E_t[s_{t+j}] + \frac{1}{(1+r)^n} E_t[d_{t+n}] \tag{2.6}$$

Third, assume the discounted sum converges and take the limit $n \to \infty$; then

$$d_t^* = \sum_{j=0}^{\infty} \frac{1}{(1+r)^j} E_t[s_{t+j}] + \lim_{n\to\infty} \frac{1}{(1+r)^n} E_t[d_{t+n}]. \tag{2.7}$$

Equation (2.7) demonstrates that initial debt equals the expected present value of future primary surpluses if and only if discounted future debt converges to zero. That is,

$$d_t^* = \sum_{j=0}^{\infty} \frac{1}{(1+r)^j} E_t[s_{t+j}] \qquad \text{(Ad hoc IBC)} \quad (2.8)$$

is equivalent to

$$\lim_{n\to\infty} \frac{1}{(1+r)^n} E_t[d_{t+n}] = 0. \qquad \text{(Ad hoc TC)} \quad (2.9)$$

Equation (2.8) is commonly known as the intertemporal budget constraint (IBC) and (2.9) as the transversality condition (TC).

The derivation highlights the arbitrariness of the discount rate r and the absence of an economic argument as to why potential buyers of government bonds should care about TC or IBC. The sustainability literature commonly interprets r as an expected return on government bonds, proxied by some historical average. Because (2.7) is an identity for any r, (2.8) has economic content only by the assertion that for the particular r-value chosen by the study's author, (2.9) describes the bondholders' transversality condition. This would make (2.9) a necessary condition for individuals to hold government bonds and would justify (2.8)–(2.9) as valid constraints on government policy.

Most empirical investigations of (2.8)–(2.9) focus on testing (2.8) by examining the unit root and cointegration properties of fiscal data.[3] In an influential paper, Trehan and Walsh (1988) show that if real revenues, real spending, and real debt have unit roots, a stationary with-interest deficit is sufficient for (2.8)–(2.9). Equivalent statements (invoking the budget identity with fixed r) are that the primary surplus and debt are cointegrated with a cointegrating vector $(1, -r)$; or that revenues, non–interest spending, and debt are cointegrated with vector $(1, -1, -r)$. Trehan and Walsh (1991) generalize this result in two directions: With variable discount rates, IBC holds if debt is difference-stationary and if the discount rate is strictly positive and bounded away from zero. Alternatively, covering the case of nonstationary with-interest deficits, IBC holds if a quasi-difference $d_t - \lambda d_{t-1}$ of debt is stationary for some $0 \leq \lambda < 1 + r$ and if debt and primary surpluses are cointegrated.

Two simple observations provide an intuition for these unit root and cointegration results. First, it is a mathematical fact that exponential decay dominates polynomial growth. If debt is difference-stationary with some finite mean δ, the expected debt n-periods ahead is approximately $E_t[d_{t+n}] \approx \bar{d}_t + n \cdot \delta$, a linear function of n, where $\bar{d}_t$ denotes the permanent component of d_t (as defined by Beveridge and Nelson 1981). Because (2.9) divides this expression by the exponential $(1 + r)^n$, the dominance of exponential decay over linear growth implies a zero limit for any $r > 0$. This explains Trehan and Walsh's result (1988) and the difference-stationarity result in Trehan and Walsh 1991. Trehan and Walsh's cointegration result (1991) derives from a second observation: exponential debt growth is consistent with (9) if the growth rate is strictly less than r (McCallum 1984). If $d_t - \lambda d_{t-1}$ is stationary as Trehan and Walsh assume, the asymptotic rate of debt growth is $\lambda - 1$, so $\lambda < 1 + r$ suffices for (2.8a, b).

Trehan and Walsh's cointegration result (1991) has a noteworthy additional implication. Cointegration between surplus and debt means that some linear combination $s_t - \alpha \cdot d_{t-1} = u_t$ is stationary, where α is a constant and u_t a stationary process. Next period's debt can then be written as $d_{t+1} = (1 + r) \cdot d_t - s_{t+1} = (1 + r - \alpha) \cdot d_t + u_{t+1}$, so $\lambda = 1 + r - \alpha$ and therefore $\alpha = 1 + r - \lambda > 0$. Trehan and Walsh's assumptions (1991) therefore imply a *strictly positive* linkage between surplus and debt $(\alpha > 0)$.[4]

From an economic perspective, one might wonder about the types of policies that might lead to (2.8)–(2.9) being satisfied or violated. Two polar scenarios are instructive. First, suppose politicians are oblivious to public debt, making exogenous decisions about taxes and about non–interest spending. Then conditions (2.8)–(2.9) are only satisfied by accident, only if the stochastic processes describing taxes and spending decisions happen to have the property that deficit-increasing shocks in one period are exactly offset in present-value terms by deficit-decreasing shocks in subsequent periods (see Hansen, Roberds, and Sargent 1991). Second, suppose politicians are instead responsive to public debt. They are more cautious about tax cuts and about spending growth whenever the debt has increased, and more willing to cut taxes and to increase spending when the debt has decreased. Such responses to debt would implement an error correction mechanism that might stabilize the debt or at least generate cointegration between debts and primary surpluses. The empirical question about sustainability is which of these scenarios better characterizes a country's political process.

A disturbing feature of ad hoc sustainability is the apparent disconnection from practical politics. While political debates about sustainability are mostly about bounds on debt-to-GDP and/or deficit-to-GDP ratios, much of the academic literature has focused on real fiscal series and treats nonstationary debt-to-GDP ratios as unproblematic.

2.4 Empirical Analysis: Unit Roots versus Stationarity

This section critically examines the time-series properties of U.S. fiscal variables, focusing on unit root tests for ad hoc sustainability. Cointegration is not examined, to save space and because the stationarity of a deficit measure and the cointegration of its nonstationary components are conceptually equivalent.[5]

Table 2.3 presents unit root tests for real variables—for public debt, the with-interest deficit, the primary deficit, revenues, noninterest outlays, and a decomposition of noninterest outlays into military and nonmilitary ones. The Phillips-Perron (PP) and Augmented Dickey-Fuller (ADF) tests examine the null hypothesis of a unit root against a trend-stationary alternative; see Hamilton 1994 for technical details. The KPSS test examines the null hypothesis of trend stationarity; see Kwiatkowski et al. 1992. PP is robust with regard to heteroskedasticity but ignores autocorrelation beyond a finite lag window. ADF includes an autoregressive correction but ignores heteroskedasticity. To accommodate short-run dependencies, all results are reported for an AR(4) in ADF and for twelve lags in PP and in KPSS. All tests allow for a deterministic time trend in the stationary alternative.

The test results in table 2.3 are statistically clear-cut. All the deficit measures appear to be stationary: ADF and PP reject a unit root while

Table 2.3
Unit root tests for real fiscal variables, 1792–2003

Variable	PP(12)	ADF(4)	KPSS(12)	Verdict
Public debt	−0.289	−0.174	0.325**	Unit root
Deficit, primary	−3.787*	−5.814**	0.076	Stationary
Deficit $(-s + r \cdot d)$	−4.143**	−5.658**	0.058	Stationary
Deficit *DEF/P*	−3.578*	−4.757**	0.134	Stationary
Revenues total	+1.614	+2.284	0.370**	Unit root
Outlays: Noninterest	+2.799	+1.692	0.380**	Unit root
Outlays: Military	−2.577	−2.804	0.349**	Unit root
Outlays: Nonmilitary	+7.144	+4.558	0.331**	Unit root
Critical values: 5%	−3.432	−3.432	0.146	
1%	−4.004	−4.004	0.216	

Notes: PP(12) = Phillips-Perron test with twelve-year autocorrelation window; ADF(4) = Augmented Dickey-Fuller test with fourth-order autocorrelation; KPSS(12) = Kwiatkowski et al. (1992) test with twelve-year autocorrelation window. Verdict = Unit root if KPSS rejects and PP/ADF does not; stationary, if ADF or PP reject and KPSS does not.
*significant at 5 percent; **significant at 1 percent.

KPSS does not reject stationarity. All other variables appear to have unit roots: KPSS rejects trend-stationarity whereas ADF and PP do not reject unit roots. Importantly, one finds a stationary with-interest deficit in a setting with nonstationary revenues, outlays, and debt, a configuration that satisfies Trehan and Walsh's sustainability condition (1988).

The results for deficits are logically inconsistent, however. The with-interest deficit is a linear function of primary deficit and debt. Given a nonstationary debt, the with-interest deficit and the primary deficit cannot both be stationary. It appears that debt has such a small weight in the with-interest deficit that the tests are not powerful enough to distinguish stationarity in $(-s_t)$ from stationarity in $(-s_t) + r_t \cdot d_{t-1}$. It is therefore unclear which of the deficit measures is stationary, that is, if Trehan and Walsh's condition is satisfied.

The real time series also suffer from an enormous nonstationarity in variances. To illustrate the problem, table 2.4 displays standard deviations of primary deficits and of the public debt for selected subsamples. The standard deviation of post-1900 real deficits exceeds the pre-1900 value by a factor of 64. Even for post–World War II data (more commonly used in the literature), standard deviations are increasing over

Table 2.4
Standard deviations of fiscal variables

Overall period:	1792–2003 sample			1960–2003 sample		
Split samples:	1792–1899 (1)	1900–2003 (2)	Ratios (3)	1960–1980 (4)	1981–2003 (5)	Ratios (6)
Real variables						
Primary deficit	1.8	114.7	64.0	48.2	184.5	3.8
Public debt	11.9	1174.3	98.3	95.2	832.4	8.7
GDP shares						
Primary deficit/GDP	2.29%	5.12%	2.2	1.15%	2.20%	1.9
Public debt/GDP	9.96%	22.44%	2.3	7.22%	6.82%	0.9

Note: Entries in columns (1)–(2) and columns (4)–(5) are standard deviations. Column (3) shows the ratio of column (2) over column (1). Column (6) shows the ratio of column (5) over column (4).

time, as illustrated by the split 1960–2003 sample. This casts some doubts on the unit root results, suggesting that the "stationary" real series in table 2.3 are not truly covariance stationary.[6] Table 2.4 also documents that the standard deviations of GDP ratios display much less growth over time, suggesting that the rising variances of real deficits and real debt are largely due to a growing economy.

Table 2.5 displays unit root tests for GDP ratios of the same variables as in table 2.3. For deficits, revenues, and nonmilitary outlays, GDP ratios have properties similar to those of the real series. All the deficit-GDP series appear stationary. Revenues and nonmilitary outlays appear to have unit roots. Different results are obtained, however, for the debt-to-GDP ratio, for outlays/GDP, and for military spending/GDP. For the debt-to-GDP ratio neither stationarity nor nonstationarity is rejected; for the outlay-to-GDP ratio both stationarity and nonstationarity are rejected; and military spending/GDP appears to be stationary.

Scaling by GDP may raise questions about the stationarity of U.S. GDP itself, the subject of an old controversy (Christiano and Eichenbaum 1990). In my real GDP series, trend stationarity is rejected for 1790–2003 (KPSS = 0.347) but not for 1868–2003 (KPSS = 0.069). A unit root is not rejected for either sample period (PP = −2.16 for 1790–2003, PP = −2.67 for 1869–2003). The evidence against stationary GDP is weak, however, because the pre-1869 GDP data may be of lower quality than the more recent data. A unit root in real GDP is also consistent with the observation that some stationary GDP-shares in table 2.5 become nonstationary when multiplied by GDP (notably public

Table 2.5
Unit root tests for GDP shares, 1792–2003

Variable	PP(12)	ADF(4)	KPSS(12)	Verdict
Public debt	−2.834	−2.861	0.118	No rejection
Deficit, primary	−5.076**	−5.587**	0.073	Stationary
Deficit $(-s + r \cdot d)$	−6.354**	−6.617**	0.075	Stationary
Deficit *DEF/Y*	−5.106**	−5.594**	0.047	Stationary
Revenues total	−2.058	−1.971	0.328**	Unit root
Outlays: Noninterest	−3.882*	−3.766*	0.236**	All rejected
Outlays: Military	−3.593*	−3.610*	0.102	Stationary
Outlays: Nonmilitary	−2.145	−1.913	0.334**	Unit root
Critical values: 5%	−3.432	−3.432	0.146	
1%	−4.004	−4.004	0.216	

Note: See table 2.3.

debt, see table 2.3). Unit roots in table 2.3 may simply reflect balanced growth without revealing much about fiscal policy.

Table 2.6 directly addresses the possibility that the time-series properties of real GDP might unduly influence the results in table 2.5. In table 2.6, the real variables are divided by a common exponential trend that captures average GDP growth for 1869–2003 (3.48 percent). The results are very similar to those of table 2.5, documenting that differences between real series and GDP ratios arise largely from reduced heteroskedasticity and are not induced by the time-series properties of GDP.

Taking logs is a common device to remove growth in the variances of strictly positive variables (e.g., debt, revenues, and outlays, but not deficits). Logarithms are not economically insightful here, however, because taking logs magnifies a series' fluctuations near zero, whereas sustainability is primarily about how fiscal policy recovers from high values of debt and outlays. To illustrate this point, figure 2.4 displays logarithms of real U.S. debt and real GDP; the gap is the log debt-to-GDP ratio. Log debt is evidently dominated by the decline to near-zero debt in the 1830s and the subsequent return to more normal values, namely, by a period that is uninformative about sustainability. Both PP and KPSS tests for log real debt are insignificant (PP = −3.08, KPSS = 0.098), so log debt provides no better statistical insights than the GDP ratio.

Table 2.6
Unit root tests for detrended real series, 1792–2003 (scaled by common exponential trend for GDP)

Variable	PP(12)	ADF(4)	KPSS(12)	Verdict
Public debt	−2.770	−3.017	0.100	No rejection
Deficit, primary	−4.942**	−5.579**	0.049	Stationary
Deficit $(-s + r \cdot d)$	−5.702**	−6.135**	0.047	Stationary
Deficit *DEF/Y*	−4.943**	−5.568**	0.068	Stationary
Revenues total	−2.321	−2.251	0.295**	Unit root
Outlays: Noninterest	−3.916*	−4.074*	0.208*	All rejected
Outlays: Military	−3.661*	−3.877*	0.098	Stationary
Outlays: Nonmilitary	−2.227	−1.813	0.330**	Unit root
Critical values: 5%	−3.432	−3.432	0.146	
1%	−4.004	−4.004	0.216	

Note: See table 2.3. In contrast to table 2.3, all variables are divided by an exponential trend with growth rate 3.48 percent, the average growth rate of real log-GDP for 1869–2003.

Figure 2.4
Logarithms of real debt and real GDP

In summary, the econometric analysis yields three main conclusions. First, GDP ratios and similarly scaled series provide more credible information about the fiscal series than raw real data. Second, there is no convincing evidence that the relationship between debt and deficits involves a unit root. All the deficit-to-GDP ratios are unambiguously stationary, and stationarity cannot be rejected for debt-to-GDP ratio. The failure to reject a unit root for the debt-to-GDP ratio does not prove a unit root. Third, certain other GDP ratios have unit roots. Revenues/GDP and nonmilitary outlays/GDP are clearly nonstationary. Unit root tests for overall noninterest outlays are contradictory, but the nonstationarity of the nonmilitary component suggests that the series for noninterest outlays/GDP is best treated as nonstationary. Because the primary deficit/GDP is found to be stationary, one may conclude that revenues and outlays are cointegrated with vector $(1, -1)$.

2.5 Model-Based Sustainability

This section returns to the first conceptual question about sustainability: which fiscal policies are sustainable? The basic economic answer is that an agent's ability to borrow is constrained by other agents' willingness to lend. The question concerning which policies are sustainable is therefore a general equilibrium question, a question of who the government's potential lenders are and what determines their behavior. Different assumptions about lenders lead to different conclusions about the set of sustainable policies.

Constraints that superficially resemble the ad hoc TC and IBC are obtained if one assumes that potential lenders are infinitely lived optimizing agents and that financial markets are complete. Such agents' asset accumulation necessarily satisfies a transversality condition. Complete markets imply that agents apply a common pricing kernel to value financial assets, so the transversality conditions aggregate. Applied to government debt, the lenders' transversality condition is

$$\liminf_{n\to\infty} E_t[u_{t,n} \cdot d_{t+n}] \leq 0, \qquad \text{(General No Ponzi Cond.)} \qquad (2.10)$$

where $u_{t,n}$ is the economy's pricing kernel for contingent claims on period $t+n$ (see Bohn 1995).

A violation of this condition (a strictly positive liminf) would mean that some of the debt's initial value would never be repaid, thereby representing a Ponzi scheme. Rational lenders would not buy such debt. Condition (2.10) is therefore a constraint on policy, a No Ponzi Condition. While (2.10) does not rule out debt policies without a proper limit or policies that imply large surpluses leading to a negative limit, such "odd" policies would be distracting here. To limit the scope of analysis, it seems reasonable to assume that debt is non-negative and that the limit in (2.10) exists. Then (2.10) specializes to

$$\lim_{n\to\infty} E_t[u_{t,n} \cdot d_{t+n}] = 0. \qquad \text{(Simple No Ponzi Cond.)} \quad (2.11)$$

From (2.11), one obtains the intertemporal budget constraint

$$d_t^* = \sum_{n=0}^{\infty} E_t[u_{t,n} \cdot s_{t+n}], \qquad \text{(IBC)} \quad (2.12)$$

by combining the Euler equations

$$E_t\left[u_{t,n} \cdot \prod_{k=0}^{n-1}(1 + r_{t+k})\right] = 1 \quad \forall(t, n), \qquad (2.13)$$

with the debt dynamics in (2.5). Equations (2.10)–(2.13) apply to real variables, nominal variables, or GDP-shares if the $u_{t,n}$ is appropriately growth-adjusted.

The intertemporal budget constraint (2.12) and the No Ponzi (a.k.a. transversality) Condition (2.11) are, by construction, consistent with optimizing bondholder behavior. They differ from the ad hoc conditions (2.8)–(2.9) whenever the pricing kernel is stochastic; then (2.13) does not yield a scalar value for $u_{t,n}$ that could be used in (2.11)–(2.12).

These differences reflect an economic intuition that is fundamental for an understanding of budget constraints under uncertainty. The key point is the distinction between uncertainty about specific debt securities and uncertainty about the future path of total public debt. Because government bonds typically promise essentially safe returns, (2.13) implies relatively low interest rates. The debt d_{t+n} in a transversality condition, in contrast, is the outstanding debt in various states of nature. This includes debt issues resulting from budget deficits and any refinancing of debt along a particular sample path (as described in [2.5]). The resulting stock of debt can be quite variable and is often correlated with major sources of systematic risk—for example, output growth and military spending. The total debt in (2.11), the surpluses in (2.12), and the security returns in (2.13) follow very different stochastic processes. An important implication is that bond returns are unsuitable as discount rates—not just technically wrong, but also misleading about the economic interpretation of transversality conditions and IBCs.

The ramifications of the sustainability conditions (2.11)–(2.12) as compared with the ad hoc conditions (2.8)–(2.9) are best illustrated in examples.

Example 1 (Risk Neutrality): Suppose lenders are risk-neutral and have a constant rate of time preference $r = 1/\beta - 1$. Then the pricing kernel reduces to the deterministic discount factor $u_{t,n} = \beta^n = 1/(1+r)^n$ and (2.11)–(2.12) reduce to (2.8)–(2.9) with the time preference as discount rate. The time preference can be estimated from average returns because (2.12) implies $E[r_t] = r$.

The ad hoc conditions (2.8)–(2.9) can thus be interpreted as special cases of (2.11)–(2.12). Now consider stochastic pricing kernels.

Example 2 (Motivated by Ahmed and Rogers 1995): Suppose $u_{t,n} = \beta^n \cdot \mu(c_t/c_{t+n})$ is the product of a time-preference factor β^n and a marginal rate of substitution $\mu(c_t/c_{t+n})$ with $\mu' > 0$ (homothetic preferences with declining marginal utility). Suppose $E_t[\mu(c_t/c_{t+n})] = 1$ for all t; and suppose marginal rates of substitution have time-invariant conditional covariances with s_{t+n} in real terms, $\text{cov}_t(\mu(c_t/c_{t+n}), s_{t+n}) = \sigma_n \ \forall t$. Then $\beta^n = E_t[u_{t,n}] = 1/(1+r)^n$ can be interpreted as the safe discount factor and

$$E_t[u_{t,n} \cdot s_{t+n}] = E_t[u_{t,n}] \cdot E_t[s_{t+n}] + \beta^n \cdot \sigma_n = (E_t[s_{t+n}] + \sigma_n)/(1+r)^n$$

is an expected value plus a covariance term. If $\sigma = \sum_{n \geq 0} \beta^n \sigma_n$ is finite (e.g., for bounded σ_n and $\beta < 1$), (2.12) reduces to

$$d_t^* = \sum_{n=0}^{\infty} \frac{1}{(1+r)^n} \cdot E_t[s_{t+n}] + \sigma, \tag{2.8*}$$

which is equivalent to (2.8) plus a constant.

Example 2 demonstrates why the ad hoc constraint (2.8) does not provide credible information about sustainability. If (2.8*) is satisfied with nonzero σ, a researcher "testing" (2.8) would naturally conclude that public debt includes a "bubble" of size σ. Conversely, finding (2.8) satisfied or violated in empirical data provides no information about

(2.12) unless one can reliably estimate the covariances between surpluses and discount factors.

Example 2 is motivated by Ahmed and Rogers (1995), who examine sustainability in a setting similar to example 2—namely, with constant $\text{cov}_t(u_{t,n}, s_{t+n})$ for all t and n. Ahmed and Rogers argue that a stationary real with-interest deficit is necessary and sufficient for (2.12), which would make stationarity restrictions important. Example 2 serves to demonstrate the opposite, however. Following Ahmed and Rogers's necessity proof, it is straightforward to show that both (2.8) and (2.8*) imply a stationary with-interest deficit. (The constant term in [2.8*] does not affect unit root considerations.) Ahmed and Rogers's sufficiency proof imposes various auxiliary assumptions on the stochastic process for debt. Example 2 suggests that these assumptions are unduly restrictive.[7] Because stationarity conditions are uninformative about covariance terms, they are not useful for testing model-based conditions like (2.11)–(2.12).

Note that (2.8*) does not restrict debt management; namely, it allows bonds with stochastic real returns. If bond returns are correlated with $\mu(c_t/c_{t+n})$, they include risk premiums and cannot serve as a proxy for r in (2.8*). This illustrates the general intuition that risk premiums in bond returns (in [2.13]) are unrelated to risk premiums associated with uncertain future surpluses (in [2.12], here σ_n).

To what extent are differences between (2.8) and (2.8*) quantitatively important? Recall from table 2.1 that U.S. primary deficits were positive on average for 1792–2003. If the deficit process is ergodic, one must conclude that U.S. primary surpluses have a negative unconditional expectation, making a zero or negative contribution to the right-hand side of (2.8*). Table 2.1 suggests therefore that U.S. public debt is backed entirely by the covariance components in (2.8*) and (2.12). The next example provides an interpretation.

Example 3 (Stochastic Growth, adapted from Bohn 1995): For the same pricing kernel as in example 2, suppose consumption and government outlays are fixed fractions of GDP ($c_t/Y_t = \bar{c}$, $G_t/Y_t = \bar{G}$), real GDP growth γ_t is i.i.d. with mean γ, public debt consists of safe securities with return r, tax revenues vary with output growth to maintain a constant end-of-period debt-to-GDP ratio $d_t/Y_t = \bar{d}$. Assume zero inflation to avoid nominal/real distinctions.

A constant debt-to-GDP ratio requires real primary surpluses that are negatively correlated with GDP growth,

$$s_{t+n} = T_{t+n} - \bar{G} \cdot Y_{t+n} = (1+r) \cdot d_{t+n-1} - \bar{d} \cdot Y_{t+n}$$
$$= \bar{d}Y_{t+n-1} \cdot (1 + r - \gamma_{t+n}). \tag{2.14}$$

Because $\mu(c_{t+n-1}/c_{t+n}) = \mu[1/(1+\gamma_{t+n})]$ and s_{t+n} are both decreasing in γ_{t+n}, this policy features a positive covariance between the pricing kernel and the primary surplus. More specifically, real debt in the No Ponzi Condition must be discounted at the discount rate on GDP-indexed claims,

$$E_t[u_{t,n} \cdot d_{t+n}] = \bar{d} \cdot E_t[u_{t,n} \cdot Y_{t+n}] = \bar{d}\frac{(1+\gamma)^n}{(1+R)^n} Y_t = \frac{(1+\gamma)^n}{(1+R)^n} d_t,$$

where $1/(1+R) \equiv E_t[u_{t,1} \cdot (1+\gamma_{t+1})]/(1+\gamma)$. Dynamic efficiency implies $R > \gamma$ and ensures that discounted real debt converges to zero, demonstrating that a policy with constant debt-to-GDP ratio satisfies (2.11)–(2.12).

Nothing in the preceding argument depends on the relationship between growth rates and the interest rate r. Because $u_{t,1}$ and γ_{t+1} are negatively correlated, the safe rate is unambiguously below the discount rate on GDP-indexed claims, $r < R$, and it may be below γ. If $E[(1+r)/(1+\gamma_t)] < 1$, then $E_t[s_{t+n}] < 0$ for all (t, n). Despite negative expected surpluses, the policy is sustainable.

The motivation for example 3 is that debt-to-GDP and surplus-to-GDP ratios are stationary in economies that display balanced growth. At long horizons, debts and surpluses must therefore include about as much systematic risk as GDP, and will therefore be discounted like GDP-indexed claims. The example makes the link between debt and GDP instantaneous.

In relation to example 2 and to Ahmed and Rogers 1995, note that example 3 exhibits a positive covariance between primary deficit and pricing kernel, matching the assumptions of example 2. But (2.8*) is not well defined for $E[(1+r)/(1+\gamma_t)] < 1$ because the surplus term in (2.8*) diverges to minus infinity whereas the covariance term diverges to plus infinity. This demonstrates the importance of risk premiums and the distinction between the discount rate on total debt (R) and the return on specific bonds (r). $E[(1+r)/(1+\gamma_t)] < 1$ essentially requires a safe interest rate below the average growth rate (apart from a Jensen's inequality term). Table 2.2 indicates that U.S. data satisfy this condition, suggesting that risk adjustments are practically important.

Example 3 also illustrates the interaction between debt management and primary surpluses. In the example, the safety of government bonds is so highly valued that the government can run negative surpluses on average, provided it promises positive payouts in "bad" states of nature, meaning states where the ex post realization of GDP growth is low enough such that $(1+r)/(1+\gamma_t) > 1$. If the government were to issue, say, GDP-indexed bonds instead, example 3 would require positive primary surpluses on average, with less variation across states of nature. Or, if risk aversion were to become smaller, government bonds would have higher yields and policy (2.14) would require higher surpluses. These considerations suggest that to determine the complete set of sustainable government policies (necessary and sufficient), one would have to specify fiscal policy in a complete way, including a specification of debt management and of state-contingent variations in primary surpluses; and the results would rely critically on asset pricing assumptions.

Unfortunately, finance theory does not provide an empirically successful model for discounting safe and risky payment streams. The leading asset pricing theory—consumption CAPM (capital asset pricing model) is a dismal failure when it comes to explaining empirical risk premiums (Mehra and Prescott 1985). An empirically credible, complete characterization of sustainable policies is therefore an impossible task. A more promising agenda is to strive for sufficient conditions that are robust with respect to asset pricing and debt management.

Finally, note that this section's critique of (2.8)–(2.9) also applies to more general ad hoc conditions—for example, the discounted-debt conditions in Wilcox 1989 and Uctum and Wickens 2000. Wilcox and Uctum and Wickens use bond returns to define discount factors $\delta_{t,n} = 1/[\sum_{k=1}^{n}(1+r_{t+k})]$ and show that an IBC-type condition $d_t^* = \sum_{j=0}^{\infty} E_t[\delta_{t,j}s_{t+j}]$ holds if and only if $\lim_{n\to\infty} E_t[\delta_{t,n}d_{t+n}] = 0$. Like (2.8)–(2.9), these conditions have economic content only by the assertion that a zero limit on debt discounted by $\delta_{t,n}$ represents the bondholders' transversality condition. However, discounting by $\delta_{t,n}$ is generally inconsistent with conditions (2.11) and (2.13).[8] The use of bond-linked discount factors like $\delta_{t,n}$ is also unfortunate because it reinforces the flawed economic intuition that confuses uncertainty about future indebtedness with uncertainty about the returns on debt securities. As noted earlier and as highlighted in the examples, the relevant uncertainty in the transversality condition is about the level of future debt and not about the riskiness of particular debt securities.

2.6 Testing Model-Based Sustainability

The second main question about sustainability is how to test whether an observed policy is on a trajectory consistent with (2.11)–(2.12).

Because testing requires a well-defined alternative hypothesis, the first follow-up question is how to think about policies that violate (2.10)–(2.12). There are at least three relevant interpretations. First, fiscal policy may operate in an economy where (2.10) does not apply. In an overlapping generations (OG) economy, for example, lenders have finite planning horizons and do not impose transversality conditions. If interest rates are sufficiently low, reasonable policies will not satisfy (2.10)–(2.12). These conditions may also be inapplicable in economies with incomplete markets where liquidity arguments enter into the pricing of government bonds. Bohn (1999) provides an example where government bonds have lower transactions costs than private loans; for low levels of public debt, the government bond rate is below the GDP growth rate, leading to a violation of (2.10) in a dynamically efficient economy with rational, infinitely lived agents. It is therefore an empirical question as to whether (2.10) is a constraint on government policy.

Second, fiscal policy may be constrained by (2.10), but a continuation of the policy observed during the sample period would violate (2.11) in the direction of too low surpluses. This may be called an empirical violation of the sustainability conditions, or more succinctly, a nonsustainable policy. If rational investors nonetheless buy government bonds, they must be expecting a policy shift that will support the debt. An empirical violation of sustainability can therefore be interpreted as signaling a policy shift. The shift may be an increase in taxes, a reduction in outlays, or—because revenues include transfers from the Federal Reserve—an increased reliance on seigniorage.[9]

Third, an empirical violation of (2.10)–(2.11) in the direction of too low surpluses may signal that the government will eventually default on its debt. If government bonds are traded, this scenario raises questions about the rationality of investor expectations. Rational investors should never buy the public debt at a price above the right-hand side of (2.12), and they should never buy new government bonds, or refinance maturing ones, unless the government provides credible assurances that (2.10) is satisfied.[10] Though default considerations may explain minor violations of (2.12) if debt is measured at face value, a scenario that requires irrational investors seems implausible. In summary, empirical violations of sustainability are best interpreted as indicating either a future shift in policy or an economic environment in which policy is not constrained by (2.10).

Turning to the search for robust sustainability conditions, a key insight is that the Euler equations (2.13) apply in any economy with a well-defined pricing kernel. Combining them with (2.11) and (2.5), one can see that a fiscal policy of *zero* primary surpluses always yields a limiting value of debt equal to initial debt. That is, if $s_{t+k} \equiv 0 \ \forall k$, then $\lim_{n\to\infty} E_t[u_{t,n} \cdot d_{t+n}] = d_t^*$. The key point here is not that a Ponzi scheme violates the No Ponzi Condition—a reassuring fact—but that the limit value can be computed even if one does not know the true pricing kernel or how to discount specific stochastic claims. Because the Euler equations apply to all financial assets, including government liabilities of any type—long-term and short-term, nominal and inflation-indexed—they impose no restrictions on debt management. Using the Ponzi scheme limit as a reference point, analogous reasoning helps prove the sustainability of policies with systematically less debt accumulation.

A second key insight is that robustness with respect to debt management requires a feedback rule for the primary surplus—a rule that makes surpluses a function of initial debt. To see this, suppose primary surpluses were unresponsive to initial debt and consider a slight variation in debt management. If the policy was sustainable before, a change in debt management that increases the return on debt in one state of nature and reduces the return in another state (respecting the Euler equation) will raise initial debt in the high return state. Without a policy response, the extra debt would be unbacked by future surpluses, thus violating the No Ponzi Condition.

The most simple feedback rule that ensures sustainability is a linear one:

PROPOSITION 1 (BOHN 1991a, 1998): Suppose the primary deficit-to-GDP ratio is an increasing linear function of the initial debt-to-GDP ratio

$$s_t = \rho \cdot d_t^* + \mu_t \tag{2.15}$$

for all t, where $\rho > 0$ is a constant and μ_t is a composite of other determinants. If μ_t is bounded as a share of GDP and if the present value of GDP is finite, then fiscal policy satisfies (2.11)–(2.12).

Proposition 1 suggests that sustainability can be tested by estimating a policy rule (or reaction function) for the primary surplus/GDP. The idea of the proof is that debt growth is reduced by $(1-\rho)$ relative to a Ponzi scheme, reducing the n-period ahead debt by about a factor $(1-\rho)^n$. For any (small) $\rho > 0$, this implies $E_t[u_{t,n} \cdot d_{t+n}] \approx (1-\rho)^n \cdot d_t^* \to 0$; the μ_t part turns out to be asymptotically irrelevant.[11]

The assumptions of proposition 1 can be weakened in various ways, for example by allowing for nonlinearity and for time-varying coefficients. A nonlinear feedback rule ensures sustainability if the slope is bounded away from zero at high debt-to-GDP ratios. That is, if there is a finite value $\hat{d}$ and a function $f(d)$ such that $f(d) \geq \rho \cdot (d - \hat{d})\ \forall d \geq \hat{d}$, then the policy rule $s_t = \rho \cdot f(d_t^*) + \mu_t$ is also sustainable (Bohn 1998). A time-varying policy rule $s_t = \rho_t \cdot d_t^* + \mu_t$ ensures sustainability if $\rho_t \geq 0\ \forall t$ and if $\rho_t > 0$ applies infinitely often (Canzoneri, Cumby, and Diba 2001). Nonlinearities and time variation may, however, raise questions about the stability of policy and hence about the plausibility of extrapolating it into the future. Proposition 1 can also be strengthened by excluding seigniorage from s_t, to ensure that sustainability is not attained through monetization.

Some conceptual points about policy functions should be noted before turning to estimating equation (2.15):

Policy functions implicitly assume stationarity and ergodicity. Stationarity is commonly assumed in applied economies, but it is unusually important here because sustainability can only be evaluated by extrapolating current policies into the indefinite future. In practical terms, the entire history of U.S. fiscal policy displays no more than three to five big movements in the debt-to-GDP ratio, suggesting that even decades of data are potentially unrepresentative or dominated by a single event. For this reason, my estimates below are based on the longest available sample, 1792–2003.

Ergodicity is critical because one only observes a single realization of history from which one must infer how policy responds to disturbances and how it would respond under various contingencies. This may be impossible. A nonlinear rule may, for example, show no evidence of a feedback from debt primary surpluses if debt happens to be below $\hat{d}$ throughout the sample; or in the case of a time-varying rule, all the within-sample ρ_t-values may equal zero. The ergodicity problem reinforces the notion that proposition 1 is sufficient but not necessary. A stable, positive feedback from debt to surplus would justify calling fiscal policy sustainable, whereas a missing or seemingly unstable feedback would be consistent with either a nonsustainable policy or with a data set insufficient for identification. The implicit stationarity and ergodicity assumptions apply analogously to unit root, cointegration, and VAR-based tests. They seem unavoidable because sustainability constraints are inherently forward-looking.

Policy functions raise unit root issues. First, if the debt-to-GDP ratio in (2.15) had a unit root and μ_t was stationary, $\rho > 0$ would imply cointegration between debt and primary surplus. Equation (2.15) would then satisfy Trehan and Walsh's sustainability conditions. Table 2.5 indicates a stationary primary surplus, however, ruling out the case of cointegration. Second, a stationary primary surplus/GDP combined with a unit root in debt might be considered evidence against $\rho > 0$. It is therefore important that there is no credible evidence for a unit root in U.S. debt/GDP. Third, unit roots require attention because their (alleged) presence can serve as a convenient excuse to leave out stationary regressors—here, to avoid modeling μ_t. But because the debt-surplus linkage seems to involve stationary variables, one cannot ignore μ_t without creating omitted variables problems.

Policy functions like (2.15) are of interest even in economies where (2.11)–(2.12) do not apply. My intuition for such economies is that lack of convergence in (2.10)–(2.12) signals an inefficiently low level of public debt. This intuition clearly applies to dynamically inefficient OG economies. Higher public debt would raise interest rates and increase welfare. In such economies, if public debt has declined because of some disturbance, a positive response of surpluses (as in [2.15]) would help restore a higher, more efficient level of debt. The same intuition applies to models with transactions cost where public debt is prized for its liquidity (e.g., Bohn 1999). If the public's demand for liquidity is so high that the government can run Ponzi schemes at low levels of debt, an increase in public debt would be Pareto-improving. A positive response of surpluses to declines in debt should again help avoid an inefficiently low public debt.

Policy functions are of interest in economies where fiscal policy is subject to additional, more stringent constraints than (2.10)–(2.12). Additional constraints may apply, for example, because the government has a limited ability to tax, or because of other practical or political-economy reasons. A feedback rule like (2.15) is promising in this context because it naturally stabilizes the debt-to-GDP ratio. If μ_t and r_{t+1}

are stationary, the debt-to-GDP ratio will fluctuate around a mean of $E[d_t^*] \approx -\bar{\mu}/[\rho - \bar{r}(1-\rho)]$. The feedback rule is thus not inconsistent with additional constraints that imply upper bounds on debt.[12]

2.7 Estimating the Determinants of the Primary Surplus

This section estimates policy functions for 1792–2003 U.S. data. The approach is similar to that of Bohn (1998) but applied to a longer data set. Guidance for the regression specification is obtained from tax-smoothing theories of optimal taxation. Tax smoothing suggests that temporary government outlays and temporary declines in income (i.e., in the tax base) trigger higher than normal budget deficits. This suggests an empirical specification for the primary surplus of the form

$$s_t = \rho \cdot d_t^* + \beta_0 + \beta_g \cdot \tilde{g}_t + \beta_y \cdot \tilde{y}_t + \varepsilon_t, \tag{2.16}$$

where $\tilde{g}_t$ is a measure of temporary outlays, $\tilde{y}_t$ measures temporary output, ε_t is a mean-zero error term, and $(\rho, \beta_0, \beta_g, \beta_y)$ are regression coefficients.

Finding empirical proxies for $\tilde{y}_t$ and $\tilde{g}_t$ for a long sample is a challenge, but important in order to identify the marginal effect of public debt. Individuals living at the time presumably had better information about business-cycle conditions than a researcher can obtain from historical data. For economic fluctuations, I simply assume that individuals were able to distinguish trends from cycles in real time as well as an economist can do so looking back, using an HP filter to extract the trend component of log real GDP. The gap between actual value and trend is taken as a proxy for $\tilde{y}_t$ (with positive values indicating above-trend output). Fluctuations in government outlays are dominated by wartime military spending. Because an HP-filter would impute an implausible degree of foresight about the start, end, and intensity of wars, the permanent component of military outlays/GDP is computed from an estimated AR(2) process.[13] Nonmilitary outlays are well approximated by a random walk; namely, they have no significant temporary component. The difference between actual and estimated permanent military outlays is used as a proxy for $\tilde{g}_t$.

Table 2.7 presents the main policy function estimate in column (1) and several alternatives in columns (2)–(5). All estimates are OLS. To account for heteroskedasticity and autocorrelation in residuals, both ordinary and robust t-statistics are shown (both in brackets).[14] Column

Table 2.7
Determinants of the primary surplus/GDP, 1793–2003 (dependent variable: s_t as percent of GDP)

Model:	Main model (1)	With debt squared (2)	With time trend (3)	With AR(1) for outlays (4)	Surplus excluding seigniorage (5)
Initial debt d_t^*	0.121 (11.3; 5.7)	0.094 (11.6; 4.7)	0.116 (10.1; 5.5)	0.117 (11.3; 5.7)	0.119 (11.3; 5.6)
Constant	−0.030 (−10.6; −5.6)	−0.030 (−10.4; −5.8)	−0.033 (−8.7; −5.4)	0.0003 (0.1; 0.1)	−0.031 (−10.9; −5.8)
Temporary output $\tilde{y}_t$	0.088 (2.2; 1.1)	0.087 (2.1; 1.1)	0.091 (2.2; 1.2)	0.085 (2.1; 1.1)	0.090 (2.2; 1.2)
Temporary outlays $\tilde{g}_t$	−0.815 (−19.6; −7.0)	−0.817 (−19.6; −7.0)	−0.823 (−19.5; −7.2)	−0.742 (−20.0; −7.2)	−0.818 (−19.9; −7.2)
Squared debt $(d_t^* - \bar{d})^2$		0.020 (0.8; 0.5)			
Time trend			$3 * 10^{-5}$ (1.0; 0.8)		
R-squared	0.689	0.691	0.691	0.690	0.697
DW	0.39	0.39	0.39	0.37	0.40

Notes: Estimates of equation (2.16). Entries are coefficient estimates. Entries in parentheses are the ordinary t-statistics and robust t-statistics, respectively. The robust t-statistics recognize the autocorrelation in residuals by allowing for two leads/lags in the autocovariance matrix. Temporary outlays are computed as the difference between actual military outlays and the permanent component implied by an AR(2) process; except column (4) uses actual military outlays as regressor, as explained in the text.

(1) displays estimates of specification (2.16). The coefficient on initial debt is significantly positive, as consistent with sustainability. The coefficients on temporary output and on temporary spending are positive and negative respectively, as consistent with tax smoothing. Taking sample means of the regressors, all five regressions imply a stationary debt-to-GDP ratio with a mean of around 25 percent, far below the historical peak of above 100 percent, suggesting a substantial margin of safety against unexpected shocks.

To examine robustness, column (2) adds the squared deviation of public debt from its mean to explore a potential nonlinearity in the surplus-to-debt relationship, finding no significant effect. Column (3) adds a time trend, also finding no significant effect. Column (4) replaces $\tilde{g}_t$ by actual military spending to document that the benchmark results are insensitive to alternative specifications for $\tilde{g}_t$. As motivation, note that for any Markov process, temporary and permanent components are linear in the current value. Hence column (4) yields consistent estimates for ρ for any Markov specification for military outlays. Column (5) replaces the primary surplus by the primary surplus excluding seigniorage (transfers from Federal Reserve to Treasury); the essentially unchanged coefficients document that the debt-to-surplus feedback is not due to monetization.

Quite different results are obtained if one omits proxies for $\tilde{y}_t$ and $\tilde{g}_t$. This is documented in table 2.8. Column (1) displays a VAR-style estimate of the surplus-debt relationship, in the spirit of Canzoneri, Cumby, and Diba (2001). Initial debt still has a positive impact on the surplus, but the impact is smaller and less significant. In column (2), which displays a simple bivariate regression, the coefficient on debt is near zero and insignificant. The small coefficients in columns (1)–(2) are suggestive of an omitted variables bias. To reinforce this point, column (3) returns to specification (2.16) but with the lagged primary surplus and lagged debt as additional regressors. Though the lagged surplus is significant, the estimates are similar to table 2.7 and the coefficient on debt is above 0.10.

An omitted variables problem may also explain the failure to reject a unit root for the debt-to-GDP ratio in table 2.5. If one includes $\tilde{y}_t$ and $\tilde{g}_t$ in an ADF-regression for the debt-to-GDP ratio (not tabulated), the t-statistic on lagged debt jumps to -4.0 in an otherwise identical specification (vs. -2.86 in table 2.5). The latter indicates significant mean reversion even at Dickey-Fuller critical values. The impact of $\tilde{y}_t$ and $\tilde{g}_t$ suggests omitted variables bias in the standard ADF regressions—not

Table 2.8
The implications of omitted variables (dependent variable: S_t as percent of GDP)

Model:	VAR style regression (1)	Bivariate regression (2)	Equation (16) and VAR-style regressors (3)
Initial debt d_t^*	0.028 (2.8; 2.5)	−0.018 (−1.3; −0.5)	0.104 (10.8; 4.5)
Lagged surplus s_{t-1}	0.957 (10.0; 3.0)		0.366 (4.2; 2.0)
Change in debt $d_t^* - d_{t-1}^*$	0.217 (2.3; 0.9)		−0.007 (−0.1; −0.05)
Constant	−0.007 (−2.3; −2.2)	0.001 (0.3; 0.2)	−0.026 (−9.8; −4.3)
Temporary output $\tilde{y}_t$			0.099 (2.8; 1.8)
Temporary outlays $\tilde{g}_t$			−0.600 (−12.9; −4.1)
R-squared	0.568	0.008	0.763
DW	1.71	0.54	1.04

Notes: Specifications as in table 2.7 unless noted. The VAR-style regressions show the change in debt $d_t^* - d_{t-1}^*$ as regressor instead of the lagged debt d_{t-1}^* to highlight the permanent effects of debt on surpluses and to avoid collinearity. If d_{t-1}^* were entered instead of $d_t^* - d_{t-1}^*$ in columns (1) and (3), neither would be individually significant, but the sum would be as significantly positive as the initial debt coefficients here.

under the unit root null, but under the alternative, leading to a lack of power.

All specifications with $\tilde{y}_t$ and $\tilde{g}_t$ yield estimates for ρ in the 0.10 to 0.12 range. This is substantially above my previous 1916–1995 estimates of about 0.05 (Bohn 1998). A closer examination of the time series suggests that the higher coefficients here are due to the interaction of public debt and military spending during the cold war era (narrowly defined, 1954–1964; more broadly, 1954–1989). Because twentieth-century samples are dominated by this period, the longer sample helps to put it in perspective.

The cold war era is important empirically because it displays both a major decline in the debt-to-GDP ratio—the key phenomenon for sustainability—and a persistently above-average level of military outlays. Military outlays exceeded 10 percent of GDP for 1951–64 and remained above 6 percent until 1989, far above the 4 percent sample mean. These persistently above-average outlays are in contrast to the quick declines in military outlays after previous wars.

In their classic articles on tax smoothing, Barro (1986a, b) and Sahasakul (1986) follow Barro's modeling (1981) of military outlays as nonstationary. Using 1932–1978 data, Barro (1981) regressed the first difference of military outlays on the casualty rate in major wars and on military capital. The implied series for permanent military outlays tracks actual outlays quite closely in the post-1953 period. That is, cold war military outlays are treated as permanent and not as temporary spending that might justify budget deficits. The above-average surpluses during 1955–64 are then interpreted as a modest response to a far-above-average debt-to-GDP ratio, consistent with $\rho \sim 0.05$.

In table 2.7, in contrast, temporary outlays are based on a stationary model for the military outlays-GDP ratio, as is consistent with the unit root tests in table 2.5.[15] The estimated mean reversion is fast enough that above-average outlays are interpreted as largely temporary. If interpreted as temporary, the high outlays during the cold war should have triggered below-average surpluses. Then the observed above-average surpluses can only be interpreted as a strong response to the high post–World War II debt-to-GDP ratios, consistent with $\rho \sim 0.12$.

Table 2.9 documents the implications of different measures for $\tilde{g}_t$. Column (1) uses Barro's measure for 1916–1995 (a sample limited by

Table 2.9
Alternative measures of temporary outlays (dependent variable: s_t as percent of GDP)

Model:	Barro's $\tilde{g}_t$ 1916–1995 (1)	AR(2) for $\tilde{g}_t$ 1916–2003 (2)	Spliced $\tilde{g}_t$ 1793–2003 (3)
Initial debt d_t^*	0.072 (5.8; 3.8)	0.147 (6.2; 3.8)	0.069 (11.7; 7.3)
Constant	−.032 (−6.3; 4.0)	−.041 (−4.8; −2.8)	−.027 (−15.2; −13.1)
Temporary output $\tilde{y}_t$	0.122 (2.5; 2.6)	0.120 (1.4; 1.0)	0.112 (4.2; 3.6)
Temporary outlays $\tilde{g}_t$	−0.875 (−19.6; −17.1)	−0.830 (−10.4; −5.2)	−0.900 (−33.7; −19.5)
R-squared	0.873	0.654	0.863
DW	1.45	0.34	1.25

Notes: Estimates of equation (2.16) in the text. Entries are coefficient estimates. Entries in parentheses are the ordinary t-statistics and robust t-statistics, respectively. Regressors are as in table 2.7. Column (1) uses Barro's GVAR variable (1986a) for temporary outlays, as updated in Bohn 1998. Column (2) uses the same specification as table 2.7, column (1), for a shorter estimation period. Column (3) combines Barro's (1986a) GVAR variable for 1916–1995 with the AR(2) estimate from table 2.7 for other years.

data availability). For comparison, column (2) displays results for my benchmark specification restricted to the same sample. The Barro-style specification yields a much smaller response to initial debt, $\rho \sim 7$ percent in column (1) versus $\rho \sim 14$ percent in column (2).

It is an open question as to whether the stationary representation or Barro's measure better represents public perceptions of cold war outlays. If the cold war was perceived as a regime switch, it may be appropriate to use different estimates for $\tilde{g}_t$ for different subsamples. In this spirit, column (3) uses Barro's $\tilde{g}_t$-measure for 1916–1995 and my AR(2) measure for all other years. This yields a full sample estimate for ρ of 6.9 percent. (Using Barro's measure for 1946–1965 only yields a similar value, 7.2 percent.)

Overall, reasonable estimates for the surplus-to-debt response range from 6.9 percent to 12.1 percent (using table 2.9, column 3 and table 2.7, column 1), depending on the interpretation of cold war spending. The cold war interpretation is just a quantitative issue, however. Sustainability is satisfied for either interpretation because all estimates for ρ are significantly positive.

2.8 Conclusions

The chapter examined the sustainability of U.S. fiscal policy, finding substantial evidence in favor. I first summarized the U.S. fiscal record from 1792–2003 and showed that growth effects had historically covered the entire interest cost of the U.S. debt. I then reviewed sustainability conditions based on expected-value budget constraints and provided a unified presentation of the implied unit root tests. I concluded that fiscal series not scaled by GDP were misleading in the context of unit root testing and that there was no credible evidence of a unit root in the U.S. debt-to-GDP and deficit-to-GDP ratios. The main evidence in favor of sustainability is the finding of a robust positive response of primary surpluses to variations in initial debt. The policy functions for primary surpluses are similar to those of Bohn (1998), but the longer 1793–2003 sample places less emphasis on World War II and on the cold war.

Notes

1. Public debt should not be confused with gross federal debt, which is sometimes discussed in the popular press. The latter far exceeds the public debt ($7,355 billion vs.

$4,296 billion as of September 2004) because it includes intragovernmental obligations to social security and other trust funds. Such internal transactions cancel out in the unified budget. I follow the sustainability literature and disregard the U.S. government's ownership of real and financial assets. This is in effect asking if U.S. policy is sustainable without asset sales. Otherwise, (2.2a) would have to be modified to equate the deficit to the change in government liabilities minus the change in assets. Treasury cash balances should also be deducted from public debt, but they are small enough to be ignored.

2. Column (1) uses the ratio of net interest outlays over public debt as a measure of interest rates. Because post-1930s data on net interest outlays are somewhat contaminated by interest income on U.S. financial assets, I have also calculated average interest rates as gross interest over gross debt. This yields a 4.66 percent average interest rate for 1916–2003 versus the 4.4 percent shown in table 2.2. Differences are even smaller for other sample periods.

3. Notable exceptions are Hamilton and Flavin 1986 and the discounted debt conditions in Wilcox 1989 and Uctum and Wickens 2000. Hamilton and Flavin (1986) test (2.9) directly against the alternative of a "speculative bubble" by regressing a time series of U.S. real debt against an exponential term of the order $(1+r)^n$ and examine the significance of the exponential; they find no bubble in U.S. debt for 1960–1984. Section 2.5 comments on Wilcox 1989 and Uctum and Wickens 2000.

4. To anticipate, this linkage is consistent with the policy reaction function examined later. Wickens and Uctum (1993) have derived similar linkages between external debt and the current account.

5. Conceptually equivalent unit root and cointegration tests may still yield different results because different methods are used to distinguish short- from long-run relationships in the data and because the equivalence is exact only if the return on debt is constant and if all variables are measured consistently. An examination of such subtle differences is beyond the scope of this paper and would distract from more important issues. See Bohn 1991b for cointegration results about U.S. fiscal policy.

6. The highly unequal variances imply that the OLS estimates underlying the unit root tests essentially disregard most of the sample—all but the most recent, most volatile observations. Phillips-Perron's heteroskedasticity correction is based on a small number of autocorrelations; its ability to correct for this trend type of heteroskedasticity is unclear.

7. Importantly, Ahmed and Rogers assume debt has an absolutely summable moving average (MA) representation, and they take differences of various infinite sums of innovations. In the setting of example 2, Ahmed and Rogers's constant covariance assumption would imply $\sigma = \infty$, suggesting that summability is a questionable assumption.

8. To document that $E_t[\delta_{t,n} d_{t+n}]$ differs from (2.11) and a zero limit is not a necessary condition for sustainability, consider the setting of example 3 where discounted debt (scaled by GDP as in Uctum and Wickens 2000) is $E_t[\delta_{t,n} d_{t+n}] = \bar{d} \cdot E_t[\delta_{t,n}] = \bar{d} \cdot (1+\gamma)^n/(1+r)^n$. It diverges to infinity whenever the interest rate lies below the average growth rate even though (2.11) holds.

9. See Bohn 1991b for tax and spending responses to deficits. See section 2.7 for evidence that monetization is unimportant. Note that a violation of (2.11)–(2.12) in the direction of too high surpluses is consistent with (2.10) and cannot be ruled out.

10. This point is neglected by the fiscal theory of the price level (FTPL). FTPL treats equations like (2.8) and (2.12) as equilibrium conditions rather than constraints (e.g., Cochrane

1998). FTPL unfortunately starts off with a preexisting nominal debt and disregards the conditions under which debt can be issued. Once a debt is outstanding, the government has obvious incentives to default, not only on nominal debt through inflation, but on any type of sovereign debt. The No Ponzi Condition (2.10) is precisely the commitment the government must make for rational lenders to buy government bonds; namely, it is a constraint at the time of debt issue. (Lack of commitment would mean that the government would have to balance its budget on a period-by-period basis.) By disputing this constraint, the FTPL implicitly allows the government to pursue time-inconsistent policies.

11. Proposition 1 is asserted in Bohn 1998. The formal statement and proof were placed in an unpublished appendix (now available at http//econ.ucsb.edu/~bohn) at the editors' request. Canzoneri, Cumby, and Diba (2001) present a remarkably similar sustainability proposition, equivalent to proposition 1 in all respects except that ρ is replaced by a time-varying coefficient (see section 2.7). Proposition 1 and its proof were first circulated in Bohn 1991a and presented at Georgetown University in January 1992.

12. Additional restrictions such as boundedness are not examined here because a rigorous analysis would require substantial elaboration that would distract from the chapter's focus on the IBC. See Blanchard 1984, Uctum and Wickens 2000, and Polito and Wickens 2005 for insightful analyses of shorter-run constraints on debt policy. A stationary debt-to-GDP ratio is not a necessary condition for the IBC because, as shown by McCallum (1984), the No Ponzi Condition can be satisfied by policies that let the debt-to-GDP ratio and the tax-to-GDP ratio increase exponentially at a rate just marginally below the discount rate.

13. The estimated AR(2) process is $g_t^{mil} = 0.59\% + 1.28g_{t-1}^{mil} - 0.43g_{t-2}^{mil}$ plus error term. The permanent component is computed with a discount rate of 2 percent.

14. The residuals display substantial heteroskedasticity associated with war periods and some autocorrelation. OLS results are reported because the wartime outliers are too idiosyncratic to be corrected convincingly by weighted least squares (WLS) or other standard methods. (I explored a variety of simple adjustments, e.g., various ways of downweighting the war years, AR corrections, and combinations thereof. The results were substantively similar to OLS; most important, ρ remained significantly positive.)

15. Apart from the stationarity issue, Barro's specification (1981) for military outlays becomes unworkable when applied to sample periods that include the civil war. Civil war casualties were so high that Barro's regression coefficients would predict negative outlays, or, if one constrained the coefficients to avoid negative values, casualty rates would become essentially irrelevant for all other periods.

References

Abel, A., N. G. Mankiw, L. Summers, and R. Zeckhauser. 1989. Assessing dynamic efficiency: Theory and evidence. *Review of Economic Studies* 56:1–20.

Ahmed, S., and J. Rogers. 1995. Government budget deficits and trade deficits: Are present value constraints satisfied in long-term data? *Journal of Monetary Economics* 36:351–374.

Barro, R. J. 1981. Output effects of government purchases. *Journal of Political Economy* 89:1086–1121.

Barro, R. J. 1986a. U.S. deficits since World War I. *Scandinavian Journal of Economics* 88:195–222.

Barro, R. J. 1986b. The behavior of United States deficits. In *The American Business Cycle: Continuity and Change*, ed. R. Gordon, 361–387. Chicago, Ill.: University of Chicago Press.

Beveridge, S., and C. Nelson. 1981. A new approach to decomposition of economic time series into permanent and transitory components with particular attention to measurement of the business cycle. *Journal of Monetary Economics* 7:151–174.

Blanchard, O. 1984. Current and anticipated deficits, interest rates and economic activity. *European Economic Review* 25:7–27.

Bohn, H. 1991a. Testing the sustainability of budget deficits in a stochastic economy. Mimeo., University of Pennsylvania.

Bohn, H. 1991b. Budget balance through revenue or spending adjustments? Some historical evidence for the United States. *Journal of Monetary Economics* 27:333–359.

Bohn, H. 1995. The sustainability of budget deficits in a stochastic economy. *Journal of Money, Credit, and Banking* 27:257–271.

Bohn, H. 1998. The behavior of U.S. public debt and deficits. *Quarterly Journal of Economics* 113:949–963.

Bohn, H. 1999. Fiscal policy and the Mehra-Prescott puzzle: On the welfare implications of budget deficits when real interest rates are low. *Journal of Money, Credit, and Banking* 31:1–13.

Canzoneri, M., R. Cumby, and B. Diba. 2001. Is the price level determined by the needs of fiscal solvency? *American Economic Review* 91:1221–1238.

Christiano, L., and M. Eichenbaum. 1990. Unit roots in real GNP: Do we know, and do we care? *Carnegie-Rochester Conference Series on Public Policy* 32:7–62.

Cochrane, J. 1998. A frictionless view of U.S. inflation. In *NBER Macroeconomics Annual*, ed. B. Bernanke and J. Rotemberg, 323–384. Cambridge, Mass.: MIT Press.

Hamilton, J. 1994. *Time Series Analysis.* Princeton: Princeton University Press.

Hamilton, J., and M. Flavin. 1986. On the limitations of government borrowing: A framework for empirical testing. *American Economic Review* 76:808–819.

Hansen, L., W. Roberds, and T. Sargent. 1991. Time series implications of present value budget balance and of martingale models of consumption and taxes. In *Rational Expectations Econometrics*, ed. L. Hansen and T. Sargent, 121–161. Boulder: Westview Press.

Kwiatkowski, D., P. Phillips, P. Schmidt, and Y. Shin. 1992. Testing the null hypothesis of stationarity against the alternative of a unit root. *Journal of Econometrics* 54:159–178.

McCallum, B. 1984. Are bond-financed deficits inflationary? A Ricardian analysis. *Journal of Political Economy* 92:125–135.

Mehra, R., and E. Prescott. 1985. The equity-premium: A puzzle. *Journal of Monetary Economics* 15:145–162.

Polito, V., and M. Wickens. 2005. Measuring fiscal sustainability. Mimeo., University of York.

Sahasakul, C. 1986. The U.S. evidence of optimal taxation over time. *Journal of Monetary Economics* 18:251–275.

Trehan, B., and C. Walsh. 1988. Common trends, the government budget constraint, and revenue smoothing. *Journal of Economic Dynamics and Control* 12:425–444.

Trehan, B., and C. Walsh. 1991. Testing intertemporal budget constraints: Theory and applications to U.S. federal budget and current account deficits. *Journal of Money, Credit and Banking* 23:210–223.

Uctum, M., and M. Wickens. 2000. Debt and deficit ceilings, and sustainability of fiscal policy: An intertemporal analysis. *Oxford Bulletin of Economics and Statistics* 62:197–222.

Wickens, M., and M. Uctum. 1993. The sustainability of current account deficits. *Journal of Economic Dynamics and Control* 17:423–441.

Wilcox, D. W. 1989. The sustainability of government deficit: Implications of the present-value borrowing constraint. *Journal of Money, Credit, and Banking* 21:291–306.

3 Sustainability and Determinants of Italian Public Deficits before and after Maastricht

Emma Galli and Fabio Padovano

3.1 Introduction

Article 1 of the Italian Constitution reads: "Italy is a Democratic Republic based on labor." A more accurate description of the country's fiscal history would be: "Italy is a Democratic Republic based on public debt." In its 145-year history since unification, Italy has experienced only thirty years during which its debt-to-GDP ratio remained below the 60 percent threshold. In 1861, one of the first policy decisions of the newly enacted Kingdom of Italy was to endorse the public debt of the preunitary states. The kingdom thus began its financial life with a debt-to-GDP ratio that had already soared above 100 percent by 1871 and kept fluctuating within the 100–150 percent range until World War I. At the beginning of the Fascist regime (1922) the ratio was 128 percent, touching a minimum of 80 percent in 1928, only to grow again to a hefty 122 percent in 1938, the last nonwar year. In 1948, when the Republican Constitution was promulgated, public debt was only 39 percent of GDP, mainly because of the hyperinflation that characterized the aftermath of World War I, and remained below 60 percent until 1974. Following that, debt continuously rose more rapidly than GDP, attaining the one-to-one ratio again in 1990 and reaching a maximum of 126 percent in 1994. The Maastricht Treaty brought some fiscal discipline afterward, but the one-to-one ratio has yet to be broken through.[1]

Such a tormented financial history, together with the international obligations that Italy endorsed by signing the Maastricht Treaty, calls for a verification of the sustainability of Italian public finances. This chapter thus first performs a Trehan and Walsh sustainability test (1988, 1991) of Italian public finances in the post–World War II period. These tests, however, can only indicate the presence, or the absence, of "forces" that eventually reestablish the long-run equilibrium in the fiscal choices of a country; they cannot identify what factors ultimately cause the dynamics and sustainability of the fiscal policies. Hence, this chapter analyzes the determinants of the evolution of Italian public deficits to point out which are the most relevant. The theoretical literature provides several alternative explanations as to why individuals prefer debt to taxes when financing public expenditures and, as is usually the case for general theories, leaves specification of the appropriate dynamics of the relationship to empirical analysis. Moreover, the remarkable cross-country differences in debt accumulation show that certain explanations are most relevant for some countries and less for others, and that different countries react to changes in the determinants of debt creation at a different speed.

We estimate a cointegration-error correction model of the determinants of Italian public deficits in the post–World War II period. This estimating technique has three advantages: first, it collapses the variables relevant to the alternative theories into a single equation, thereby making it possible to assess which theory, or theories, carries the greatest explanatory power in the given sample. Second, the evaluation of the appropriate dynamic specification of the cointegration-error correction is based on the same nonstationarity analysis of the Trehan and Walsh test (1988, 1991) for sustainability. Third, the estimation of this model on two sample periods, a "pre-Maastricht" (1950–1990) and a "post-Maastricht" (1950–2002) one, offers preliminary evidence of whether the constraints imposed by the Maastricht Treaty affected both the deficit level and its determinants. Our previous research (Galli and Padovano 2002, 2004) indicates that 1991, the year the Maastricht Treaty was signed, is a major breakpoint in the data. A series of Chow forecast tests (available upon request) reveals that the null hypothesis of no structural change in the series is rejected for seven consecutive years in the 1988–1994 time interval.[2] A CUSUM of squares test yields similar results, as it suggests parameter or variance instability for a somewhat longer time interval (1981–1998). Because 1991 lies in the middle of both these intervals and there is the a priori of the Maastricht Treaty to suggest the choice of that year as the structural breakpoint, we elect to estimate the cointegration-error correction model in a pre-Maastricht and a post-Maastricht sample.

The preliminary evidence thus obtained is used in the third step of the analysis as the basis for the specification of a "dummy variable" model that takes advantage of identifying the most relevant determinants of debt creation in Italy. Specifically the "dummy variable" model disaggregates the multivariate qualitative variables used in the cointegration-error correction into a series of dummies to refine our understanding of how institutional changes have affected the dynamics of the deficit in Italy.

There are two main conclusions to these analyses. First, and predictably, in the period under consideration Italian public finances fail the sustainability tests. Second, compared to the pre-1991 period, debt creation has become much more sensitive to external constraints, chiefly the numerical rules imposed by the Maastricht Treaty itself, and to institutional factors, such as the budget approbation rules and the relative political power of the Minister of the Economy over the spending ministers. Other economic and political factors seem to play a less important role.

The rest of the chapter is organized as follows. Section 3.2 illustrates the evolution of the fiscal variables in the sample period under investigation, 1950–2002, presents the test of the sustainability of these variables and discusses the results. In section 3.3 we turn to the analysis of the determinants of fiscal policy variables in Italy, chiefly public deficit, with section 3.4 surveying the competing theories of debt creation to be tested and compared. Section 3.5 describes the specification of the cointegration-error correction model and discusses the results emerged from the estimates on the pre-Maastricht sample (1950–1990) and the post-Maastricht (1950–2002) one. In section 3.6 we highlight the main changes in the determinants of Italian public deficit that emerged from the estimation of the error correction model on the two samples and estimate the "dummy variable" model. Section 3.7 summarizes the main findings of the analysis and offers some considerations for (institutional) policy.

3.2 Evolution and Sustainability of Fiscal Variables

Figures 3.1 and 3.2 illustrate the evolution of the GDP ratios of the main fiscal indicators (total and primary surplus, public debt and total interest outlays), while figure 3.3 shows that of the public expenditures and revenues of the general government in real terms from 1951 to 2003. All variables appear stable at moderate levels until the early 1960s; the mid-1960s marked the beginning of a period of increasing fiscal imbalances that tapered off around 1994, as the deadline for joining the European Monetary Union (May 1997) approached. A

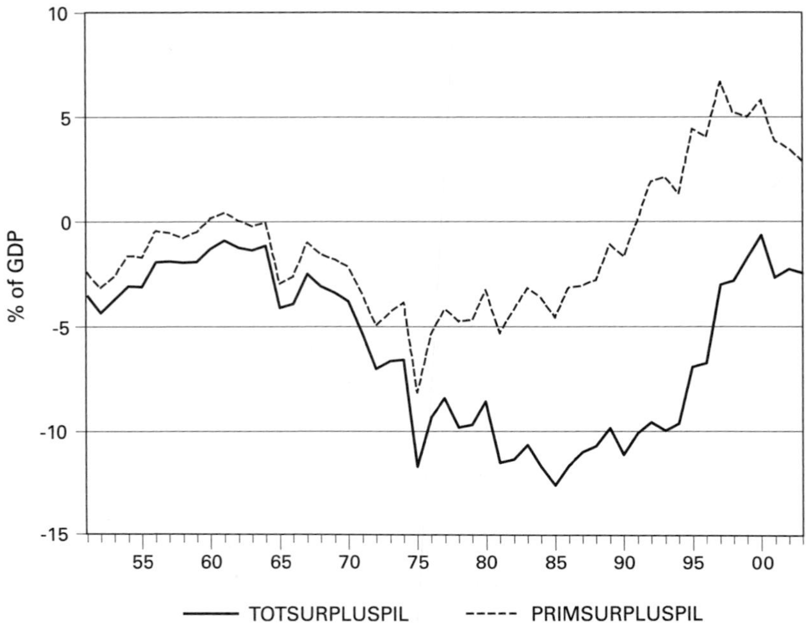

Figure 3.1
Total and primary surplus (1951–2003)

comparison of figure 3.3 with figures 3.1 and 3.2 (as well as a comparison of the original series) shows that fiscal disequilibria are not the product of the dynamics of GDP. If anything, the nominal debt is greater than the real debt and its GDP ratio, since the 1970s and 1980s saw increasing and high levels of inflation, while in the 1990s and 2000s inflation steadily declined and is now below the EU average. The evolution of Italian public finances thus provides quite an interesting sample for sustainability analysis.

To this end, we follow the methodology developed by Trehan and Walsh (1988, 1991) and described by Bohn (chapter 2), which is based on the idea of "ad hoc sustainability." This approach assesses the sustainability of a particular fiscal policy by verifying whether it is on a trajectory path such that the expected present value of future primary surpluses equals the initial debt. Examining the unit roots and/or cointegration properties of fiscal data can test satisfaction of the intertemporal budget constraint implied by this condition. In particular, Trehan and Walsh (1988) show that if real revenues, real public expen-

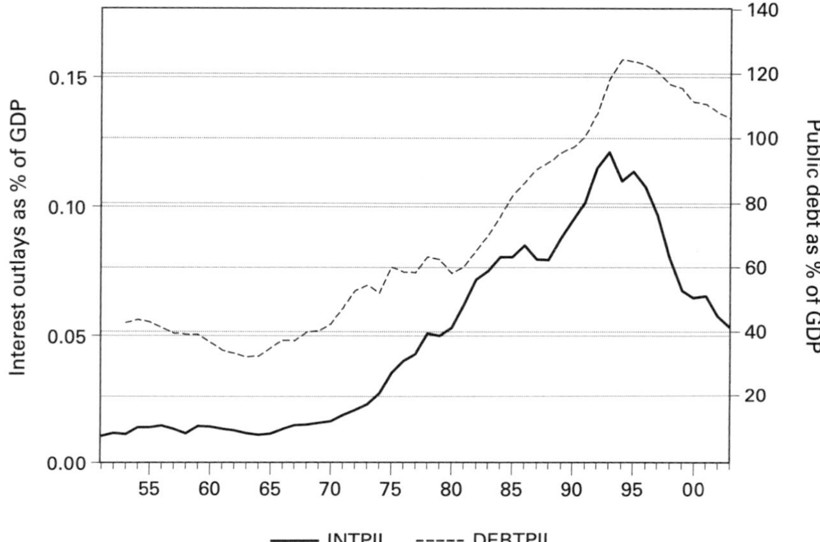

Figure 3.2
Public debt and interest outlays (1951–2003)

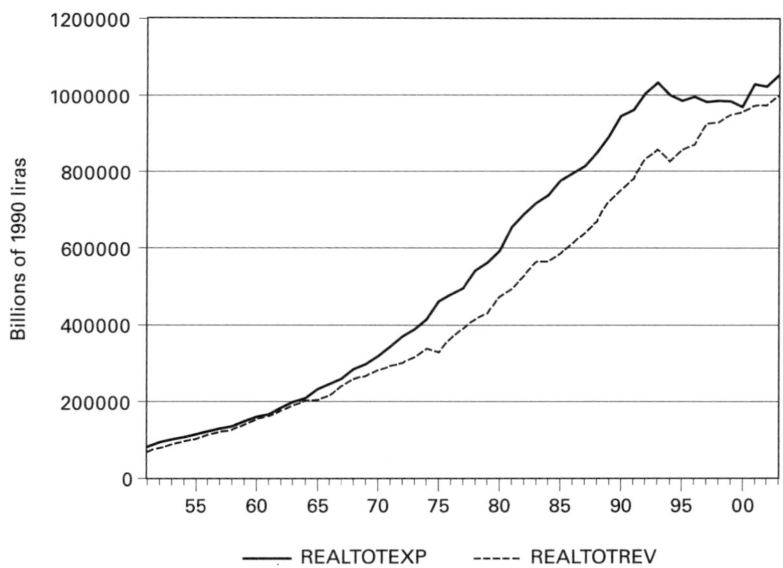

Figure 3.3
Real total expenditures and revenues: General government (1951–2003)

Table 3.1
Unit root tests for real fiscal variables

Sample period:	1951–2002				1951–1975				1976–2003			
Variable	ADF	PP	KPSS	Verdict	ADF	PP	KPSS	Verdict	ADF	PP	KPSS	Verdict
Public debt	−2.478**	−1.708**	2.5020**	Unit root	0.213**	−0.440**	1.1188**	Unit root	−1.892**	−0.757**	1.3902**	Unit root
Primary surplus	−2.442**	−1.543**	0.9566**	Unit root	1.236**	3.219**	0.9185**	Unit root	−1.608**	−1.933**	1.2689**	Unit root
Total surplus	−2.263**	−0.954**	1.3504**	Unit root	2.141**	3.065**	0.9506**	Unit root	−1.116**	−1.357**	0.7278*	Unit root
Total revenues	−2.074**	−2.045**	2.5945**	Unit root	−2.308**	−2.303**	1.2836**	Unit root	−1.085**	−1.349**	1.4223**	Unit root
Total outlays	−2.513**	−2.011**	2.6218**	Unit root	1.739**	3.499*	1.2406**	Unit root	−0.738**	−0.870**	1.3038**	Unit root
Noninterest outlays	−2.724**	−2.293**	2.6394**	Unit root	−0.690**	1.929**	1.2533**	Unit root	−1.397**	−1.638**	1.3617**	Unit root
Interest outlays	−2.153**	−1.575**	2.3114**	Unit root	3.106**	7.145	0.9703**	Conflict	−0.290	0.023	0.7881**	Unit root
Critical values 1%	−4.158	−4.142	0.463		−4.158	−4.394	0.463		−4.322	−4.394	0.463	
Critical values 5%	−3.504	−3.496	0.739		−3.659	−3.612	0.739		−3.579	−3.612	0.739	

Notes: ADF = Augmented Dickey-Fuller test with fourth-order autocorrelation; PP = Phillips-Perron test with two-year autocorrelation window; KPSS test with two-period lag structure. Verdict: Unit root if ADF and PP fail to reject and KPSS rejects; stationary if ADF or PP reject and KPSS fails to reject.

*significant at 5 percent; **significant at 1 percent.

Table 3.2
Standard deviations of fiscal variables

Variable	1951–1975	1976–2003	Ratio
GDP shares			
Primary surplus	7.38	23.45	3.17
Total surplus	3584.15	46292.78	12.91
Public debt	7.39	23.45	3.17
Real variables			
Primary surplus	21866.54	68629.64	3.14
Total surplus	30481.03	54968.44	1.80
Public debt	174821.77	627490.78	3.59

ditures, and real debt have unit roots, a stationary with-interest deficit is sufficient to satisfy the ad hoc sustainability condition. Equivalent statements (as demonstrated by Bohn in chapter 2), based on budget identities with fixed interest rate r, are that the primary surplus and debt are cointegrated with a cointegrating vector $(1, -r)$; or that revenues, noninterest outlays and debt are cointegrated with the vector $(1, -1, -r)$. We use the original Trehan and Walsh methodology (1988), as an examination of the stochastic properties of the series is also required by the cointegration-error correction analysis of the determinants of fiscal choices.

Table 3.1 reports the results of the Augmented Dickey Fuller (ADF) and Phillips-Perron (PP) tests of the null hypothesis of a unit root against the trend-stationary alternative, as well as the results of the KPSS test of the (opposite) null hypothesis of trend-stationarity against the alternative of a unit root. The fiscal variables being tested are public debt, primary deficit, total deficit, total revenues, total outlays, and noninterest and interest outlays. All the series, including the primary deficit, present a unit root; this implies that the Trehan and Walsh sustainability condition (1988) is not satisfied in the Italian case.[3] Interestingly, the results are also logically consistent, since the with-interest deficit, which is a linear function of the primary deficit and public debt, is nonstationary, just like its components. This is a further condition of the Trehan-Walsh test that is often violated, as in the case of the U.S. sample (chapter 2).

The real time series, however, suffer from a noticeable nonstationarity in variances. Table 3.2 illustrates the problem by reporting the standard deviation of primary deficit, total deficit, and public debt for the

1951–1975 and 1976–2003 subsamples. The standard deviations of the 1976–2003 variables exceed those of the 1951–1975 subsample by a factor that varies from about 2 to about 13. Such unequal variances cast some doubts on the unit root results, as they imply that the OLS estimates underlying the unit root tests essentially disregard most of the samples—namely, all but the most recent and, in our case, more volatile observations. Table 3.2 also documents that the standard deviations of GDP ratios display greater growth over time than real variables, suggesting that the rising variances in the real fiscal variables are largely due to a slowdown in the growth of the economy.

To shed light on these doubts, we repeat the Trehan-Walsh sustainability test on the same variables as those in table 3.1 normalized by GDP; table 3.3 reports the results. Again, for no series can nonstationarity be rejected; this corroborates the interpretation of a lack of sustainability of Italian fiscal policies derived from the stochastic properties of the real variables.[4]

In summary, the Trehan-Walsh tests yield three main results. First, real raw data provide more credible information about fiscal series than GDP ratios. Second, there is evidence that the relationship between debt and deficits involves a unit root. Third, since the primary deficit is not found to be stationary, either in real terms or when scaled by GDP, one cannot conclude that revenues and outlays are cointegrated with vector $(1, -1)$. Italian fiscal policies are thus not ad hoc sustainable in the sample period under consideration.

3.3 An Overview of the Evolution of the Main Determinants of the Italian Public Deficit

Rejecting fiscal sustainability naturally leads to questioning what the determinants of the evolution of the Italian fiscal variables are and why these determinants place fiscal policies on an unsustainable path.

The theoretical literature on debt creation points to factors such as the deviation of economic indicators (like output, public expenditures, and unemployment levels) from their usual dynamics, the internal cohesion of governments facing adverse fiscal shocks, the struggles between spending and finance ministers within the cabinet, the binding force of the budget approbation procedures, the demands for intra- and intergenerational redistribution triggered by demographic devel-

Table 3.3
Unit root tests for GDP shares

Sample period:	1951–2002				1951–1975				1976–2003			
Variable	ADF	PP	KPSS	Verdict	ADF	PP	KPSS	Verdict	ADF	PP	KPSS	Verdict
Public debt	−2.595**	−2.083**	1.6402**	Unit root	0.125**	1.570**	0.66*	Unit root	−1.193**	−0.623**	1.2488**	Unit root
Primary surplus	−1.969**	−1.753**	0.9792**	Unit root	−0.566**	0.860**	0.8013**	Unit root	−1.146**	−1.186**	1.3009**	Unit root
Total surplus	−1.632**	−1.105**	0.9141**	Unit root	0.380**	1.039**	0.8339**	Unit root	−1.206**	−1.526**	1.0238**	Unit root
Total revenues	−2.241**	−1.987**	1.7086**	Unit root	0.323**	−2.060**	1.0998**	Unit root	−1.039**	−0.604**	1.2803**	Unit root
Total outlays	−1.932**	−1.119**	1.6363**	Unit root	−0.924**	−2.636**	1.2060**	Unit root	−0.811**	0.610**	0.5442*	Unit root
Noninterest outlays	−1.308**	−2.026**	1.6722**	Unit root	−2.023**	−3.450**	1.225**	Unit root	−1.288**	−1.573**	0.571*	Unit root
Interest outlays	−1.943**	−1.178**	1.4507**	Unit root	2.225**	2.828**	0.7868	Unit root	−0.523**	−0.256**	0.4377*	Unit root
Critical values 1%	−4.158	−4.142	0.739		−4.158	−4.394	0.739		−4.322	−4.394	0.739	
Critical values 5%	−3.504	−3.496	0.463		−3.659	−3.612	0.463		−3.579	−3.612	0.463	

Note: ADF = Augmented Dickey-Fuller test with fourth-order autocorrelation; PP = Phillips-Perron test with two-year autocorrelation window; KPSS test with two-period lag structure. Verdict: Unit root if ADF and PP fail to reject and KPSS rejects; stationary if ADF or PP reject and KPSS fails to reject.

*significant at 5 percent; **significant at 1 percent.

opments, and participation in international agreements that constrain the country's monetary and fiscal policies (Alesina and Perotti 1999).

In Italy, all these factors underwent dramatic changes in the post-Maastricht years. Real output growth came to a virtual standstill during the 1990s, while unemployment reached a peak in the second half of the 1990s and then started to decrease for the first time after several years. Political and institutional equilibria, which had lasted more or less unchanged since the end of World War II, were upset by the combined effects of the change in the electoral system from proportional representation to majority rule and of the judicial inquiries that led to the disappearance of old parties and the birth of new ones. In turn, these new (or relaunched) parties are slowly aggregating in two coalitions that, for the first time in the history of the country, are alternating in government. More recently, a series of institutional reforms has more than halved the number of spending ministers (from 25 to 10) and concentrated the government's financial choices in the hands of a "Superminister" of the Economy. Budget rules became much more stringent after the "constitutionalization" of the fiscal provisions of the Maastricht Treaty and the adoption of a budgetary reform that restricted the possibility of the legislature to amend government proposals.

On the other hand, demands for income redistribution and government spending owing to the demographic evolution of the Italian population have probably become more pressing, as the combined effects of a negative balance between births and deaths and the smoothing of the social impact of firms' restructuring through early retirement schemes has increased the share of the population dependent on income-producing individuals. Finally, the Maastricht Treaty itself strengthened the external constraints that have historically driven all the major policy decisions in Italy during the last few decades.

These historical developments warrant an empirical analysis "before and after Maastricht" in order to assess whether the Stability and Growth Pact (SGP) affected not only the deficit levels (figure 3.1) but also the processes that determine Italian fiscal choices. We thus estimate a model of the determinants of public deficits first on a sample period from 1950 to 1990, one year before the signing of the Maastricht Treaty, and then on a sample period from 1950 to 2002, the last year for which a complete data set is available. By comparing the results we aim to highlight structural changes in the processes of debt creation related to the need to comply with the Maastricht criteria.

It is important to stress that the convergence process has influenced fiscal performance both *directly*, through the adoption of restrictive policies, and *indirectly*, for example, by forcing the adoption of institutional reforms and by conditioning the election results and political equilibria, which in turn affected fiscal choices. These indirect effects require that the econometric model allow for a comprehensive consideration of the various determinants of public deficits, hence the choice of a cointegration-error correction model. This estimation technique imposes the lightest structure on the data, as it lets the dynamics of the relationships emerge from the stochastic properties of the data themselves. As a dependent variable we choose the total, with-interest public deficit over primary deficit, because the accounting definition of the primary deficit changed more frequently during the period under scrutiny whereas that of total deficit remained by and large the same. In addition, we focus on deficits rather than debt, as variations in the stock of the debt derive from changes in the flux of deficits. Finally, we focus on the accounting of the general, rather than central government, since Italy was a highly centralized state throughout the sample.

Previous empirical analyses of the evolution of Italian public deficits can be divided into two strands. An extensive body of literature follows a historical approach based mainly on descriptive statistics. The *Storia Monetaria d'Italia* (Monetary History of Italy) by Fratianni and Spinelli (1991) is one of the outstanding works in this line of research; Brunila, Buti, and Franco 2001 and Giudice and Montanino 2003 are recent contributions focusing on the Stability and Growth Pact. The second approach is based on econometric estimates of the determinants of Italian public deficits (Balassone and Giordano 2001; Padovano and Venturi 2001; Galli and Padovano 2002). Balassone and Giordano (2001) find evidence that compromises between different ideological motivations within multiparty governments result in a bias toward running budget deficits, even if all parties within the coalition prefer balanced budgets. Padovano and Venturi (2001) instead show that measures of ideological polarization lose their explanatory power once estimated alongside indicators of political fragmentation of government coalitions. This suggests that Italian parties as members of government coalitions tend to behave opportunistically rather than ideologically.

Finally, Galli and Padovano (2002) open the analysis to a comparison of a larger set of economic, demographic, and politico-institutional theories of the determinants of Italian public deficits. In a sample that covers the 1950–1998 interval, they find that deficits are sensitive to interest groups' preferences (especially those of the elderly), government fragmentation, changes in the degree of stringency of budget rules, and external economic constraints. Data instead provide weak or no support to the hypotheses that deficits respond to output growth and electoral events. In this chapter we exploit the availability of a longer time span after the Maastricht Treaty to reconsider and extend the analysis of our previous work.

3.4 Short Survey of the Theories under Investigation

3.4.1 Keynesian Approaches to Fiscal Policy

While there is a tendency to consider Keynesian macroeconomics as a falsified and outdated theory, in Italy at least it still constitutes *the* cultural background of economic policymakers. Furthermore, as Buchanan and Wagner (1977) point out, when it did represent the scientific mainstream, Keynesianism provided the theoretical justification for debt financing. Hence, whatever its current standing in economics, Keynesian macroeconomic policy holds an explanatory potential for both past and present Italian fiscal policy choices.

Keynesian macroeconomic policy sees deficits as a tool for counter cyclical policy. New Keynesian theories stress the importance of nominal and real rigidities as the vehicle for policy-induced changes in nominal variables to produce real effects. Deviations in indicators of unemployment and output levels from their long-run trends seem the most appropriate empirical variables for these theoretical models, since prices and wages adjust slowly to changes in economic conditions (Romer 1993). The empirical tests of old Keynesian macroeconomics were often less refined, because the levels of unemployment or even the growth rate of output were considered relevant meters of the state of the economy (Schlitzer 1994; Goff and Tollison 2002).

Because our analysis covers periods when policy decisions were taken according to both old and new Keynesian visions of the economy (Fratianni and Spinelli 1991), we choose a battery of the state of economy variables and let the data indicate the most appropriate:

1. Deviations in the unemployment rate around a time-varying trend, approximated as a Hodrick-Prescott filter of the annual series. This

variable (labeled *TRU*) is consistent with the New Keynesian Phillips curve interpretation of unemployment, which implies that politicians respond only to its cyclical component.

2. The rate of unemployment (*U*). This specification presupposes that policymakers try to reduce the social and political problems that high unemployment engenders, irrespective of the position of the economy through the cycle or of the structural component of unemployment exceeding the cyclical one.

3. The deviations in output level around a time-varying trend, again approximated as a Hodrick-Prescott filter. Taken alone, this variable (labeled *TRY*) is consistent with the New Keynesian theory of the business cycle. Together with the deviations in public expenditure from their trend, as we shall see, it offers a joint hypothesis of the optimal finance theory.

4. Finally, the growth rate of real output (*GY*), calculated as the first differences of the logs of real gross domestic product. Lower growth levels are conceived as a downward position with respect to the expansion path of the economy and vice versa. A significant coefficient on this variable suggests that fiscal policy is essentially aimed at stimulating output (Schlitzer 1994). The presence of GDP measures among the independent variables is an additional reason to specify the dependent variable in real terms rather than in GDP ratios.

3.4.2 The Optimal Finance Theory

The fundamental difference between the Keynesian and the optimal finance approach to public debt is that, in the neo-Ricardian framework, individuals do not consider government bonds as net wealth. Barro (1974, 1979) holds that whenever a government chooses to deficit-finance a given level of expenditures, individuals save the equivalent of the debt issues (and their rates of return) to meet the taxes levied to pay the interest and eventually retire the principal. Since debt issues do not impact aggregate consumption, deficits are no longer a useful tool to ease countries out of recessions. Still, deficits can be used to smooth tax rates over time, despite fluctuations in government expenditures and GDP (tax base). A constant fiscal pressure requires budget deficits when government spending is above its trend value (as in times of war) and budget surpluses when it is below (as in peacetime). Similarly, business cycle-induced fluctuations of the tax base require deficits in downturns and surpluses in upswings to keep the tax rate and government expenditures constant.

We measure deviations in public expenditures from their normal level (labeled *TREXP*) and of income from its normal level (labeled *TRY*) as the ratio of their current value and trend (Hodrick-Prescott filtered) value at time *t*. While a significant (negative) coefficient on *TRY* alone may be consistent with New Keynesian-style fiscal stabilization policies, Barro (1979) stresses that tests supportive of the optimal finance theory require a joint significance of *TREXP* and *TRY*.

3.4.3 The Special Interest Group Explanation

A class of public choice models explains the choice of financing public expenditures through debt rather than taxation by evaluating the political influence of interest groups that stand to gain from deficit spending (Rowley, Shughart, and Tollison 1988). While some controversy exists over which group fits in this characterization, Cukierman and Meltzer (1988), Rowley, Shughart, and Tollison (1988), and Goff (1993), among others, agree that elderly people who do not leave bequests to future generations are the most obvious candidates. The political influence of this group is supposed to increase with its percentage share of the total population. This "special interest group theory" predicts a positive correlation between the percentage of the population represented by elderly people and deficit levels. The association between elderly people and special interest groups is quite appropriate for Italy, where more than 50 percent of unions members are retired people (as opposed to 20 percent in France and Germany) and the median union member is forty-four years old, four years above the European average (Boeri, Brugiavini, and Calmfors 2001).

Incidentally, the special interest group theory is also observationally equivalent, and conceptually similar, to Tullock's "malevolent parents" explanation (1982) of debt creation. The same variable can then be used to test both theories.

3.4.4 Wars of Attrition

A line of research (Alesina and Drazen 1991; Kontopoulos and Perotti 1999) identifies coalition or divided governments as an explanation for the creation and persistence of fiscal disequilibria. After an exogenous fiscal shock, coalition governments tend to delay stabilization and accumulate debt because each member of the coalition seeks to transfer the political costs of the adjustment onto the other(s). Padovano and Venturi (2001) argue that it is important to take the fragmentation of the opposition coalition into account too, as it may affect the cost of the government coalition delaying fiscal stabilization and, by that, the equilibrium deficit level. A government coalition of, say, three parties will find it easier to stabilize the budget when it has to overcome the opposition of several poorly coordinated political forces rather than a single monolithic party.

Several power indices measure political fragmentation (Huber, Kocher, and Sutter 2003), but there is no clear reason to prefer one over the others. We choose the standard Herfindahl index, because it shows higher variability when applied to the Italian government data. On the other hand, measures of ideological polarization do not seem convincing; Padovano and Venturi (2001) show that the impossibility of the Communist Party and parties on the extreme right entering into government (at least until the 1990s) made it rational for the other parties to behave opportunistically rather than ideologically.

We measure the Herfindahl index of the parliamentary seats of the parties that did not vote against the government in the initial confidence debate and term this variable *GOVFRAG*. Similarly, we estimate the concentration of the opposing coalition (*OPFRAG*) as the Herfindahl index of the parliamentary seats of the parties that voted against the government in the initial confidence. These indices are distributed in the $(0, 1]$ interval: they equal 1 when there is one single party in the coalition (minimum fragmentation), and approach 0 when the number of parties tends to infinity (maximum fragmentation). According to the logic of war of attrition models, more fragmented coalitions tend to delay stabilizations more; *GOVFRAG* should be negatively related to budget deficits. Conversely, since more fragmented opposing coalitions can be more easily used to solve struggles within the government majority, we expect a positive partial correlation between *OPFRAG* and the dependent variable.

A variant of this model suggests that debt is created as a by-product of a war of attrition within the government (Alesina and Perotti 1999). Finance and spending ministers hold opposite objective functions and become increasingly opposed when the economy needs to be stabilized. The ratio of the spending ministers to the finance ministers

(*SPENDMIN*) indicates the intensity of this type of war of attrition within the government.

3.4.5 *Political Budget Cycles*

The rational political budget cycles literature argues that, inasmuch as it ensures a boom, an expansionary fiscal policy before elections raises the probability of the incumbent government majority winning the elections. That is because voters perceive the boom as a sign of competence and reward it accordingly (Rogoff 1990; Alesina, Roubini, and Cohen 1997). We use a dummy variable to test the hypothesis that governments manipulate fiscal policies before the elections to maximize the probability of reelection. The standard specification in the literature (Alesina, Roubini, and Cohen 1997) is a variable (labeled *ELE*) that equals 1 in the election year if the elections occur in the second half of that year; 1 in the election year and in the year *before* the election if the polling day occurs in the first half of the year; and 0 otherwise.

Alternatively, we construct a variable *ELC* that takes the value of 1 in the election year if the elections occur in the first half of that year; 1 in the election year and in the year *after* the election if the polling day lies in the second half of the year; and 0 otherwise. This variable takes into account the time interval (roughly one year) that the Italian budget rules open between the moment when funds for a given expenditure are appropriated (*bilancio di competenza*) and the moment when they are actually spent (*bilancio di cassa*). The electorate is likely to respond to the appropriation of funds (first moment) but data on deficits are registered only after expenditures are made and revenues collected (the second moment).

3.4.6 *Budgetary Procedures*

Recent contributions to the literature on the determinants of public deficits focus their attention on the procedures that discipline the approbation of the budget bill to explain the considerable cross-country differences in fiscal performances within highly interconnected and similarly developed economies (Alesina and Perotti 1999). The general idea is that democratic institutions allow policymakers to partially internalize the political costs of their spending decisions, with a consequent deficit. Different budget procedures, however, put similarly deficit-biased policymakers under different sets of constraints. Budget outcomes thus vary according to the degree of stringency of these constraints (von Hagen 1992; von Hagen and Harden 1995).

During the sample period, Italy reformed its budgetary rules twice. First, in 1978, the introduction of the *Legge Finanziaria* (Financial Bill) effectively circumvented the original provision for a budget balanced on a yearly basis enshrined in Article 81 of the constitution. Second, in 1988, law 362/1988 introduced two corrections that limit the deficit drift engendered in the *Legge Finanziaria*. First, it broke the set of provisions of the original *Finanziaria* into a plurality of financial bills to be approved at different times of the year, thereby limiting the possibilities of logrolling, and the associated tendencies toward deficit spending, that the comprehensive structure of the *Finanziaria* allows. Second, it imposed voting on the budget totals at the beginning of the approbation of the budget rather than at the end, as foreseen in the original *Legge Finanziaria*. In doing so, the deficit is set at the beginning and cannot be increased by the parliamentary struggles that occur during the budget session. The literature (da Empoli, De Ioanna, and Vegas 2000) agrees to interpret the reform of 1978 as a major reduction in the degree of stringency of Italian budget rules; the reform of 1988 is evaluated as a partial correction that failed to fully restore the constraining power of the pre-1978 procedures.

In the cointegration-error correction model we capture the different binding forces of Italian budget rules by means of a qualitative variable *BUDRULE* that takes the value of 2 between 1950 and 1977, 0 between 1978 and 1987 and 1 between 1988 and 2002; in the "dummy variable" model we will disaggregate this variable further.

3.4.7 Economic Constraints

Changes in economic conditions may place more or less binding constraints on the tendency of fiscal decision makers to go into debt. We use two different regressors to control for the effects of the state of the economy on the wars of attrition: (1) the budget costs of high interest rates, and (2) the external constraints imposed on discretionary fiscal policies.

1. In a high public debt country like Italy, interest rate shocks, even of relatively small magnitude, imply a significant rise in the cost of servicing the debt. It has been observed that policymakers may decide to finance this higher cost of servicing the debt through new debt,

rather than taxes (Alesina 1988). Unexpectedly high levels of interest rates should then be positively correlated with deficits. Following Alesina, Roubini, and Cohen (1997), we measure the budgetary costs of higher interest rates as the debt-to-GDP ratio multiplied by the change in the differential between real interest rates and the output growth rates. We call this variable *COSTDEBT*. As policymakers may adjust the deficit to the budgetary costs of higher interest rates after one year, we lag *COSTDEBT* once in the estimates.

2. Multilateral exchange rate agreements may force governments to stabilize the economy to avoid the budget costs and crowding out effects of high interest rates. The provisions of the Maastricht Treaty are a case in point. We represent the effects of these external constraints on the fiscal choices of the government by means of a qualitative variable, *EXTCONST*: the higher the potential of the external constraint to restrain discretion in fiscal policy, the larger the value of the variable (Obstfeld 1997). Specifically, *EXTCONST* takes the value of 0 in the years when the exchange rate of the lira is totally flexible (1972–1973), 1 if the currency abides by a somewhat loose exchange-rate regime (like the "Snake-in-the-Tunnel" from 1973 to 1979), 2 if the exchange rate system has a well-developed set of rules (like Bretton Woods until 1971 and the European Monetary System from 1980 to 1990), and 3 if the regime sets explicit limits to deficits and debt levels en route to the creation of a single currency, as in the Maastricht Treaty (from 1991 onward).[5] The expected sign is negative. Again this variable will be further disaggregated in the dummy variable model.

The appendix provides definitions of all the variables used in the estimates.

3.5 Cointegration and Error Correction Analysis

3.5.1 Tests for Nonstationarity

An analysis of the stochastic properties of the series allows us to establish whether the deficit and each explanatory variable share a long- or a short-run relationship; and to identify the appropriate lag structure for each variable. This information leads to the specification of a structural model of the determinants of public deficits devoid of spurious regression problems. Table 3.4 reports the results of the Augmented Dickey-Fuller (ADF) and Phillips-Perron (PP) test of nonstationarity of

Table 3.4
Tests of nonstationarity of the series

Sample period:	1950–1990			1950–2002		
Variable	ADF(4)	Phillips-Perron (12)	Test specification	ADF(4)	Phillips-Perron (12)	Test specification
DEF	−0.099	−0.10	Trend and constant	−0.616	−0.910	None
d(DEF)	−4.25***	−6.54***	Trend and constant	−3.695***	−8.488***	None
POP65	−3.15	−3.32*	Trend and constant	−0.518	−0.687	Trend and constant
d(POP65)	−4.183***	−6.08***	Trend and constant	−3.132*	−4.427***	Trend and constant
U	−1.71	−1.597	None	−2.3406	−2.283	Trend and constant
d(U)	−3.07***	−4.4***	None	−3.710***	−4.618***	Trend and constant
TRU	−3.403***	−3.185***	None	−4.308***	−3.344***	None
GY	−4.759***	−6.665***	Trend and constant	−5.232***	−7.04***	Trend and constant
TREXP	−2.924***	−2.518**	None	−4.022***	−3.594***	None
TRY	−3.682***	−3.122***	None	−4.785***	−4.009***	None
GOVFRAG	−4.527***	−7.17***	Trend and constant	−3.910**	−5.361*	Trend and constant
OPFRAG	−3.12***	−4.704***	Trend and constant	−2.595*	−4.748***	None
d(OPFRAG)	—	—	Trend and constant	−6.915***	−12.265***	None
COSTDEBT	−1.728*	2.134**	None	−2.240**	−4.741***	None
d(COSTDEBT)	−5.45***	−7.11***	None	—	—	—

the normally distributed series. A significant test statistic rejects the null hypothesis of nonstationarity of the series in their levels. The test specification is with a constant, a trend and a constant or none of the two, as appropriate for each series. Finally, the test is performed for the 1950–1990 and 1950–2002 sample periods to find the appropriate specification for the pre- and post-Maastricht models.

Nonstationarity can be rejected at the 1 percent level in both periods for *TRU, GY, TREXP,* and *TRY,* as one would expect from growth rates and series that capture deviations from a trend. Nonstationarity can also be rejected for *GOVFRAG* and *OPFRAG,* consistent with the erratic nature of Italian government coalitions. As for *COSTDEBT,* nonstationarity can be rejected only for the 1950–1990 interval but not for the sample that also includes the Maastricht years. This is the first piece of evidence that joining the EMU stabilized both the interest rate and the output growth rate component of the variable. For all the other series—dependent variable included—the null hypothesis of nonstationarity cannot be rejected at the 1 percent level in either period.

3.5.2 Tests for Cointegration

Since the dependent variable is nonstationary in its levels, the next step is to test the dynamic nature of its relationship with each nonstationary independent variable: *POP65, U, SPENDMIN,* and *COSTDEBT* for the 1950–1990 period and the former three for the 1950–2002 sample. Table 3.5 presents the results of the Johansen cointegration tests. The null hypothesis is that there is no cointegration, namely, that the two series have no equilibrium condition that keeps them in proportion to each other in the long run. The lag structure of the series and the assumption about the presence of an intercept and/or of a deterministic trend in the cointegrating equation are as the dynamics of the series suggests.

The likelihood ratio test statistics indicate one cointegrating equation between deficits and the size of the elderly population with a 95 percent level of confidence. This result is plausible given the long-run implications of demographic phenomena. As expected, *U, SPENDMIN,* and *COSTDEBT* do not result as cointegrated with public deficits, which is consistent with the short-run dynamics of the Keynesian, war of attrition, and economic constraints models, respectively.

Table 3.5
Johansen cointegration test

Sample period:	1950–1990				
Variable	Lag structure	Eigenvalue	Likelihood ratio	5 percent critical values	1 percent critical values
POP65	1	0.327	26.323	25.32	30.45
U	1	0.235	16.677	25.32	30.45
COSTDEBT	1	0.302	23.819	25.32	30.45
Sample period:	**1950–2002**				
Variable	Lag structure	Eigenvalue	Likelihood ratio	5 percent critical values	1 percent critical values
POP65	1	0.4652	34.016	19.96	24.6
U	1	0.2443	16.95	25.32	30.45

3.5.3 *Error Correction Model*

The assessment of the stochastic properties of the series and the identification of one cointegrating equation between deficits and elderly population allow us to specify and estimate an error correction model. We regress the first difference of the endogenous variable *DEF* on a one-period lag of the cointegrating equation and on all the other independent variables.

We estimate the following system of equations:

$$DEF_{t-1} = \alpha_0 POP65_{t-1} + \eta_{t-1}$$

$$d(DEF)_t = \beta_1 ECTPOP65_{t-1} + \beta_2 TRY_t + \beta_3 TREXP_t + \beta_4 EXTCONST_{t-1} + \beta_5 BUDRULE_t + \beta_6 ELE_t + \beta_7 SPENDMIN_t + \beta_8 d(U)_t + \beta_9 COSTDEBT_{t-1} + \upsilon_t. \tag{3.1}$$

Table 3.6 reports the estimates of the error correction model, where the best fitting models (evaluated stepwise on the basis of the Schwarz criterion) are estimated for the 1950–1990 pre-Maastricht sample and for the 1950–2002 post-Maastricht sample.

The first result that deserves attention is the coefficient on *EXTCONST*. While it is not significant in the 1950–1990 sample, it

Table 3.6
Error correction models

Sample period:		1950–1990		1950–2002	
Dependent variable:		Cointegrating equation DEF_{t-1}		Cointegrating equation DEF_{t-1}	
Variable		Coefficient	t-stat.	Coefficient	t-stat.
$POP65_{t-1}$		5.92^{-06}	8.44	6.11^{-06}	5.53
Dependent variable:		Vector error correction $d(DEF_t)$		Vector error correction $d(DEF_t)$	
Variable		Coefficient	Prob.	Coefficient	Prob.
$ECTPOP65_{t-1}$		−0.348	0.03	−0.873	0.00
$TREXP_t$		0.0003	0.02	0.0004	0.00
TRY_t		−0.0001	0.04	−0.0001	0.3
$EXTCONST_t$		−0.439	0.8	−4.126	0.05
ELE_t		−1.302	0.5	3.641	0.4
$BUDRULE_t$		−13.634	0.00	−16.25	0.00
$SPENDMIN_t$		0.605	0.00	0.834	0.00
$d(U)_t$		−1.04	0.58	−1.317	0.7
$COSTDEBT_{t-1}$		−173.41	0.00	−142.93	0.00
Adj. R^2		0.44		0.51	
S.E. of regression		5.47		14.79	
Breusch-Godfrey	F stat.	0.871		0.182	
LM test	$N \cdot R^2$	2.192		0.498	
Log likelihood		−110.0		−196.56	
Schwarz criterion		6.837		8.737	
No. of obs.		40		52	

Note: The operator *d* indicates first differences.

becomes so and with the expected negative sign in the 1950–2002 sample. This evolution captures the direct effect of the Maastricht Treaty on the deficit. Previous exchange rate agreements were not so binding on the country's fiscal choices; the "Maastricht numbers" are.

Other indirect effects of the Maastricht Treaty are captured by the evolution of the coefficients on *BUDRULE* and *SPENDMIN*. While significant and with the expected negative sign in both samples, the coefficient on *BUDRULE* is greater in the full sample. The constitutionalization of the Maastricht Treaty might have induced a greater respect for budget approbation procedures by policymakers.

Similarly, the greater political weight of the Minister of the Economy relative to the spending ministers following the reduction in their number has a distinct impact on fiscal imbalances; the size of the coefficient on *SPENDMIN* increases by 25 percent. This regressor proves multicollinear with *GOVFRAG* and *OPFRAG*, but holds a greater explanatory power than the latter two variables, which have therefore been excluded from the final specification of the regression model.

We infer that the relevant locus of wars of attrition within Italian government coalitions is the cabinet, rather than the parliament. The reunification of the previous three financial ministries (Treasury, Finances, and Budget) into one Ministry of the Economy means that only one party is responsible for such a ministry and, consequently, that the other government coalition members hold spending portfolios. Hence, the Council of Ministers is where the parties fight and strike deals over fiscal choices.

Only one of the four Keynesian variables turns out to be significant—namely, *TRY* and only in the pre-Maastricht sample. Neither the rate of growth of real output nor the various specifications of unemployment are ever statistically different from zero. A possible interpretation for the negative and significant coefficient on *TRY* until 1990 is that the external constraint imposed by the Maastricht Treaty forced Italian politicians to diminish their attempts to use fiscal policy actively over the cycle. As for the lack of significance on unemployment measures throughout both samples, it would be excessive to infer that Italian fiscal authorities never took it as a target; instead, they apparently did not do so in the countercyclical manner postulated by the functional finance theory. The political conveniences of deficit spending outweighed the welfare maximization logic of Keynesian fiscal policy, in line with the arguments of Buchanan and Wagner (1977).

As for the optimal finance variables, in all regressions *TREXP* shows the correct sign and is strongly significant, whereas the coefficient on *TRY* is significant only in the pre-Maastricht sample. The large deviations from the trend of Italian public expenditures mainly depend on the large share of entitlement programs in the budget outlays. A negative fiscal shock is automatically transmitted to public expenditures and deficits must be raised to keep the fiscal pressure constant; this may explain the steady significance of *TREXP*. Conversely, the loss of significance of *TRY* when the 1990–2002 period is also considered may be the result of the lower distortionary effect of the Italian tax system in the 1990s with respect to the previous years. This in turn makes the fundamental hypothesis of the Barro model (1979) less plausible in the full sample period. The 1970s and 1980s saw a dramatic increase in the deadweight costs of taxation owing to reforms that raised the effective progressivity of the system and owing to the fiscal drag resulting from the high inflation rates; the 1990s, instead, witnessed, on the one hand, tax reforms that slowly made the rates more proportional and, on the other hand, a sharp decline in inflation with a lower fiscal drag. In this scenario, shocks to the tax base affect the excess burden of taxation less, with a lower need to intervene by issuing debt.

Elections do not seem to have a significant direct effect on the dynamics of budget deficits in any sample, although the coefficient acquires the correct sign and becomes closer to being significant once the recent years, when two coalitions alternate in government, are considered. Nevertheless, the lack of explanatory power of the *ELE* regressor (as well as on *ELC*, although the results on this variable were not reported) is largely owing to the fact that elections did not occur at regular, predictable intervals. This reduces the possibility of organizing an expansion of the budget before, and a contraction after, the polls.

The lagged value of *COSTDEBT*, which measures the budgetary cost of high interest rates, is always significant and presents the expected negative sign. The size of the coefficient is smaller for the full sample, a sign that the stabilization of the interest rate on the Italian public debt after joining the EMU made public deficits less sensitive to the financial costs of servicing the debt.

Finally, the percentage of the elderly in the total population holds the expected positive sign and is always significant. The coefficient grows in the overall sample, in line with the larger and rising share of expenditures on pensions and social security in the Italian budget. This result is coherent with Galasso and Profeta's explanation (2004) of the postwar dynamics of social security expenditures in Italy, where the aging of the electorate and union members made office-seeking policymakers more sensitive to pension spending. On the other hand, it is quite possible that the increasing costs of raising revenues and the weakening of intergenerational linkages pushed the preferences for financing these expenditures toward deficits and away from taxation. The error correction term is negative and significant and shows a faster return to normal values once the 1990s are taken into account, probably because of the effects of the pension reforms that were introduced in 1993, 1995, and 1997.

Overall, the models explain approximately 44 percent (1950–1990) and 51 percent (1950–2002) of the total variation of the dependent variable, with considerable precision, as the log likelihood functions indicate. In both samples, the Breusch-Pagan Lagrange multiplier test statistics fail to reject the null hypothesis of no serial correlation in the residuals.

3.6 Dummy Variable Model

The results of the error correction models reported in table 3.6 indicate that the variables that change their explanatory power the most between the pre-Maastricht and the post-Maastricht sample are the binding force of external constraints and budget approbation rules; the war of attrition within the cabinet; and the cost of high debt levels and the demands for deficit spending from the rising share of the elderly among the total population. A series of t-tests, reported in table 3.7, confirms such a conclusion. Figure 3.4 illustrates the percentage changes of the estimated coefficients. The results of the error correction model suggest focusing the analysis on these four theories out of the seven originally considered.

Table 3.7
t-tests on the estimated coefficients of the error correction models H_0: $\hat{\beta}_{1950-2002} = \hat{\beta}_{1950-1990}$

Variable	t-test
$POP65_{t-1}$	0.118
$ECTPOP65_{t-1}$	−3.343***
$TREXP_t$	0.793
TRY_t	0.372
$EXTCONST_t$	−2.23***
ELE_t	1.118
$BUDRULE_t$	−8.099***
$SPENDMIN_t$	1.74*
$d(U)_t$	0.579
$COSTDEBT_{t-1}$	6.13***
Critical values 1%	2.704
Critical values 5%	2.021
Critical values 10%	1.68

Note: t-test critical values two-sided, 41 degrees of freedom.

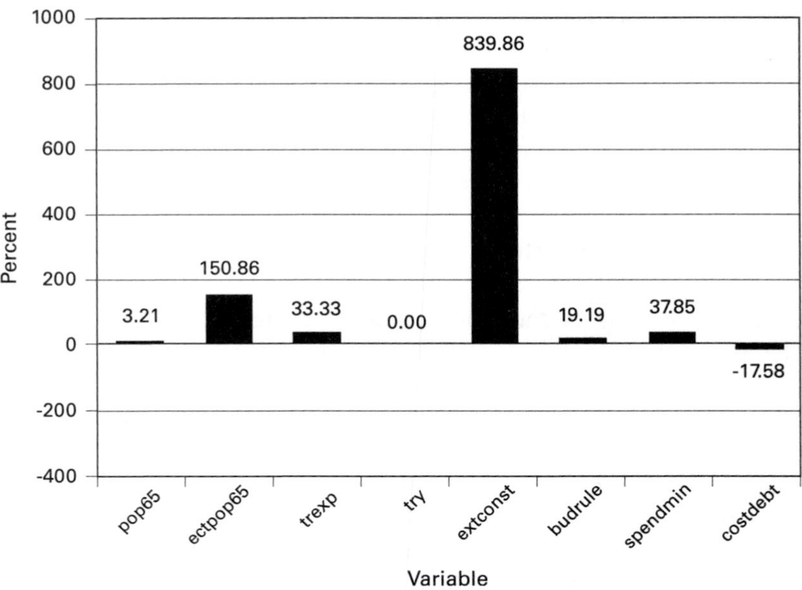

Figure 3.4
Percentage change of the estimated coefficients

In order to deepen our understanding of the impact of these factors on the evolution of Italian public deficits we estimate the following model on the entire 1950–2002 sample:

$$d(DEF)_t = \beta_1 ECTPOP65_{t-1} + \beta_2 EXTCONST_t + \beta_3 BUDRULE_t + \beta_4 COSTDEBT_{t-1} + \beta_5 SPENDMIN_t + \upsilon_t. \tag{3.2}$$

Because of its more parsimonious nature, this model allows us to decompose the qualitative multivariate variables *EXTCONST* and *BUDRULE* used in the error correction model into their single components by a series of dummy variables. Specifically, they are *dummyBRETTONWOODS*, *dummySNAKETUNNEL*, *dummyEMS*, and *dummyMAASTRICHT* in place of *EXTCONST*, and *dummyFINANZIARIA* and *dummy1988REFORM* in place of *BUDRULE*. Each variable equals 0 in the years when the characteristic is absent and 1 in the years when it is present. This decomposition allows us to indicate which of these specific institutional changes affected the dynamics of the deficit most.

Table 3.8
"Dummy variable" model (1950–2002)

Dependent variable: Variable	DEF_t Coefficient	Prob.
$ECTPOP65_{t-1}$	−0.613	0.02
$dummyMAASTRICHT_t$	−24.041	0.05
$dummyFINANZIARIA_t$	13.218	0.007
$COSTDEBT_{t-1}$	−84.878	0.42
$SPENDMIN_t$	0.024	0.06
Adj. R^2	0.30	
S.E. of regression	18.40	
Log likelihood	−209.613	
Schwarz criterion	8.952	
No. of obs.	49	

Table 3.8 reports the best estimate of equation (3.2), the one with all the continuous variables and the dummies with significant coefficients—namely, *dummyMAASTRICHT* and *dummyFINANZIARIA*, at the 5 percent and 1 percent level, respectively. Debt creation appears to be (1) negatively correlated with the constraints imposed by the Maastricht Treaty, which implies a downward shift of the function; (2) positively correlated with the introduction of the *Legge Finanziaria* in the procedure of budget approbation favoring debt financing of public expenditures, which marks an upward shift of the function; (3) positively correlated with pressures to spend in deficit coming from elderly people, although with a seemingly built-in reversion to the mean; (4) negatively correlated with the political power of the spending ministers with respect to the finance one(s) within the cabinet. Interestingly, other institutional factors embedded in the *EXTCONST* and *BUDRULE* multivariate variables used in the error correction models, like the exchange rate agreements in place before Maastricht or the 1988 budgetary reform, do not carry any statistically appreciable explanatory power. Moreover, Italian public deficits seem less sensitive to traditional "sustainability" criteria, such as the differential between output growth rates and interest rates, captured by the variable *BUDRULE*, which is not statistically significant.

The estimates of equation (3.2) suggest that prospects of (future) sustainability of Italian public finances appear to be tied mainly to the resilience of these institutional constraints. If the procedures to approve the budget are slackened and the Stability and Growth Pact softened, as has apparently been the case after the EU summit of March 2005, Italian deficits will soar more than in the case of an increase in the interest rates that raise the costs of servicing the debt. Instead, if these institutional reforms were applied by a sequence of alternating coalitions and supported by public opinion, and if new reforms were introduced in this direction, Italy might slowly cease to be a financial concern for its European partners.[6]

3.7 Conclusions

The analysis described in this chapter indicates that the determinants of Italian public deficits have remained by and large the same before and after Maastricht, but the way in which fiscal policy reacts to each of these determinants has changed considerably since the treaty was signed. Institutional constraints, be they internal, such as the budget approbation rules, or external, like the Maastricht Treaty, have always been the main condition for Italian public finances to be in equilibrium. Our analysis also suggests that the sensitivity of Italian budget deficits to these institutional constraints has increased since 1991. The recent weakening of the Stability and Growth Pact is therefore not good news for the sustainability of Italian public finances.

These results are quite similar to, and therefore corroborate, the findings of previous analyses based on similar explanatory techniques but on a more limited time span, where the effects of the Maastricht Treaty were not completely manifest. The Maastricht years have produced a wealth of new facts in the economic, political, and fiscal history of the country, but in a sense the driving forces behind Italy's public deficits remain the same. This suggests that the investigation of the determinants of Italian public deficits is probably complete, and the potential of the explanatory approach pursued in this chapter has been exhausted.

The main limit to this analytical approach is that it may explain the dynamics of fiscal *totals*. Yet, as budget deficits are the difference between total expenditures and total revenues, and these two totals often result from a bottom-up process of aggregating single expenditure programs and tax instruments, we believe that progress in the explanation (and control) of the dynamics of the fiscal performance of a country will come from an investigation of the determinants of the *composition* of public expenditures and taxation—that is, from more disaggregated analyses based on models of the political economy of public spending and taxation.

Appendix

In table 3A.1, the variables used in the empirical study are defined.

Table 3A.1
Definitions of the variables

Variable	Definition
BUDRULE	Budgetary discipline variable. Equals 2 between 1950 and 1977; 0 between 1978 and 1987; 1 between 1988 and 2002
COSTDEBT	Budgetary cost of interest rates. Equals the debt-to-GDP ratio multiplied by the change in differentials between the real interest rate and real output growth rate
DEF	Total with interest public deficit measured at par value
dummy1988REFORM	Component of BUDRULE. 0 between 1950 and 1987, 1 onward
dummyBRETTONWOODS	Component of EXTCONST. 1 between 1950 and 1971, 0 onward
dummyEMS	Component of EXTCONST. 1 between 1980 and 1991, 0 otherwise
dummyFINANZIARIA	Component of BUDRULE. 0 between 1950 and 1978, 1 onward
dummyMAASTRICHT	Component of EXTCONST. 1 between 1992 and 2002, 0 otherwise
dummySNAKETUNNEL	Component of EXTCONST. 1 between 1973 and 1979, 0 otherwise
ECTPOP	Error correction mechanism
ELC	Political business-cycle dummy (1 in election year if the election occurs in the first half of that year; 1 in the election year and in the year after the election if the election occurs in the second half of the year; 0 otherwise)
ELE	Political business-cycle dummy (1 in election year if election occurs in the second half of the year; 1 in election year and year before if election occurs in the first half of the year; 0 otherwise)
EXTCONST	External constraint on fiscal choices of the government. Equals 0 between 1972 and 1973, 1 between 1974 and 1979, 2 between 1950 and 1971 and between 1980 and 1991, and 3 from 1992 onward
GOVFRAG	Fragmentation of government coalition (Herfindahl index of the parliamentary seats of the parties that did not vote against the government in initial confidence debate)
GY	Growth rate of real gross domestic product.

Table 3A.1
(continued)

Variable	Definition
OPFRAG	Fragmentation of opposition coalition (Herfindahl index of the parliamentary seats of the parties that voted against the government in initial confidence debate)
POP65	Percent of the population aged 65 and over
SPENDMIN	Ratio of spending ministers to finance minister(s)
TREXP	Deviation of total with interest public expenditures rate around the time-varying trend (Hodrick-Prescott filter)
TRU	Deviation of the unemployment rate around the time-varying trend (Hodrick-Prescott filter)
TRY	Deviation of gross domestic product around the time-varying trend (Hodrick-Prescott filter)
U	% rate of unemployment
Y	Real gross domestic product

Notes

This chapter was presented at the XVIth Scientific Meeting of the Società Italiana di Economia Pubblica, the CESifo–LBI Conference on Sustainability of Public Debt, the workshop on Italian Institutional Reforms: A Political Economy Perspective held by the Department of Political Institutions and Social Sciences of the University Roma Tre, and the EPCS 2005 Meeting. We thank the participants to these conferences and especially Reinhard Neck, Jan-Egbert Sturm, Roberto Ricciuti, Daniela Monacelli, Ilde Rizzo, John Ashworth, Massimo Bordignon and two anonymous referees for useful comments on previous versions of this chapter. The usual caveat applies.

1. Data on the debt-to-GDP ratio are taken from Fratianni and Spinelli 1991.

2. There is evidence of another structural break in the mid-1970s around the first oil shock which is less significant to our purpose.

3. The results for public expenditures and tax revenues are in line with previous sustainability tests carried out by Ricciuti (2004) for the 1861–1998 time period.

4. Scaling by GDP may raise questions about the stationarity of GDP itself. In the Italian sample under consideration, a unit root is not rejected at the 1 percent level in neither the whole time interval, or in the 1951–1975 and 1976–2003 subsamples.

5. We tried the alternative specification of a dummy variable that takes the value of 1 from 1991 onward and 0 otherwise without getting substantially different results. Since, however, many events took place in Italy in the early 1990s (changes in the electoral rules, political scandals), we prefer to adopt the more roundabout procedure of a multivariate qualitative variable in the error correction models and of a series of simple qualitative variables in the dummy variable model. By that we are better able to identify the most important structural changes in the series and disentangle their effects on the deficits.

6. Based on dummy or multivariate qualitative variables, our analysis does not allow us to assess the likely impact of reforms to the Maastricht Treaty on the sustainability of Italian public finances. Such an insight might be gathered, as time goes by, through an evaluation of how these revisions will affect the spreads and the levels of interest rates in the EU zone and, by that, the cost of servicing the Italian debt. See Faini 2004 for an early treatment of these issues.

References

Alesina, A. 1988. The end of large public debts. In *High Public Debt: The Italian Experience,* ed. F. Giavazzi and L. Spaventa, 34–79. Cambridge: Cambridge University Press.

Alesina, A., and A. Drazen. 1991. Why are stabilizations delayed? *American Economic Review* 81:1170–1188.

Alesina, A., and R. Perotti. 1999. Budget deficits and budget institutions. In *Fiscal Institutions and Fiscal Performance,* ed. J. M. Poterba and J. von Hagen, 13–36. Chicago: University of Chicago Press.

Alesina, A., N. Roubini, and G. D. Cohen. 1997. *Political Cycles and the Macroeconomy.* Cambridge, MA: MIT Press.

Balassone, F., and R. Giordano. 2001. Budget deficits and coalition governments. *Public Choice* 106:327–349.

Barro, R. J. 1974. Are government bonds net wealth? *Journal of Political Economy* 82:1095–1117.

Barro, R. J. 1979. On the determination of the public debt. *Journal of Political Economy* 87:941–971.

Boeri, T., A. Brugiavini, and L. Calmfors, eds. 2001. *The Role of the Unions in the Twenty-first Century.* Oxford: Oxford University Press.

Brunila, A., M. Buti, and D. Franco, eds. 2001. *The Stability and Growth Pact. The Architecture of Fiscal Policy in EMU.* Basingstoke: Palgrave.

Buchanan, J. M., and R. E. Wagner. 1977. *Democracy in Deficit.* New York: Academic Press.

Camera dei Deputati della Repubblica Italiana. 2001. *Notiziario della Camera dei Deputati. Compendio Statistico dalla Ia alla XIIIa Legislatura. Dati Statistici e Quantitativi.* Rome: Camera dei Deputati della Repubblica Italiana.

Cukierman, A., and A. H. Meltzer. 1989. A political theory of government debt and deficits in a neo-Ricardian framework. *American Economic Review* 79:713–732.

da Empoli, D., P. De Ioanna, and G. Vegas. 2000. *Il bilancio dello Stato. La Finanza Pubblica tra Governo e Parlamento.* Milano: Ed. Il Sole-24 Ore.

Faini, R. 2004. Fiscal policy and interest rates in Europe. In *Public Debt,* ed. Banca d'Italia, 481–511. Rome: Bank of Italy.

Fratianni, M., and F. Spinelli. 1991. *La Storia Monetaria d'Italia: 1860–1980.* Milan: Mondadori.

Galasso, V., and P. Profeta. 2004. Lessons for an ageing society: The political sustainability of social security systems. *Economic Policy* 19:63–115.

Galli, E., and F. Padovano. 2002. A comparative test of alternative theories of the determinants of public deficits. *Public Choice* 113:37–58.

Galli, E., and F. Padovano. 2004. The determinants of Italian public deficits before and after Maastricht. Working paper. Società Italiana di Economia Pubblica, Pavia (SIEP).

Giudice, G., and A. Montanino. 2003. Il patto di stabilità e crescita. *Rivista di Politica Economica* 7–8:185–273.

Goff, B. L. 1993. Evaluating alternative explanations of postwar federal deficits. *Public Choice* 75:247–261.

Goff, B. L., and R. D. Tollison. 2002. Explaining U.S. federal deficits, 1889–1998. *Economic Inquiry* 40:457–469.

Huber, G., M. Kocher, and M. Sutter. 2003. Government strength, power dispersion in governments and budget deficits in OECD countries: A voting power approach. *Public Choice* 116:333–350.

Kontopoulos, J., and R. Perotti. 1999. Government fragmentation and fiscal policy outcomes. In *Fiscal Institutions and Fiscal Performance*, ed. J. M. Poterba and J. von Hagen, 81–102. Chicago: University of Chicago Press.

IMF. Various years. *Government Financial Statistics*. Washington, DC: IMF.

ISTAT. Various years. *Annuario Statistico Italiano*. Rome: ISTAT.

Obstfeld, M. 1997. Destabilizing effects of exchange rate escape clauses. *Journal of International Economics* 43: 61–77.

OECD. Various years. *Economic Outlook*. Paris: OECD.

OECD. Various years. *Historical Statistics*. Paris: OECD.

Padovano, F., and L. Venturi. 2001. Wars of attrition in government coalitions and fiscal performance: A test on Italian 1948–1994 data. *Public Choice* 109:15–54.

Ricciuti, R. 2004. A nonlinear characterisation of fiscal sustainability. Royal Holloway University of London Discussion Papers in Economics, no. 2004-06.

Rogoff, K. 1990. Equilibrium political budget cycles. *American Economic Review* 80:21–36.

Romer, D. 1993. The new Keynesian synthesis. *Journal of Economic Perspectives* 7:5–22.

Rowley, C. K., W. F. Shughart, and R. D. Tollison. 1988. Interest groups and deficits. In *Deficits*, ed. J. M. Buchanan, C. K. Rowley, and R. D. Tollison, 263–280. London: Blackwell.

Schlitzer, G. 1994. Nuovi strumenti per la valutazione e la previsione del ciclo economico in Italia. *Rivista di Politica Economica* 2:3–34.

Senato della Repubblica Italiana. Various years. *Atti Parlamentari*. Rome: Senato della Repubblica Italiana.

Trehan, B., and C. Walsh. 1988. Common trends, the government budget constraint and revenue smoothing. *Journal of Economic Dynamics and Control* 12:425–444.

Trehan, B., and C. Walsh. 1991. Testing intertemporal budget constraints: Theory and applications to U.S. federal budget and current accounts deficits. *Journal of Money, Credit and Banking* 23:210–223.

Tullock, G. 1982. *The Economics of Income Redistribution*. Boston: Kluwer-Nijhoff.

von Hagen, J. 1992. Budgeting procedures and fiscal performance in the European Community. Commission of the European Communities, Economic Paper no. 96.

von Hagen, J., and J. Harden. 1995. Budget processes and commitment to fiscal discipline. *European Economic Review* 39:771–779.

Woldendorp, J., H. Keman, and I. Budge. 1993. Political data 1945–1990: Party government in twenty democracies. *European Journal of Political Research* 24:1–119.

Woldendorp, J., H. Keman, and I. Budge. 1998. Party government in twenty democracies: An update (1990–1995). *European Journal of Political Research* 33:1–119.

4 Policy Adjustments and Sustainability of Public Finances in the Netherlands

Jakob de Haan, Jan-Egbert Sturm, and Olaf de Groot

4.1 Introduction

Following the oil shocks of the 1970s many OECD countries had large and persistent deficits, which in turn resulted in an unprecedented peacetime rise in the public debt-to-GDP ratio. The Netherlands was no exception. In 1982 the general government budget deficit in the Netherlands amounted to 6.2 percent of GDP, the highest level in decades. The general government debt-to-GDP ratio increased from a postwar low of 39 percent in 1976 to 78 percent in 1993.

Various coalition governments—differing substantially in terms of the parties participating—aimed to reduce the budget deficit in the 1980s and 1990s since fiscal policy at the time was generally perceived as unsustainable. Over time, the financial position of the public sector improved substantially. In 2000 the Dutch government even had a surplus of 2.2 percent of GDP. However, in more recent years the fiscal situation deteriorated rapidly, even to such an extent that the ECOFIN Council, in its meeting of June 2, 2004, decided that the Netherlands had an excessive deficit according to the rules of the Stability and Growth Pact. However, in 2004, the deficit was reduced to 2.3 percent and was forecast to decrease further to 1.6 percent in 2006. In June 2005 the ECOFIN Council therefore decided to abrogate the excessive deficit procedure.

This chapter analyzes fiscal policy in the Netherlands over the period 1948–2003 from two perspectives. First, we draw on the fiscal sustainability literature, testing whether the intertemporal budget constraint of the public sector would have been satisfied had fiscal policy in the sample been pursued indefinitely and were the relevant macro and structural features of the economy stable over time. We conclude that fiscal policy in the Netherlands was sustainable.

Second, we analyze to what extent recent fiscal policy was in line with policy recommendations coming from the so-called fiscal adjustment literature. According to this line of research, which started with the seminal paper by Alesina and Perotti (1995b), successful fiscal policy adjustments are characterized by (large) spending cuts. Notably, spending on government wages and transfers ought to be cut in order to permanently improve the government's financial position. In contrast, fiscal adjustments that rely primarily on tax increases and cuts in public investment tend not to last. However, we find that successful fiscal adjustments in the Netherlands were often not in line with these prescriptions.

The remainder of this chapter is organized as follows. In section 4.2 the sustainability of fiscal policy in the Netherlands is examined. In section 4.3 the policy adjustments during the period 1970–2003 are analyzed in some detail, following the fiscal adjustment literature. The final section offers our conclusions.

4.2 Sustainability of Fiscal Policy

As pointed out by Bohn in chapter 2, most previous studies consider fiscal policy sustainable if it is on a trajectory such that the expected present value of future primary surpluses equals the initial debt. The period-by-period government budget constraint can be written as

$$\Delta B_t = rB_{t-1} + G_t - T_t, \tag{4.1}$$

where B_t denotes the real value of government debt at the end of the period, r is the interest payable on that debt, G_t is real government expenditures exclusive of debt interest payments, and T_t denotes real tax revenues. Reformulating equation (4.1) and performing recursive substitution for all future debt yields

$$B_t = \sum_{j=1}^{n} [1/(1+r)^j] S_{t+j} + 1/(1+r)^n B_{t+n}, \tag{4.2}$$

where S (the primary deficit) is defined as

$$S_t = T_t - G_t. \tag{4.3}$$

If the second term on the right-hand side of equation (4.2) converges to zero as n becomes large, the outstanding stock of government debt equals the present value of future government surpluses:

$$\lim_{n\to\infty} 1/(1+r)^n B_{t+n} = 0. \tag{4.4}$$

In that case the government budget is intertemporally balanced. If the limit term is higher than zero, the government is "bubble-financing" its expenditures. It is important to point out that the solvency constraint can be satisfied by an infinite series of conventional budget deficits.

Various tests have been proposed in the literature to examine sustainability.[1] Hamilton and Flavin (1986), who were—as far as we know—the first to examine this issue, assume that the real interest rate is constant and that the deviation of the debt from the sum of discounted future surpluses grows at rate r. In that case, one can write

$$B_t = c(1+r)^t + \sum_{s=1}^{\infty}(1+r)^{-s}E_t S_{t+s}, \tag{4.5}$$

where E_t denotes the expectation operator conditional on information at time t. The intertemporal budget constraint would only be satisfied if $c = 0$. If both the debt and the sum of discounted surpluses are stationary, $c = 0$. Hamilton and Flavin examined the order of integration of B_t and S_t using annual data for the United States and found that the data favor the rejection of the null hypothesis of nonstationarity in both cases, which led them to conclude that the government budget is balanced in present value terms.

Trehan and Walsh (1988) argue that if debt and deficits are integrated, and if interest rates are constant, then a necessary and sufficient condition for sustainability is that debt and primary balances are cointegrated. This can easily be seen by writing equation (4.1) as

$$B_{t+1} - B_t = rB_t + S_t. \tag{4.1a}$$

If B_t is integrated of order one (I(1)), then $B_{t+1} - B_t$ is stationary by definition, which, in turn, implies that the overall balance $D = rB_t + S_t$ is stationary, and that, if the interest rate r is constant, B_t and S_t are cointegrated with a cointegrating vector $(1, -r)$.

Trehan and Walsh (1991) show that an alternative way to examine sustainability is to test whether the deficit inclusive of interest payments (D_t) is stationary. The attractive feature of this test is that its derivation does not depend on the assumption of a constant interest rate. As Trehan and Walsh (1991) show, stationarity of D_t is a sufficient condition for intertemporal budget balance for positive (not necessarily constant) real interest rates.

Alternatively, one can test whether expenditures including interest payments are cointegrated with tax revenues (Trehan and Walsh 1991; Hakkio and Rush 1991). If the series G_t, T_t, and rB_{t-1} are I(1) variables, the deficit inclusive of interest payments is a zero mean stationary process if and only if $T_t - G_t - r_tB_{t-1}$ is a cointegration relationship. Ahmed and Rogers (1995) test this for the United States and the United Kingdom and accept it. Likewise, Trehan and Walsh (1991) accept this condition for the United States, but Hakkio and Rush (1991) reject cointegration.

Table 4.1 shows the outcomes of the unit root and cointegration tests using data for the Netherlands over the period 1948–2001. The left-hand side shows that the Dickey-Fuller unit root test suggests that general government debt (B_t) contains a unit root. Hence, according to the test of Hamilton and Flavin (1986), we cannot reject that general government debt in the Netherlands is on a nonsustainable path. The failure to reject a unit root does not, however, prove the existence of a unit root. The three sustainability tests of Trehan and Walsh (1991) clearly point in that direction. First, as shown in the left-hand side of table 4.1, the deficit including interest payments (D_t) is stationary. Furthermore, as shown in the right-hand side of table 4.1, general government debt is—according to the Engle-Granger test—cointegrated with the primary deficit (S_t), while expenditures including interest payments ($G_t + rB_t$) are cointegrated with tax revenues.[2] Hence, overall, the data indicate that fiscal policy in the Netherlands has been sustainable over the past five decades.

Some previous studies on the sustainability of Dutch fiscal policy sometimes came to different conclusions.[3] One obvious difference between our study and previous papers is the time period taken into account. Except for de Haan and Siermann 1993, most studies summarized in the appendix focus on a shorter time period (normally covering around 30 years) than we do. These differences in sample size and periods might explain the diverging conclusions. The lower part of table 4.1 therefore shows the outcomes of the unit root and cointegration tests for the period 1970–2001. For this period all tests conclude that fiscal policy in the Netherlands was on an unsustainable path, suggesting that the differences between our findings and those of some previous studies may reflect differences in sample periods.

Table 4.1
Sustainability of fiscal policy: Unit root and cointegration tests

Sample: 1948–2001

Dickey-Fuller test		Engle-Granger cointegration test	
Variable	test-statistic	Variables	test-statistic
B_t	−1.56	B_t & S_t	−6.44
D_t	−4.44	T_t & $(G_t + rB_t)$	−5.50

Notes: All variables are expressed as percentages of GDP.
Except for B_t—where 3 lags of the dependent variable are included—no lagged dependent variables are included in the tests.
The 1 percent critical value of the D-F test equals −3.57.
The 1 percent critical value of the E-G cointegration test equals −4.11.

Sample: 1970–2001

Dickey-Fuller test		Engle-Granger cointegration test	
Variable	test-statistic	Variables	test-statistic
B_t	−2.99	B_t & S_t	−1.38
D_t	−1.91	T_t & $(G_t + rB_t)$	−3.44

Notes: All variables are expressed as percentages of GDP.
Except for B_t—where 3 lags of the dependent variable are included—no lagged dependent variables are included in the tests.
The 1 percent critical value of the D-F test equals −3.70.
The 1 percent critical value of the E-G cointegration test equals −4.27.

In our view, it is preferable to use long sample periods for two reasons. First, sustainability is a long-term phenomenon, and second, the power of unit root and cointegration tests is rather low for short time spans.

The unit root and cointegration tests have been criticized by Bohn (1998; see also chapter 2). As he points out, unit root analysis is suitable for testing what he calls "ad hoc sustainability," but it is not informative about model-based conditions. Tax smoothing, for instance, suggests that temporary declines in income and temporary government outlays trigger higher than normal budget deficits. Sustainability tests should allow for these kinds of effects to take place and then check whether or not there is sufficient feedback of government debt on the primary balance. Also in contrast to most other tests, the proposed alternative methodology of Bohn does not rest on the assumption of a constant discount rate. He suggests estimating the following equation:

$$S_t = \beta_o + \beta_1 B_{t-1} + \beta_2 Z_t + u_t, \tag{4.7}$$

Table 4.2
Sustainability of fiscal policy: Augmented Bohn tests, 1948–2001 (dependent variable: *S/GDP*)

	(1)	(2)	(3)	(4)	(5)
Constant	−2.913 (−5.39)	−3.092 (−3.96)	−3.126 (−3.88)	−3.253 (−4.17)	−0.268 (−0.14)
S_{-1}	0.285 (2.94)	0.231 (2.43)	0.230 (2.40)	0.230 (2.45)	0.184 (1.88)
B_{-1}	0.076 (6.64)	0.077 (7.07)	0.078 (7.00)	0.077 (7.13)	0.078 (7.22)
π		0.126 (1.55)	0.124 (1.50)	0.115 (1.42)	0.078 (0.90)
G_{temp}		−0.406 (−2.47)	−0.406 (−2.45)	−0.440 (−2.68)	−0.426 (−2.62)
U		−0.277 (−1.30)	−0.280 (−1.30)	−0.272 (−1.29)	−0.335 (−1.57)
EL			0.139 (0.21)		
REGEL				1.070 (1.44)	
PC					−0.516 (−1.55)
NPART					
NMIN					
POLSUP					
POLFRAC					
POPSH65					
R^2 (adj.)	0.737	0.792	0.787	0.796	0.798
No. of obs.	53	53	53	53	53
Durbin h	0.78	0.45	0.46	0.18	0.48

(6)	(7)	(8)	(9)	(10)	(11)
−3.380	−2.338	−3.212	−3.881	−6.888	−2.352
(−2.51)	(−1.03)	(−3.57)	(−4.68)	(−3.60)	(−0.69)
0.224	0.240	0.232	0.156	0.199	0.126
(2.25)	(2.42)	(2.42)	(1.61)	(2.15)	(1.22)
0.077	0.079	0.077	0.079	0.087	0.082
(6.93)	(6.76)	(6.92)	(7.52)	(7.59)	(6.72)
0.117	0.138	0.127	0.141	0.148	0.102
(1.29)	(1.55)	(1.54)	(1.79)	(1.86)	(1.19)
−0.404	−0.404	−0.409	−0.381	−0.377	−0.396
(−2.43)	(−2.43)	(−2.46)	(−2.41)	(−2.37)	(−2.49)
−0.229	−0.265	−0.264	−0.357	−0.683	−0.500
(−0.81)	(−1.22)	(−1.20)	(−1.72)	(−2.45)	(−1.57)
					−0.439
					(−1.31)
0.078					
(0.26)					
	−0.059				
	(−0.35)				
		0.172			
		(0.28)			
			0.623		0.474
			(2.23)		(1.13)
				0.357	0.100
				(2.15)	(0.39)
0.788	0.788	0.788	0.808	0.807	0.809
53	53	53	53	53	53
0.57	0.33	0.50	0.40	−0.10	0.32

and testing whether β_1 is positive. A positive β_1 coefficient indicates that fiscal policymakers react to an increased stock of debt by increasing the primary surplus. Z_t is a vector of additional variables like the output gap and temporary public expenditures.

We estimated this model for the Netherlands for the period 1948–2001. All fiscal variables are measured relative to GDP. In addition to the debt ratio, we also include the lagged primary deficit in our model. Column (1) of table 4.2 shows the results. It is clear that β_1 differs significantly from zero, suggesting that fiscal policy was sustainable. Column (2) shows the outcome if we add temporary government spending (G_{temp}),[4] inflation (Π), and unemployment (U) as explanatory variables.[5] We find that β_1 remains significantly positive, strengthening the robustness of our conclusion concerning the results in column (1).

In line with our previous findings, these results suggest that fiscal policy in the Netherlands after World War II was sustainable. To check to what extent this conclusion is different if a shorter time period is considered, we reestimated our model for a moving window of thirty years. Figure 4.1 shows the β_1 coefficient using rolling regressions. For

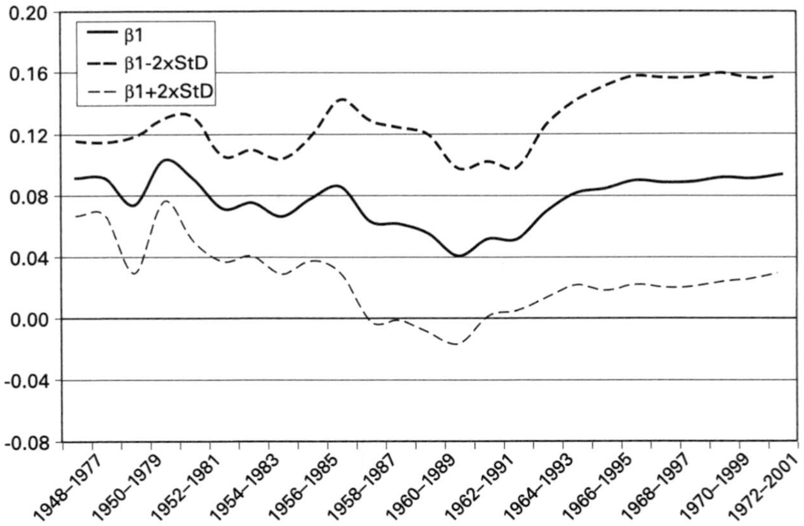

Figure 4.1
Rolling regression results for β_1 using a fixed window of thirty years and the specification as in column (1) of table 4.2

the thirty-year samples around 1960–1990, the tests suggest that fiscal policy in the Netherlands was unsustainable. This might explain why Corsetti and Roubini (1991), Artis and Marcelino (2000) and Vanhorebeek and van Rompuy (1995) found that Dutch fiscal policy was non-sustainable. The results for other sample periods clearly indicate the opposite.[6]

Our conclusion is that despite some prolonged periods with high budget deficits, the institutional budgetary setting in the Netherlands ensured that some kind of adjustment occurred, which ensured that fiscal policy remained on a sustainable path. This is a remarkable finding because the Dutch political system has many features that, according to recent cross-country-based research, are likely to lead to budget deficits.[7] For instance, the results of Perotti and Kontopoulos (2002) suggest that fragmented governments, namely, governments consisting of various political parties, are inclined to have deficits. The Netherlands has always been governed by cabinets consisting of sometimes as many as five or six parties. To test to what extent these and other political-institutional factors that, according to various studies, may influence fiscal outcomes (see, e.g., Alesina and Perotti 1995a; Kirchgässner 2001) affected fiscal policy in the Netherlands, we added the following political-institutional variables to the model:

- an election variable *EL*, which is defined as $EL_t = [(M-1) + d/D]/12$, where M is the month of year t in which an election takes place, d is the day of the election, and D is the number of days in that month; $EL_{t-1} = 1 - EL_t$. Since there are both regular and irregular elections, we constructed two versions of the election variable. The first one only takes regular elections (*REGEL*) into account; the other (*EL*) includes all elections. This variable has been used by Franzese (2002) to test for political budget cycles;
- the ideological position of the government (*PC*) on a scale from 1 (left) to 10 (right), defined as $PC = \sum_i (NMIN_i \times COLOUR_i/NMIN)$, where $COLOUR_i$ is the political position of party i.[8] This variable is included since the partisan theory suggests that the ideological composition of the government may affect fiscal policy outcomes (see, e.g., Franzese 2002);
- the number of political parties in the government (*NPART*);
- the number of ministers in the government (*NMIN*).[9] Perotti and Kontopoulos (2002) argue that government fractionalization—measured by the number of political parties or the number of spending

ministers in government—affects fiscal policy. The more fragmented the government, namely, the higher the number of parties or spending ministers, the higher the budget deficit will be. There is significant support for this view (see, e.g., Volkerink and de Haan 2001);

• support for the government in parliament (*POLSUP*), defined as the number of seats of the coalition in parliament divided by the total number of seats, taking into account the number of months in a year that the government is in power. The rationale of this variable is that the more seats the parties in the government have in parliament, the stronger the government will be (see also Volkerink and de Haan 2001); and

• the degree of political fractionalization *POLFRAC*, defined as $POLFRAC = \sum_i [NMIN_i/NMIN \times (COLOUR_i - PC)^2]$. Volkerink and de Haan (2001) suggest that political fractionalization may affect fiscal policy outcomes: the more similar the parties forming a coalition are from an ideological perspective, the easier it will be to keep fiscal policy on track.

Finally, we included the elderly population share, defined as the number of persons aged 65 and over relative to the total number of persons in the population (*POPSH65*). From a political economy perspective, the share of the elderly may be an important determinant of budget deficits. Cukierman and Meltzer (1989) argue that bequest-constrained individuals, namely, individuals who would like to leave a negative bequest to their descendants but who lack the opportunity to do so, will favor a fiscal policy that increases their lifetime income at the expense of future generations even when the present value of the tax change is zero. Thus the higher the share of bequest-constrained individuals in the population, the higher the likelihood of budget deficits. Cukierman and Meltzer show that under majority rule, budget deficits will be greater the larger the expected growth rate of the economy and the higher the longevity. The higher the expected rate of future economic growth, the more the current generation will expect future generations to be relatively better off, thereby increasing the number of individuals who are bequest-constrained. Higher expected longevity tends to increase the length of time an individual spends in retirement, raising the required amount of resources necessary to sustain consumption. Likewise, Chen (2004) argues that a rise in the number of retired persons will increase the population share of bequest-constrained individuals.

It follows from columns (3)–(11) of table 4.2 that the political variables are not significantly different from zero if added one by one, or have the "wrong" sign if significant.[10] None of them is significant if the significant variables are included together (column [11]). Interestingly, β_1 remains fairly constant and is significantly different from zero in all these specifications. In conclusion, our results suggest that fiscal policy in the Netherlands was sustainable during the period under consideration. Sustainability was not undermined by political-institutional and demographic characteristics of the Netherlands.

4.3 Fiscal Policy Adjustments in the Netherlands, 1970–2003

Our finding that fiscal policy was sustainable may surprise some observers, since the Netherlands had substantial deficits and a steeply rising debt ratio, especially during the 1980s. Figure 4.2 shows the general debt-to-GDP ratio (right-hand side) and the general government financial balance for the period 1969–2003. The decline in national economic performance in the late 1970s and early 1980s triggered a financial crisis in the Dutch welfare state. As follows from figure 4.2, annual budget deficits were quite high since 1975, reflected in a subsequent upsweep of the debt ratio, which reached a peak in 1993. Afterward, a

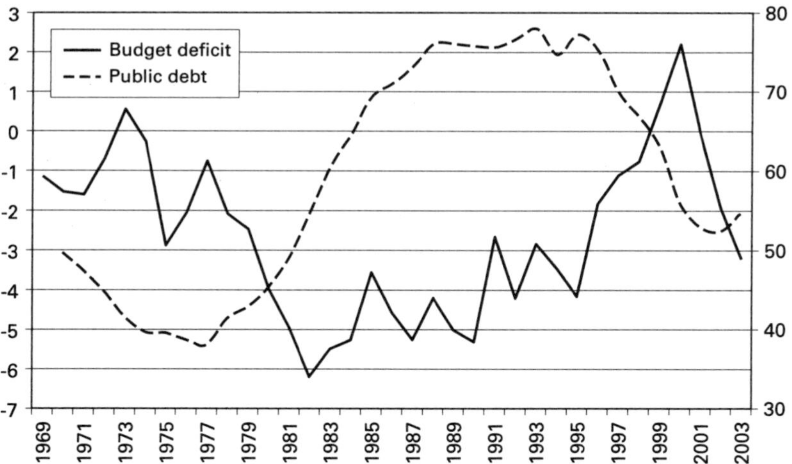

Figure 4.2
Government debt (right-hand side) and government financial balance (left-hand side), 1969–2003 (% GDP)

steep decline in the debt ratio set in, which leveled off in more recent years.

After the second oil shock hit the Netherlands, unemployment shot up. Since transfers to strongly rising numbers of benefit recipients were, at the time, fully linked to contractual wages, general government spending was in fact out of control. It took quite a while before the budget deficit was reduced to levels compatible with a constant debt-to-GDP ratio.

It is quite interesting that various coalition governments all aimed to reduce budget deficits, independent of their composition. Much of the improvement in the financial position was realized by reducing government spending. Figure 4.3 shows total government spending as a share of GDP, as well as government transfers and government wages. The latter are also shown since the fiscal adjustment literature suggests that especially reductions in these categories of spending are needed for a permanent improvement in the government's financial position. Figure 4.3 indicates that the time patterns of total government spend-

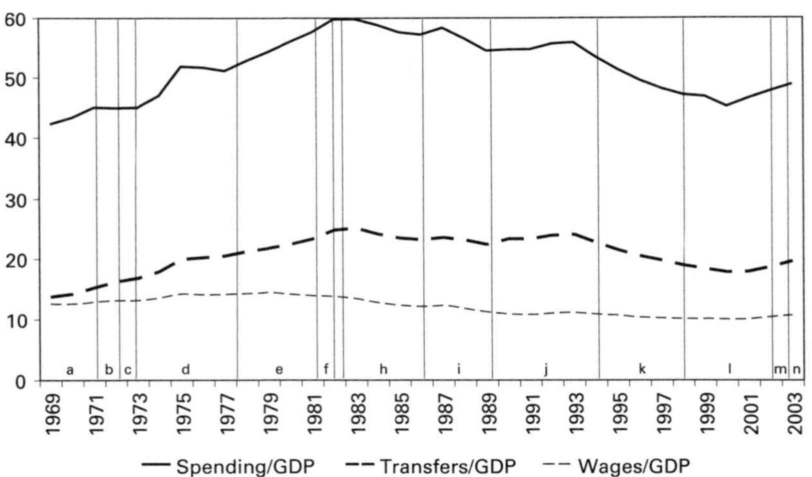

Figure 4.3
Total government spending, government transfers to households and government wages, 1969–2003 (% GDP)
Cabinets: (a) De Jong, (b) Biesheuvel I, (c) Biesheuvel II, (d) Den Uyl, (e) Van Agt I, (f) Van Agt II, (g) Van Agt III, (h) Lubbers I, (i) Lubbers II, (j) Lubbers III, (k) Kok I, (l) Kok II, (m) Balkenende I, (n) Balkenende II. Each vertical line shows the starting date of the subsequent cabinet.

ing and government transfers are much alike (the correlation coefficient of both variables is 0.96). The degree of concordance between total government spending and government wages is much less (correlation coefficient of 0.25).

When a policymaker must redress a fiscally unbalanced position, he can raise taxes and/or cut expenditures. Which should be used in order to permanently improve the fiscal position? And which type of expenditure or tax should be changed? Various studies have addressed the question of whether the composition of the fiscal adjustment matters enough for it to lead to a long lasting improvement in the government's fiscal position. Alesina and Perotti (1995b, 1997), McDermot and Wescott (1996), Alesina, Perotti, and Tavares (1998), and Alesina and Ardagna (1998) find that fiscal adjustments that concentrate on the spending side, and in particular on public wages and social welfare spending, are more successful (i.e., long lasting) than adjustments that rely primarily on tax hikes.[11] There is less agreement on other determinants of successful fiscal adjustments, although the size and persistence of the adjustment are often found to matter as well (see, e.g., von Hagen, Hughes Hallett, and Strauch 2001).[12]

In the remainder of this section, we analyze the fiscal adjustments of the Netherlands in some detail to examine whether the Dutch policy experience is in line with the main conclusions of the fiscal adjustment literature. In defining a successful fiscal adjustment, the literature normally proceeds in two steps: (1) identify periods with a fiscal adjustment, and (2) apply some criterion to differentiate between successful (i.e., long lasting) and unsuccessful adjustments.

A fiscal adjustment is generally defined as a period during which the government tries to reduce its budget deficit. We follow Alesina and Perotti (1995b) and employ two fiscal impulse indicators: (1) the change in the primary deficit as share of the previous year's GDP (FSM1), and (2) an indicator suggested by Blanchard (1993), which is an estimate of the budget deficit if the unemployment rate had remained the same as in the previous year (FSM2).[13] Following Alesina and Perotti (1995b), we regressed transfers as share of GDP on a time trend and the unemployment rate and used the estimated coefficient for the unemployment rate to estimate what transfers would be in period t if unemployment were the same as in the previous year. Finally, since FSM1 and FSM2 have certain drawbacks, we also used the change in the cyclically adjusted deficit (as share of GDP) as calculated by the OECD (FSM3).[14] Unfortunately, this reduces the sample length somewhat (1981–2003 instead of 1971–2003).

In most previous studies some absolute benchmark is applied to all countries—independent of their fiscal policy history—to identify years with a fiscal adjustment. The benchmarks chosen differ markedly across studies. For instance, Alesina and Ardagna (1998) include years in which the cyclically adjusted primary balance (CAPB) improves by at least 2 percent of GDP, or a period of two years in which the CAPB improves by at least 1.5 percent of GDP each year, while von Hagen et al. (2001) select episodes in which the cyclically adjusted government budget balance increased by at least 1.25 percent of GDP in two consecutive years, or when the change in the cyclically adjusted budget balance exceeded 1.5 of cyclically adjusted GDP in one year and was positive but less than 1.25 percent in the preceding year and in the subsequent year.[15]

In contrast, we selected years with a fiscal adjustment in terms of deviations from the average for the Netherlands during the period under consideration. Let u and σ be the average and the standard deviation of our fiscal stance measure (FSM), which is the change in the primary deficit, the Blanchard impulse measure, or the change in the cyclically adjusted deficit. In a given year fiscal policy is

- neutral if FSM $\in (u - 0.5\sigma, u + 0.5\sigma)$
- loose if FSM $\in (u + 0.5\sigma, u + 1.5\sigma)$
- very loose if FSM $\geq u + 1.5\sigma$
- tight if FSM $\in (u - 1.5\sigma, u - 0.5\sigma)$
- very tight if FSM $\leq u - 1.5\sigma$.

We consider years with either a tight or very tight fiscal policy, according to one of the fiscal stance measures, to be years with a fiscal adjustment.

It is hard to give a precise definition of a successful adjustment, but there is a broad consensus that a reasonable indication might be if the ratio of public debt to GDP starts to decline after the adjustment and continues to do so. Following McDermott and Wescott (1996), we consider a reduction of at least 3 percentage points in the ratio of gross public debt to GDP by the end of the third year *after* the fiscal tightening began as a workable criterion for judging success. Since years with a fiscal adjustment are determined on the basis of the three fiscal stance measures outlined previously, the use of a particular fiscal stance measure also influences the selection of fiscal adjustments that are considered to be successful. To ensure that our results are not driven by the selection of one particular fiscal stance measure, we employ three such measures.

Now let's turn to the characteristics of successful adjustment. According to the fiscal adjustment literature, successful adjustments are characterized by lower spending on government wages and transfers, while unsuccessful ones rely more on tax increases to decrease the government budget deficit.

Table 4.3 contrasts successful and unsuccessful fiscal adjustments in the Netherlands. It is clear from the table that the Dutch experience is hardly in accordance with the general conclusions of the fiscal adjustment literature. Take, for instance, transfers to households. If the measure FSM1 is used to identify years with tight fiscal policy, it follows that transfers were reduced in unsuccessful fiscal adjustments, while they were increased in successful ones. If we use FSM3, transfers were reduced in successful adjustment, but more so in unsuccessful ones. Under the FSM2 measure, transfers increased in successful and unsuccessful adjustments, while the increase was much higher during successful adjustments.

Likewise, government wages, which should decline according to the fiscal adjustment hypothesis to lead to a permanent decline in the debt ratio, did not decline in successful adjustments no matter which fiscal stance measure we took. In contrast, in unsuccessful years this category of spending did decline.

Now let us turn to the revenue side of the budget. According to the fiscal adjustment literature, fiscal adjustments that turn out to be unsuccessful often rely on tax increases. As table 4.3 shows, this is not confirmed by our evidence. Under FSM1 and FSM2, taxes were increased in successful adjustments, while under FSM3, taxes were reduced more in unsuccessful than in successful ones. Income taxes were reduced in successful adjustments according to FSM1 and FSM3, but more so in unsuccessful ones. Under FSM2 income taxes were increased (reduced) in (un)successful adjustments.

Finally, we used an alternative definition of a successful adjustment that is independent of the characterization of fiscal policy as stringent. For a year to be registered as one with a successful fiscal adjustment, we now only require that the debt ratio three years later has been

Table 4.3
Successful vs. unsuccessful adjustments

FSM1	#Obs.	Total	Investment	Transfers to households	Wages	Non-wage consumption	Rest
Successful	4	2.12	0.26	0.87	0.44	0.45	0.10
Unsuccessful	6	−1.36	−0.06	−0.71	−0.61	0.14	−0.12
	#Obs.	Total	Income taxes	Soc. sec. premiums	Indirect taxes	Business taxes	Rest
Successful	4	0.09	−0.32	−0.56	0.52	−0.02	0.46
Unsuccessful	6	−1.56	−0.37	−0.47	0.07	0.11	−0.89

FSM2	#Obs.	Total	Investment	Transfers to households	Wages	Non-wage consumption	Rest
Successful	3	5.66	0.10	2.99	0.96	0.49	1.13
Unsuccessful	9	2.41	−0.25	1.40	−0.29	0.45	1.10
	#Obs.	Total	Income taxes	Soc. sec. premiums	Indirect taxes	Business taxes	Rest
Successful	3	2.26	0.23	0.67	0.10	−0.02	1.28
Unsuccessful	9	1.22	−0.86	0.92	0.09	0.18	0.89

FSM3	#Obs.	Total	Investment	Transfers to households	Wages	Non-wage consumption	Rest
Successful	2	−0.87	0.24	−0.90	0.03	0.30	−0.54
Unsuccessful	3	−3.27	−0.08	−1.83	−0.75	0.08	−0.69
	#Obs.	Total	Income taxes	Soc. sec. premiums	Indirect taxes	Business taxes	Rest
Successful	2	−0.94	−0.46	−0.80	0.73	−0.06	−0.36
Unsuccessful	3	−2.32	−2.77	0.42	0.25	0.10	−0.32

Alternative definition of successful adjustment	#Obs.	Total	Investment	Transfers to households	Wages	Non-wage consumption	Rest
Successful	9	1.05	0.01	0.47	0.30	0.26	0.01
Unsuccessful	21	−0.06	−0.17	0.19	−0.50	0.28	0.15
	#Obs.	Total	Income taxes	Soc. sec. premiums	Indirect taxes	Business taxes	Rest
Successful	9	0.87	−0.01	0.16	0.45	−0.05	0.32
Unsuccessful	21	−0.15	−0.33	0.03	0.19	0.15	−0.18

reduced by three percentage points. In the lower part of table 4.3 we show the results using this alternative definition of successful adjustments. Again, the Dutch experience is not in line with the policy prescriptions of the fiscal adjustment literature. Transfers and wages, for instance, were not reduced more in successful adjustments than in unsuccessful ones. Unsuccessful adjustments had tax reductions, while successful ones had tax increases.

In conclusion, with respect to fiscal adjustment the Dutch experience deviates substantially from the policy advice coming from the fiscal adjustment literature. The conclusions of studies like Alesina and Perotti (1995b), McDermott and Wescott (1996), and von Hagen, Hughes Hallett, and Strauch (2001) are based on a panel of OECD countries. As a consequence, the Dutch experience may only play a minor role in these studies, especially if the chosen methodology implies that only a few fiscal adjustments in the Netherlands are included. The selection of a fiscal stance indicator, the selection criterion for deciding on the stance of fiscal policy, and the definition of a successful adjustment determine how many observations for each country are selected. It seems that our study differs from previous studies especially with respect to the selection of years with a fiscal policy adjustment in the Netherlands. McDermott and Wescott (1996) include 1982, 1983, and 1988. In contrast, Alesina and Ardagna (1998) only select 1991, which is also picked up by von Hagen, Hughes Hallett, and Strauch (2001), in addition to 1993 and 1995–1996. Of course, the selected years depend on the fiscal stance measure chosen. For FSM3, we identified the following years as ones with a fiscal adjustment: 1982, 1991, 1993, 1996, and 1999. So we identified more adjustment years for the Netherlands than did previous studies, although the years chosen are quite in line with those of other studies.

Therefore, we finally redid our analysis, selecting only years with a very restrictive fiscal policy as years with a fiscal adjustment. Unfortunately, that implied that for FSM2 and FSM3 all years selected were classified as unsuccessful ones. For FSM1 one year was successful (1996), while the other (1991) was not. For this particular case, our results are somewhat more in line with the conclusions of the fiscal adjustment literature. For instance, transfers were reduced in the successful adjustment by 2.14 percent of GDP and by only 0.62 percent of GDP in the unsuccessful adjustment. However, taxes were reduced by 0.22 percent of GDP in the successful adjustment and by 2.05 percent of GDP in the unsuccessful one.

In conclusion, our results suggest that successful fiscal adjustments in the Netherlands were different than the ones focused upon in the fiscal adjustment literature. For one thing, the adjustments were much more gradual. If we apply the methodology of the fiscal adjustment literature, it becomes clear that many successful adjustments were not based on reducing transfers and wages, but often relied on tax increases. Still, during the 1980s–1990s, the public sector in the Netherlands was trimmed: government spending as share of GDP declined substantially, and this was realized to considerable extent by cutting transfers.

4.4 Conclusions

We analyzed fiscal policy in the Netherlands over the period 1948–2003 from two perspectives. First, drawing on the fiscal sustainability literature we tested whether Dutch fiscal policy was sustainable. Our tests suggest that this was the case. We also found that many political-institutional features that are likely to lead to budget deficits according to recent cross-country-based research did not affect budget deficits in the Netherlands. So despite some prolonged periods with high budget deficits, the institutional budgetary setting apparently ensured that some kind of adjustment took place that made policy sustainable. We examined to what extent the Dutch experience is in line with policy recommendations coming from the so-called fiscal adjustment literature. According to this line of research, successful fiscal policy adjustments are characterized by spending cuts. Notably, spending on government wages and transfers ought to be cut in order to permanently improve the government's financial position. In contrast, fiscal adjustments that rely primarily on tax increases and cuts in public investment tend not to last. We conclude that successful fiscal adjustments in the Netherlands have been quite different: the adjustments were quite gradual and successful adjustments often relied on tax increases. Still, during the final two decades of the previous century, government spending as share of GDP declined substantially, and this was realized to some extent by cutting transfers.

Appendix

In table 4A.1, we summarize some results from studies of sustainability of public debt.

Table 4A.1
Summary of research on the sustainability of fiscal policy (only studies that include the Netherlands)

Study	Period and countries	Test performed	Sustainable?
Grilli, Masciandaro, and Tabellini 1991	1950–1986, 10 EU countries	Stationarity of deficit including interest payments	Nonstationarity only rejected for the United Kingdom, and, at a lower confidence level, for Germany and possibly Denmark
Corsetti and Roubini 1991	1960–1989, 18 OECD countries		Problems present in some countries, including the Netherlands
de Haan and Siermann 1993	1900–1988, the Netherlands	Stationarity of deficit including interest payments and cointegration of expenditures and revenues	Yes
Caporale 1995	1960–1991, EU countries	Stationarity of deficit and debt	Not in Italy, Greece, Denmark, and Germany
Uctum and Wickens 2000	1965–1994, 11 EU countries and the United States	Stationarity test (public debt)	Sustainable in Denmark, Ireland, and the Netherlands
Artis and Marcelino 2000	Early 1970s–1994, EU countries minus Greece and Luxembourg	Stationarity test (public debt)	Mixed evidence, depending on particular assumptions, including the Netherlands
Afonso 2005	1970–2003, EU countries	Unit root and cointegration tests of revenues and expenditures	Fiscal policy is deemed unsustainable with the possible exception of Germany and the Netherlands
Bravo and Silvestre 2002	1960–2000, 11 EU countries	Cointegration tests of expenditures and revenues	Sustainable in Austria, France, Germany, the Netherlands, and the United Kingdom
Vanhorebeek and van Rompuy 1995	1970–1994, 8 EU countries 1870–1993, Belgium	Stationarity test	No, except for France and Germany

Notes

We would like to thank the participants at the CESifo/LBI conference on Sustainability of Public Debt (October 22–23, 2004), the Annual Meeting of the European Public Choice Society (March 31–April 3 2005), our discussant Emma Galli, and three referees for their very helpful comments.

1. This part draws heavily on Artis and Marcellino 2000.

2. The conclusions do not change when lagged endogenous variables are included in the unit root test equations to correct for possible autocorrelation in the residual terms.

3. The appendix offers a summary of all papers we are aware of that perform some kind of sustainability test of fiscal policy in the Netherlands. It follows that our results deviate from some previous studies that concluded that Dutch fiscal policy was not always on a sustainable path.

4. Determined using a Hodrick-Prescott filter ($\lambda = 100$) for government expenditures net of interest payments as share of GDP.

5. It turned out that the output gap and the growth rate of real GDP were not significant, and they were therefore not included.

6. We also performed recursive regressions starting with twenty observations. These produce very stable β_1 coefficients between 0.076 and 0.097 (not shown).

7. Most research on the influence of political-institutional factors combines cross-country and time-series information; see, e.g., de Haan and Sturm 1994, 1997. A notable exception is the study by Galli and Padovano (2002) for Italy.

8. The following scores were given to parties that participated at some time in government: PPR = 2, PvdA = 3, D66 = 4, ARP = 4, CDA = 5, KVP = 5, DS70 = 5, CHU = 6, VVD = 7, LPF = 8.

9. In the case of more than one government in a particular year, we took averages using the number of months that the governments were in power when calculating *NPART* and *NMIN*.

10. We checked whether there was a multicollinearity problem, but with one exception the correlation coefficients were not very high. The exception is the correlation between *POPSH65* and *U*, which is 0.73, explaining the large change in the coefficient of *U* once *POPSH65* is included.

11. However, Heylen and Everaert (2000) reject the hypothesis that to succeed, consolidation should rely on cutting the government wage bill.

12. There is also empirical evidence showing that the quality of the institutions governing the budget process is an important determinant of the durability and success of fiscal consolidations (see, e.g., von Hagen 1992; de Haan and Sturm 1994; and the various contributions in Poterba and von Hagen 1999). As our analysis is based on time-series evidence for just one country, we discard the role of budgetary institutions.

13. Alesina and Ardagna (1998) argue that this method is simple, transparent, and straightforward. It has been used in various studies, including Alesina and Perotti 1995, Alesina and Ardagna 1998, and Alesina, Perotti, and Tavares 1998.

14. As one of the referees rightly pointed out, FSM1 cannot be considered a cyclically adjusted indicator because the change in the primary deficit is not corrected in any way.

FSM2 corrects the budget only for the cyclical effects on transfers and ignores potentially important effects on tax revenues.

15. As a consequence, the fiscal adjustment periods identified differ markedly across studies.

References

Afonso, A. 2005. Fiscal sustainability: The unpleasant European case. *FinanzArchiv* 61:19–44.

Ahmed, S., and J. H. Rogers. 1995. Government budget deficits and trade deficits: Are present value constraints satisfied in long-term data? *Journal of Monetary Economics* 36:351–374.

Alesina, A., and S. Ardagna. 1998. Tales of fiscal adjustment. *Economic Policy* 27:489–545.

Alesina, A., and R. Perotti. 1995a. The political economy of budget deficits. *IMF Staff Papers* 42:1–37.

Alesina, A., and R. Perotti. 1995b. Fiscal expansion and fiscal adjustments in OECD countries. *Economic Policy* 21:205–248.

Alesina, A., and R. Perotti. 1997. Fiscal adjustments in OECD countries: Composition and macroeconomic effects. *IMF Staff Papers* 44:210–248.

Alesina, A., R. Perotti, and J. Tavares. 1998. The political economy of fiscal adjustments. *Brookings Papers on Economic Activity* 1 (Spring): 197–266.

Artis, M., and M. Marcellino. 2000. The solvency of government finances in Europe. In *Fiscal Sustainability*, ed. Banca d'Italia, 209–241. Rome: Bank of Italy.

Blanchard, O. 1993. Suggestions for a new set of fiscal indicators. In *The Political Economy of Government Debt*, ed. H. A. A. Verbon and F. A. A. M. Van Winden, 307–325. Amsterdam: North-Holland.

Bohn, H. 1998. The behavior of U.S. public debt and deficits. *Quarterly Journal of Economics* 113:949–963.

Bravo, A., and A. Silvestre. 2002. Intertemporal sustainability of fiscal policies: Some tests for European countries. *European Journal of Political Economy* 18 (3): 517–528.

Caporale, G. M. 1995. Bubble finance and debt sustainability: A test of the government's intertemporal budget constraint. *Applied Economics* 27 (12): 1135–1143.

Chen, D. H. C. 2004. Population age structure and the budget deficit. Policy Research Working Paper no. 34235. The World Bank, Washington, DC.

Corsetti, Giancarlo, and Nouriel Roubini. 1991. Fiscal deficits, public debt and government solvency: Evidence from OECD countries. *Journal of the Japanese and International Economies* 5 (4): 354–380.

Cukierman, A., and A. Meltzer. 1989. A political theory of government debt and deficits in a neo-Ricardian framework. *American Economic Review* 79:713–32.

de Haan, J., and C. L. J. Siermann. 1993. The intertemporal government budget constraint: an application to the Netherlands. *Public Finance* 48:243–249.

de Haan, J., and J.-E. Sturm. 1994. Political and institutional determinants of fiscal policy in the European Community. *Public Choice* 80:157–172.

de Haan, J., and J.-E. Sturm. 1997. Political and economic determinants of OECD budget deficits and government expenditures: A reinvestigation. *European Journal of Political Economy* 13:739–750.

Franzese, R. J. 2002. Electoral and partisan cycles in economic policies and outcomes. *Annual Review of Political Science* 5:369–421.

Galli, E., and F. Padovano. 2002. A comparative test of alternative theories of the determinants of Italian public deficits (1950–1998). *Public Choice* 113:37–58.

Grilli, V. 1989. Seigniorage in Europe. In *A European Central Bank?*, ed. M. de Cecco and A. Giovannini, 53–79. Cambridge: Cambridge University Press.

Grilli, V., D. Masciandaro, and G. Tabellini. 1991. Political and monetary institutions and public financial policies in the industrial countries. *Economic Policy* 13: 341–392.

Hakkio, C., and M. Rush. 1991. Is the budget deficit too large? *Economic Inquiry* 59:429–445.

Hamilton, J., and M. Flavin. 1986. On the limitations of government borrowing: A framework for empirical testing. *American Economic Review* 76:808–819.

Heylen, F., and G. Everaert. 2000. Success and failure of fiscal consolidation in the OECD: A multivariate analysis. *Public Choice* 105:103–124.

Kirchgässner, G. 2001. The effects of fiscal institutions on public finance: a survey of the empirical evidence. CESifo Working Paper no. 617.

McDermott, C., and John R. F. Wescott. 1996. An empirical analysis of fiscal adjustments. *IMF Staff Papers* 43:725–753.

Perotti, R., and J. Kontopoulos. 2002. Fragmented fiscal policy. *Journal of Public Economics* 86 (2): 191–222.

Poterba, J., and J. von Hagen, eds. 1999. *Fiscal Institutions and Fiscal Performance*. Chicago: University of Chicago Press.

Trehan, B., and C. Walsh. 1988. Common trends, intertemporal budget balance, and revenue smoothing. *Journal of Economic Dynamics and Control* 12:425–44.

Trehan, B., and C. Walsh. 1991. Testing intertemporal budget constraints: theory and applications to U.S. federal budget and current account deficits. *Journal of Money, Credit, and Banking* 23:206–223.

Uctum, M., and M. Wickens. 2000. Debt and deficit ceilings, and sustainability of fiscal policies: An intertemporal analysis. *Oxford Bulletin of Economics and Statistics* 62 (2): 197–222.

Vanhorebeek, F., and R. van Rompuy. 1995. Solvency and sustainability of fiscal policies in the EU. *De Economist* 143:457–473.

Volkerink, B., and J. de Haan. 2001. Fragmented government effects on fiscal policy: New evidence. *Public Choice* 109:221–42.

von Hagen, J., A. Hughes Hallett, and R. Strauch. 2001. Budgetary consolidation in EMU. European Commission Economic Papers no. 148.

Wilcox, D. 1989. The sustainability of government deficits: Implications of the present value borrowing constraint. *Journal of Money, Credit, and Banking* 21:291–306.

5 The Long Shadow of "Austrokeynesianism"? Public Debt Sustainability in Austria

Reinhard Neck and Gottfried Haber

5.1 Introduction

After a few years during which the objective of a balanced budget was emphasized in Austria, in October 2004, the Austrian federal minister of finance announced a planned federal budget deficit of about 2 percent of GDP for the fiscal year 2005. He and other officials repeatedly argued that the soon-to-come tax reform with lower income tax rates would be necessary to promote employment, investment, and private consumption. This may be interpreted as a return to one of the basic ideas of "Austrokeynesianism," a policy-mix including activist (mostly expansionary) fiscal policy design to combat unemployment and enhance growth. It should be noted, however, that the idea of a budget balanced in the long run was not alien to Keynes himself; within the concepts of countercyclical budgetary policies, the idea of paying back incurred debt by generating a surplus in economic boom periods plays a central role.

During the 1990s and the early 2000s, the issue of public debt has increasingly become a public concern for both economists and politicians. Mounting public debt in Austria as well as in most of the OECD countries is on the daily political agenda. The Stability and Growth Pact (SGP) and the Maastricht criteria for prospective member countries of the European Economic and Monetary Union (EMU) directed fiscal policies toward sustainability, but owing to the difficulties in meeting these criteria, their interpretation has become "loose" over time, allowing for larger deviations from a balanced budget than previously agreed upon. One of the key ideas of the SGP is the prevention of spillover of unsustainable fiscal policies from individual member states—for example, via rising interest rates within the EMU, causing crowding out and higher interest rate levels in the whole Euro Area or undesirable effects on the exchange rate of the euro toward other currencies (cf., e.g., Gros and Thygesen 1998; De Grauwe 2005).

There is much debate on the question of what kind of fiscal policy is sustainable in the long run. Even if the economic position of the government is regarded as different from that of a private household, there is general agreement among economists that the government has to decide on fiscal policies in line with some long-term budget constraint. The most general guidelines for sustainability concern the relation between accumulated discounted future government budgetary surpluses and discounted future government debt, including the initial stock of debt. No rational private agent would lend money to a government if that agent expected that the debt could not be paid back (unless compensated by very high interest payments before default).

However, such an approach requires a lot of information regarding past, present, and future government budgetary policies. Several methodologies exist to test for the sustainability of fiscal policy. Two broad approaches will be applied in this chapter. First, several econometric approaches are applied to test for the stationarity of the series of discounted public debt. If the series is stationary, that is, if public debt does not increase in the long run and exceed discounted future surpluses, fiscal policy is ("ad hoc") sustainable. Second, a model is tested that takes into account the reactions of fiscal policymakers to rising public debt. If policymakers increase the primary surplus as a reaction to increased public debt in the previous period, and if this reaction is strong enough, fiscal policy is sustainable.

This chapter is structured as follows: Section 5.2 describes the present situation of the federal budget in Austria and the historical development of federal debt and deficit. Section 5.3 briefly reviews the theoretical framework of the government budget constraint. Section 5.4 presents the results of some econometric tests regarding the stationarity of the discounted public debt. Next, we apply Bohn's test for sustainability (1998) for Austria in section 5.5. Finally, section 5.6 summarizes the results of the chapter.

5.2 Public Debt and Deficit in Austria

As in most EMU member states, the current debt-to-GDP ratio in Austria is clearly above the EMU target of 60 percent for general government debt. This is mainly owing to increases in central (federal) government debt; federal provinces (states, or *Bundesländer*) and communities and municipalities account for only a relatively small part of the public sector and have even obtained budgetary surpluses in some years in the recent past. The consolidation of the federal budget, however, cannot yet be labeled successful even if the entry conditions for Austria's membership in the EMU were fulfilled (cf. Breuss 1999). Because consistent time-series data on public debt over a longer period are only available for the central (federal) government (*Bund*), in this chapter the analysis is confined to this level of the Austrian public sector. Because Austria is a federally organized country with nine federal provinces, over 2,500 communities and numerous *parafisci* and state-owned companies, a consistent fiscal policy can only be expected at the level of central government. Of course, all public debt has to be taken into account when fulfillment of the SGP criteria is evaluated.

The descriptive literature on public finances in Austria (e.g., Seidel 1985; Smekal and Gantner 1983; Neck 2005) identifies three or possibly four different periods of fiscal policies in the past:

1. From World War II until the mid-1950s, fiscal policy was mostly characterized by balanced federal budgets.

2. From 1958 to 1974, ideas of Keynesian stabilization policies influenced fiscal policy decisions in Austria. As a result, fiscal policies were designed to smooth the business cycle, aiming at a balanced budget in the medium or long run (over the cycle). This was mostly achieved; hence the federal debt-to-output ratio remained constant on average during these years. One reason for this was the high average growth of real GDP during this period (and period 1), which enabled policymakers to enjoy a considerable "growth dividend."

3. Starting with the first oil price shock, which hit Austria in 1975, Austria's growth rates were reduced and significantly higher fiscal deficits were built up. Although Keynesian policy prescriptions were losing their appeal during these years on an international level, most Austrian policymakers (especially the then dominating party SPÖ—Social Democrats) still insisted on some kind of Austrokeynesianism as their economic policy ideology, aiming at full employment by applying instruments of fiscal policy in an expansionary way. There were several attempts at consolidating the federal budget, but these efforts were only temporarily successful because they did not result in a fall in federal government debt (relative to GDP) but merely delayed further increases by a few years.

4. Possibly, a fourth fiscal policy regime exists starting with Austria's entry into the EU (and the aim of fulfilling the Maastricht criteria to

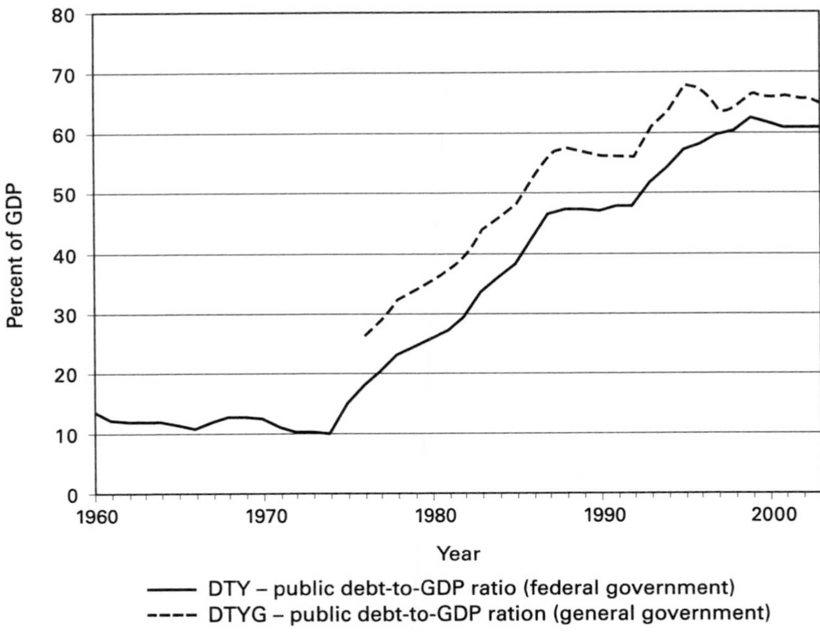

Figure 5.1
Federal and general government debt-to-GDP ratio for Austria
Source: WIFO database, earlier SNA-GDP data linked to ESA 95 data, and our own calculations.

become a member of the Euro Area) or (more likely) starting with the "center-right" government of the Austrian Peoples' Party (ÖVP; Christian Democrats) and the Freedom Party (FPÖ; right-wing) in 2000. One of the declared objectives of this government was the achievement of a balanced budget ("zero budget deficit"). Whether this really represents a regime change remains an open question.

Figure 5.1 shows the development of the federal and the central government debt in Austria relative to Austrian GDP (debt-to-GDP ratio) since 1960 and since 1976, respectively.

Although the current (net) federal government deficit-to-GDP ratio in Austria is below the critical (SGP) value of 3 percent, this is neither sufficient for stabilizing federal government debt nor fully in line with the recent budget consolidation program submitted to the European Commission. In contrast to the "gross budget surplus," the "net budget surplus" does not include payments to settle outstanding debt. Therefore, the (economically more relevant) net budget deficit is closely re-

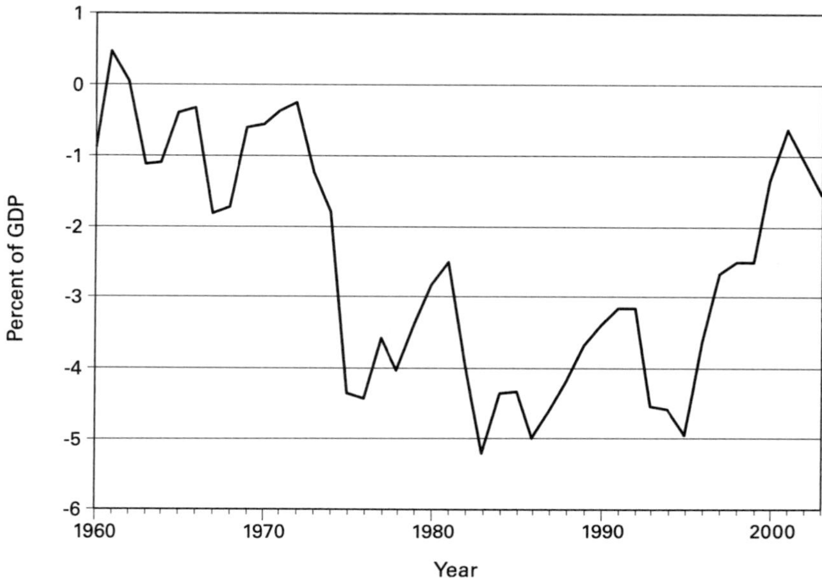

Figure 5.2
(Net) budget surplus (ratio to GDP) for Austria

lated to the increase in public debt and is also the politically more important variable. Figure 5.2 shows that the net surplus of the federal government in Austria was (with only a few exceptions) negative; that is, net federal budget deficits occurred during the last decades.

Some information about the composition of these deficits can be inferred from figure 5.3, where the primary surplus (its ratio to GDP) for the same period is presented. In spite of some subperiods with (sometimes even high) primary surpluses, interest payments on outstanding public debt have been so high (and grown so much) as to turn primary surpluses into net deficits. This may also be seen as one crucial factor associated with unsustainable fiscal policies: if, in the long run, public debt rises beyond a critical level, primary surpluses might not be sufficient even to finance interest payments. This can lead to a vicious circle of incurring additional debt in order to be able to service present debt.

5.3 Some Theoretical Considerations

The development of public debt in discrete time can be described by the accounting identity (all variables in nominal terms)

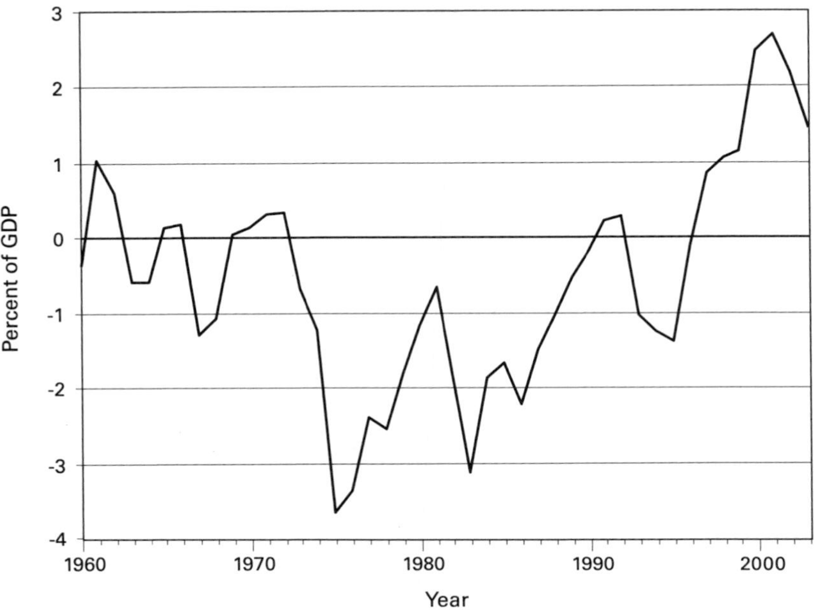

Figure 5.3
Primary budget surplus (ratio to GDP) for Austria

$$B_t = B_{t-1}(1 + r_{t-1}) - S_t, \tag{5.1}$$

where B_t denotes real public debt, r_t is the real rate of interest, and S_t denotes the real primary surplus (budgetary surplus excluding interest payments). Given interest payments, the stock of public debt increases even if government revenues are equal to government expenditures excluding interest payments (i.e., if $S_t = 0$) because the government has to finance interest payments by an increase in public debt.

Defining a discount factor d_t by

$$d_t = \prod_{j=0}^{t-1}(1 + r_j)^{-1}, \quad d_0 = 1, \tag{5.2}$$

the present value of both sides of equation (5.1) can be rewritten as

$$B_t d_t = B_{t-1} d_{t-1} - S_t d_t. \tag{5.3}$$

Defining $B_t d_t \equiv b_t$ and $S_t d_t \equiv s_t$, we get

$$b_t = b_{t-1} - s_t. \tag{5.4}$$

Reformulating equation (5.4) by recursive substitution leads to

$$b_{t+N} = b_t - \sum_{j=1}^{N} s_{t+j}. \tag{5.5}$$

If we require future discounted real public debt to go to zero in the limit, the present value of public debt has to be equal to the sum of discounted expected future primary surpluses:

$$b_t = E_t \sum_{j=1}^{N} s_{t+j}, \tag{5.6}$$

with E_t denoting the expectations operator. Equation (5.6) is the ad hoc form of the intertemporal (present value) borrowing constraint of the government in the sense of Bohn (chapter 2). The following condition is equivalent to the requirement for this budget constraint (5.6) to be fulfilled:

$$\lim_{N \to \infty} E_t b_{t+N} = 0, \tag{5.7}$$

which is commonly known as the No Ponzi Condition. This condition states that (private or public) agents cannot indefinitely accumulate debt by borrowing new money to pay back their old liabilities including interest payments. An alternative, weaker condition demands stationarity of the debt-to-GDP ratio, which is sufficient for sustainability if Ponzi games are considered admissible in the long run.

In the following sections, we apply several statistical tests to shed light on the question as to whether Austrian fiscal policy is sustainable in the sense that condition (5.6), namely, the ad hoc intertemporal government budget constraint, is fulfilled. We follow and extend the studies by Greiner and Semmler (1999) for Germany and Getzner, Glatzer, and Neck (2001) for Austria.

5.4 Tests for Stationarity of Austrian Budgetary Policies

5.4.1 The General Approach

Fulfilling the budget constraint according to equation (5.6) means that public debt b_t at time t can be paid back by surpluses in future periods. In the following, the fulfillment of this constraint is taken as the null hypothesis. We start from the equation

$$b_t = A_0 \prod_{j=1}^{t}(1 + r_j) + E_t \sum_{j=1}^{\infty} s_{t+j}. \tag{5.8}$$

The intertemporal budget constraint is fulfilled if $A_0 = 0$ which means that b_t will be stationary for any stationary series of s_t. If $A_0 > 0$, b_t will not be stationary; that is, public debt at time t cannot be paid back by expected future surpluses.

As a first empirical indication of the sustainability of Austrian budgetary policy, figure 5.4 shows real public debt and discounted real public debt for the period 1960–2003 (annual data). "Real public debt" is the time series of the central (federal) government's financial debt at 1995 prices; the series of nominal federal government's financial debt was taken from the database of the Austrian Institute of Economic Research (WIFO) and deflated with the GDP deflator. The discounted real public debt figures were calculated by using a discount factor according to equation (5.2). The annual net return of newly emitted

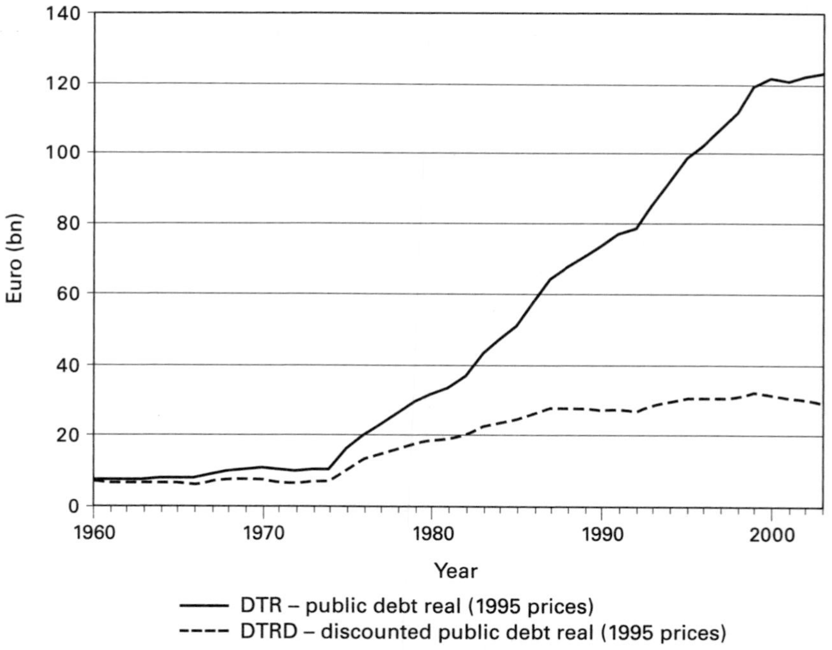

Figure 5.4
Real federal public debt and discounted real public debt in Austria, 1960–2003 (1995 prices)

bonds (without government bonds) was used as the (variable) discount rate. This procedure may be criticized as testing for ad hoc sustainability (chapter 2), but the interest rate used is the only one that is available in a consistent way for the whole period 1960–2003 and hence may be interpreted as a proxy for the theoretically adequate use of prices for contingent claims in the No Ponzi Condition and the "true" intertemporal budget constraint.

Clearly, discounted real federal government debt and particularly undiscounted real federal government debt show a sharp increase in the mid-1970s, which is consistent with the data of the debt-to-GDP ratio shown in figure 5.1. Between 1960 and 1974, the series follows a stable path without much variation. The year 1975 seems to mark a structural break in Austrian budgetary policies. From 1975 to 2003, real federal government debt increased from around EUR 16 billion to around EUR 123 billion (at 1995 prices), corresponding to an increase in the debt-to-GDP ratio from about 10 percent in 1974 to about 61 percent in 2003. A visual inspection of the data gives the impression of another structural break between 1999 and 2000, which might be related to the efforts of Austrian governments to fulfill the Maastricht criteria for entering the EMU and sticking to the SGP or the policy goal of a balanced budget proclaimed by the center-right government in the early 2000s. However, the most recent figures again show rising federal (and general) government deficits in Austria in 2004 and 2005, and the hypothesis of another structural break cannot be confirmed statistically because the period from 1999–2000 to 2003 is too short to allow for testing with annual data.

5.4.2 *Generalized Flood-Garber Test*

For estimating equation (5.8), we assume that expectations about future budgetary surpluses can be formed on the basis of surpluses of past years. To eliminate serial correlation in the residuals, lagged values of public debt are included as additional regressors. The equation to be estimated can then be written as

$$b_t = c_0 + A_0 \prod_{j=1}^{t} (1 + r_j) + c_1 b_{t-1} + \cdots + c_p b_{t-p} + a_0 s_t + a_1 s_{t-1} + \cdots + a_p s_{t-p} + \varepsilon_t. \tag{5.9}$$

The so-called generalized Flood-Garber test (Flood and Garber 1980) starts from equation (5.9). The null hypothesis for the test is $A_0 = 0$. If this condition is fulfilled, the series of public debt is stationary. Estimating equation (5.9) by OLS yields the results shown in table 5.1, estimation (1). The estimated model shows that the coefficient A_0 is significantly positive (t-statistic 2.59). Thus, the null hypothesis seems to be rejected, and this first test favors the conclusion that discounted federal government debt is not stationary. But this result is not robust: In order to reduce serial correlation in the residuals, estimation (2) of table 5.1 shows the results of an estimation including two AR-terms (using nonlinear least squares). Now the coefficient A_0 becomes insignificant with a t-value of 0.50.

As figure 5.1 shows, there might be a structural break in the series of real federal government debt and discounted real federal government debt. A Chow breakpoint test for estimation (1) indicates a structural break in the year 1975 (log-likelihood ratio 7.99(*)), but does not do so for estimation (2). To obtain more insights, we estimate both equations for the periods 1960–1974 and 1975–2003 separately.

Estimations (3)–(6) of table 5.1 show the results. For the first period, 1960–1974, the null hypothesis cannot be rejected since the coefficient A_0 is significantly different from zero neither in estimation (3) nor in (5). This means that the No Ponzi Condition may hold for the first period; that is, discounted real federal government debt is stationary. For the second period, it is less clear whether the series of discounted real public debt is stationary since the coefficient A_0 is significantly positive in estimation (4) (t-statistic 2.74) but not in estimation (6). The coefficient of b_{t-1} is close to one if this variable is included, which points toward the possibility of a unit root in the series of real federal government debt. Thus the generalized Flood-Garber test applied on the basis of past developments of the Austrian budgetary surplus does not give clear-cut results but seems to indicate that Austrian federal budgetary policy may have been less sustainable in the period since 1975 than before.

5.4.3 *Restricted Flood-Garber Test*

In order to obtain more evidence on the stationarity of Austrian public debt, we apply the so-called restricted Flood-Garber test introduced by Hamilton and Flavin (1986) and extended by Greiner and Semmler (1999). With the generalized Flood-Garber test, no restrictions are

Table 5.1
Stationarity of Austrian federal government debt: Generalized Flood-Garber test

	Estimation (1) Coefficient (t-statistic)	Estimation (2) Coefficient (t-statistic)	Estimation (3) Coefficient (t-statistic)	Estimation (4) Coefficient (t-statistic)	Estimation (5) Coefficient (t-statistic)	Estimation (6) Coefficient (t-statistic)
Constant	−0.6533 (−3.1212**)				5.9900 (5.3701**)	33.5820 (1.9289(*))
A_0	0.1041 (2.5852*)	0.3410 (0.5041)	−0.0206 (−0.1891)	0.1182 (2.7448*)	0.1439 (0.8316)	−0.1260 (−0.1672)
s_t	−1.0931 (−13.2522**)	−1.1342 (−6.1347**)	−0.6728 (−3.8425**)	−0.9998 (−13.9029**)	−0.3842 (−1.6010)	−0.8153 (−2.9183**)
s_{t-1}		−0.6090 (−3.5408**)				
s_{t-2}		−0.4614 (−2.6651*)				
b_{t-1}	0.9763 (54.8900**)		1.0010 (10.1727**)	0.9450 (39.7286**)		
AR(1)		1.8582 (14.4309**)			0.9540 (3.0817*)	1.2970 (6.4566**)
AR(2)		−0.8599 (−6.5281**)			−0.5907 (−2.1853(*))	−0.3650 (−1.9063(*))
Adj. R^2	0.9984	0.9963	0.5928	0.9951	0.5398	0.9912
Durbin-Watson	1.7166	1.9278	1.9102	1.2217	1.8523	1.3835
No. of observations	43	40	14	29	13	29
Period	1961–2003	1964–2003	1961–1974	1975–2003	1962–1974	1975–2003

Source: OLS estimation.
$^{**}p < 0.01$, $^{*}p < 0.05$, $(^{*})p < 0.1$.

imposed on the parameters $a_1, a_2, \ldots$ in equation (5.9). However, if one assumes that the primary surpluses s_t follow an autoregressive process, the following system of two equations can be derived. The first equation (5.10) describes the autoregressive process, while the second one (equation [5.11]) results from inserting the expected value of s_t derived from the first equation into equation (5.9).

$$s_t = c_1 + c_2 s_{t-1} + c_3 s_{t-2} + c_4 s_{t-3} + \varepsilon_{2t}, \tag{5.10}$$

$$b_t = A_0 \prod_{j=1}^{t}(1 + r_j) + c_5 + \frac{(c_2 a + c_3 a^2 + c_4 a^3) s_t}{(1 - c_2 a - c_3 a^2 - c_4 a^3)}$$
$$+ \frac{(c_3 a + c_4 a^2) s_{t-1}}{(1 - c_2 a - c_3 a^2 - c_4 a^3)} + \frac{(c_4 a) s_{t-2}}{(1 - c_2 a - c_3 a^2 - c_4 a^3)} + \varepsilon_{1t}. \tag{5.11}$$

For the restricted Flood-Garber test, equations (5.10) and (5.11) are estimated simultaneously by nonlinear least squares (SUR, or seemingly uncorrelated regressions).

The term $a = 1/(1 + r)$ denotes the discount factor for one period, with r being the average real rate of interest. The average real interest rate for the whole period (1960–2003) amounted to 3.42 percent. However, interest rates (and GDP growth) differed between the two periods. In period 1960–1974, real interest rates were 2.83 percent on average while in the second period, 1975–2003, real interest rates were 3.73 percent.

Table 5.2 shows the results of the simultaneous estimation of equations (5.10) and (5.11). The null hypothesis of the restricted Flood-Garber test is again $A_0 = 0$. The estimations for the whole period (1960–2003) as well as for the second period (1975–2003) yield coefficients for A_0 that are highly significantly different from zero. For the whole period, the t-statistic for A_0 is 19.35 (table 5.2, est. [7]), while for the second period, the t-statistic is 9.81 (table 5.2, est. [9]). The results for the first period (1960–1974) are reported in table 5.2, est. [8] and show a coefficient of A_0 that is much smaller and just significant at the 5 percent level (t-statistic: 2.13).

The results of the restricted Flood-Garber test give a stronger indication for Austrian federal government debt being closer to stationarity for the period before 1975 than from 1975 on. H_0 is clearly rejected for the second period, indicating that discounted real federal government debt was not stationary over the period 1975–2003.

Table 5.2
Stationarity of Austrian federal government debt: Restricted Flood-Garber test

	Estimation (7) Coefficient (t-statistic)	Estimation (8) Coefficient (t-statistic)	Estimation (9) Coefficient (t-statistic)
c_1	−0.8050 (−2.1178*)	−0.2394 (−2.5313*)	−0.0616 (−0.3881)
c_2	1.1782 (1.9258(*))	0.3427 (1.3289)	1.1433 (4.7868**)
c_3	−0.2164 (−0.2447)	−0.7534 (−3.2502**)	−0.3323 (−0.9502)
c_4	−1.5012 (−2.4559*)	−0.0753 (−0.3080)	0.0246 (0.0988)
c_5	−2.5250 (−2.0280**)	5.5025 (8.0287**)	9.4498 (5.5437**)
A_0	1.9592 (19.3540**)	0.2247 (2.1269*)	1.2023 (9.8064**)
$\bar{R}^2$ equation (5.10)	0.7049	0.2104	0.7350
$\bar{R}^2$ equation (5.11)	0.8304	0.1349	0.7421
No. of observations	42	13	29
Period	1962–2003	1962–1974	1975–2003

Source: SUR (NLS) estimation.
$^{**}p < 0.01$, $^{*}p < 0.05$, $^{(*)}p < 0.1$.

5.4.4 *Unit Root Tests*

Tests for Stationarity of b_t

Next, three unit root tests, the Augmented Dickey-Fuller (ADF) test, the Phillips-Perron (PP) test, and the Kwiatkowski-Phillips-Schmidt-Shin (KPSS) test, are applied to test for stationarity in some time series of Austrian budgetary policies. The ADF test takes the first difference of a time series as the dependent variable and regresses it on the lagged values of the same time series and on one or more lagged first differences of the series. Furthermore, a constant and a linear trend can be included as explanatory variables. If the time series has a unit root and hence is nonstationary, the estimate for the coefficient of the lagged series is non-negative. If the estimator is significantly negative, the null hypothesis H_0—namely, the hypothesis that the time series has a unit root[1]—has to be rejected. In order to apply the ADF test to the time series b_t, the following equation has to be estimated:

Table 5.3
Stationarity of Austrian federal government debt b_t: Unit root tests

	Estimation (10)	Estimation (11)	Estimation (12)
ADF test-statistic	−1.1136	−2.6512	−4.7381**
PP test-statistic	−0.5958	−2.2740	−5.0617**
KPSS test-statistic	0.7390**	0.2579	0.6334*
No. of observations	42	13	29
Period	1962–2003	1962–1974	1975–2003

$^{**}p < 0.01$, $^{*}p < 0.05$, $^{(*)}p < 0.1$.

$$(b_t - b_{t-1}) = \beta_0 + \beta_1 b_{t-1} + \beta_2 (b_{t-1} - b_{t-2}), \tag{5.12}$$

where the βs are the coefficients to be estimated.

An alternative to the ADF test is the PP test. This test does not include the lagged first difference $(b_{t-1} - b_{t-2})$ but adjusts the value of the t-statistic for serial correlation in the residuals. Another test for the presence of a unit root is the KPSS test. In contrast to the ADF and PP tests, this method can be applied to test the null hypothesis of stationarity against the alternative of the presence of a unit root (nonstationarity). The power of all these tests is limited for the small number of observations available for our time series; hence we want to check for the robustness of the results by applying all three test statistics.

Table 5.3 shows the results of the ADF, PP, and KPSS tests in different specifications. For the whole period, all of the test procedures indicate that discounted public debt is nonstationary. For the subperiods, the results are inconclusive: the ADF and PP tests cannot reject the unit root hypothesis for the first period but do so for the second period. On the other hand, the KPSS test statistic in estimation (12) does not reject the null hypothesis of stationarity for the first period but does so for the period 1975–2003 at the 5 percent significance level.

The results in table 5.3 seem to indicate that the discounted real federal government debt is nonstationary for the whole period 1962–2003, which seems astonishing, but on the other hand these tests are known to be not very powerful. The KPSS test suggests that 1962–1974 may be stationary and hence public debt was sustainable, but for 1975–2003 this may not be the case, which seems more plausible when inspecting the data. Summing up, the results for the subperiods are rather inconclusive.

Table 5.4
Stationarity of Austrian federal government primary surplus s_t: Unit root tests

	Estimation (13)	Estimation (14)	Estimation (15)
ADF test-statistic	−2.3472	−4.0291*	−1.5745
PP test-statistic	−1.8656	−2.1319	−1.1153
KPSS test-statistic	0.3300	0.3855(*)	0.6304*
No. of observations	42	13	29
Period	1962–2003	1962–1974	1975–2003

$^{**}p < 0.01$, $^{*}p < 0.05$, $^{(*)}p < 0.1$.

Tests for Stationarity of s_t

In order to further test for the stationarity of Austrian public debt, we consider the stationarity of the federal budget primary surplus. As Trehan and Walsh (1991) have shown, a stationary discounted primary surplus is a necessary and sufficient condition for stationarity of the series of discounted public debt, provided that the expected real interest rate is constant.

In order to test for the nonstationarity of the discounted real primary surplus s_t, the following equation was estimated:

$$(s_t - s_{t-1}) = [\beta_0] + \beta_1 s_{t-1} + \beta_2 (s_{t-1} - s_{t-2}) + [\beta_3 Trend]. \tag{5.13}$$

Table 5.4 shows the results for several unit root tests for s_t. The hypothesis of nonstationarity cannot be rejected for the whole period by the ADF and PP tests (estimation [13]) and the second period (estimation [15]). For the first period (estimation [14]), the ADF test rejects nonstationarity at the 5 percent level of significance (the ADF t-statistic is −4.03). The respective results for the PP tests also indicate that the hypothesis of nonstationarity of the series of the discounted real primary surplus cannot be rejected at any reasonable level of significance for all specifications (except possibly for the period 1962–1974). On the other hand, the KPSS test results give some hint of stationarity for the whole period, but not for the subperiods. In the period 1975–2003, as with ADF and PP, the series is indicated as being nonstationary.

Tests for Stationarity of si_t

Another test for the stationarity of Austrian federal government debt proceeds by testing the stationarity of the real federal budgetary

Table 5.5
Stationarity of Austrian federal government budget surplus si_t: Unit root tests

	Estimation (16)	Estimation (17)	Estimation (18)
ADF test statistic	−2.4014	−3.7403*	−2.1612
PP test statistic	−1.7415	−1.9895	−1.7094
KPSS test statistic	0.3294	0.4151(*)	0.3765(*)
No. of observations	42	13	29
Period	1962–2003	1962–1974	1975–2003

$^{**}p < 0.01$, $^{*}p < 0.05$, $^{(*)}p < 0.1$.

surplus including interest payments, si_t, namely, the real (net) budget surplus. Trehan and Walsh (1991) have also shown that the stationarity of si_t is a sufficient condition for the stationarity of public debt b_t with positive (not necessarily constant) real interest rates.

The stationarity of si_t is again tested by applying the ADF, the PP, and the KPSS tests as before. Table 5.5 shows the results for si_t.

The picture is very similar to the one obtained for the primary surplus: for no period, the ADF and PP tests reject the null hypothesis of nonstationarity at a reasonably high level of significance, the only possible exception being the ADF for the first period; hence, the federal budget surplus seems to be characterized by a unit root. The KPSS tests again give different results: no indication of a unit root for the total sample and rejection of stationarity for the two subperiods at the 10 percent significance level. Only for the second subperiod do all tests consistently indicate nonstationarity.

Summing up the tests for stationarity in the series of real federal government public debt, primary surplus, and net budget surplus, with the possible exception of the period up to 1974, we did not find much evidence that some of the time series are stationary, namely, that the Austrian budgetary policy was sustainable in the long run in the ad hoc sense as defined earlier.

5.4.5 *ARMA Processes*

Hamilton and Flavin (1986) criticized the tests applied so far regarding stationarity of the time series as being too restrictive. Following their arguments, Wilcox (1989) assumed an autoregressive moving average (ARMA) process for discounted public debt of the following form:

Table 5.6
Stationarity of Austrian federal government debt b_t: ARMA processes

	Estimation (19) Coefficient (t-statistic)	Estimation (20) Coefficient (t-statistic)	Estimation (21) Coefficient (t-statistic)
Constant	21.3277 (4.1057**)	6.9760 (57.9981**)	30.5677 (16.3865**)
AR(1)	1.9852 (30.2481**)		0.8757 (35.0219**)
AR(2)	−0.9952 (14.4468**)		
MA(1)	−0.7542 (−3.5072**)	0.9899 (51519.11**)	0.5369 (3.3209**)
MA(2)	−0.6098 (−2.9676**)		
Adj. R^2	0.9956	0.6257	0.9903
Durbin-Watson	2.2324	1.3644	1.8835
No. of observations	42	15	29
Period	1961–2003	1960–1974	1975–2003

Source: OLS estimation.
$^{**}p < 0.01$, $^{*}p < 0.05$, $(^{*})p < 0.1$.

$$(1 - \rho(L))((1 - L)^d b_t - \alpha_0) = (1 - \theta(L))e_t, \tag{5.14}$$

where α_0 is the unconditional expected value of the stationary time series $(1 - L)^d b_t$. In order to follow an ad hoc sustainable budgetary policy, b_t has to be stationary; that is, d and the unconditional expected value of b_t have to be equal to zero ($\alpha_0 = 0$).

The unit root tests applied in the previous subsections have mostly shown that the null hypothesis of nonstationarity of Austrian public debt cannot be rejected. However, these tests are not very selective. In order to apply additional tests for stationarity of Austrian public debt, we hypothesize that describing the time series of discounted real public debt b_t with an ARMA process is adequate and that the series is stationary.

We test for several specifications according to the following approach. We start with a more general specification in the form of an ARMA $(3, 3)$ process and then eliminate all terms that are not significant at the 10 percent significance level. We first try to estimate an ARMA process for the whole period and then separately for the first and second period. Table 5.6 shows the results.

As mentioned earlier, stationarity of the series of federal government debt requires that the term α_0 is not significantly different from zero. Estimation (19) in table 5.6 shows the result of estimation for the whole period. Looking at the characteristic equation of the autoregressive part of this equation shows that it is statistically indistinguishable from a unit root process, implying possible nonstationarity of this process. For the first period 1960–1974, the unconditional expected value is estimated to be 6.98 with a high t-value of 58.0 (est. [20], table 5.6). However, the period includes only fifteen observations and the resulting moving average specification is statistically not very attractive, hence the result of nonstationarity is not too reliable. Estimation (21) shows that the intercept is much larger for the second period (1975–2003) and significantly positive with a value of 30.57 (t-value: 16.39). This result may be interpreted to mean that Austrian fiscal policy was less sustainable in the second than in the first period.

5.5 Bohn's Sustainability Test

In the previous section, the stock of discounted real federal government debt and the different budget surplus measures were tested for stationarity. The tests show a slight tendency toward stationarity in the first period (1960–1974), while the series does not seem to be stationary in the second period but rather follows some kind of growth process. A conclusion that could be derived from such tests is that Austrian fiscal policy has not been sustainable since 1975. However, all tests applied so far are based on assumptions about the "adequate" discount rate. Variations in the discount rate might alter the results because discounted public debt is very sensitive with respect to the interest rate used for discounting. Such a sensitivity of results is a major disadvantage of the stationarity tests applied in the previous sections. In addition, as Bohn (chapter 2) points out, when using some (more or less arbitrary) rate of discount, one is testing for ad hoc sustainability instead of for public debt sustainability based on the true intertemporal budget constraint.

This section provides the results of testing for sustainability of Austrian federal government debt with a methodology developed by Bohn (1998) in the context of U.S. fiscal policy. This methodology does not rest on assumptions about the discount rate. For such an approach, the following equation is estimated:

$$ps_t = \rho d_{t-1} + \alpha_0 + AZ_t + \varepsilon_t, \tag{5.15}$$

where ps_t denotes the primary surplus of period t, d_t is the stock of central government debt in period t, and Z_t is a vector of additional variables influencing the budgetary surplus. For example, Barro (1979) included deviations of GDP and of public expenditures from their trend, which proved, however, not to be significant for Austrian data. All variables are measured as ratios to GDP (in percent; primary surplus-to-GDP ratio, debt-to-GDP ratio). Bohn has shown that fiscal policy is sustainable if equation (5.15) mirrors a mean-reverting process. In this case, we require ρ to be significantly positive, indicating that fiscal policymakers react to an increased stock of debt at the beginning of period t by increasing the primary surplus (reducing the primary deficit) in period t. This is a sufficient condition for "true" sustainability of the debt process d_t (see also chapter 2).

As a first step before empirically estimating equation (5.15), we apply the ADF and PP methodology to test whether the primary surplus-to-GDP ratio has a unit root. We cannot reject the hypothesis of a unit root at the 1 percent significance level, while at the 5 percent (ADF test) and 10 percent (PP test) levels, we can reject the hypothesis of a unit root. This is again an inconclusive result; hence, t-tests suffer from a possible bias toward rejecting null hypotheses too easily. Nevertheless, for the following results, we denote significance as being when the t-distribution holds (stationarity); however, most t-values are high enough to indicate significance under the Dickey-Fuller distribution as well.

Table 5.7 shows several estimations of equation (5.15). As it turns out, an estimation of equation (5.15) without accounting for the structural break in 1974–1975 is not correctly specified; we start with estimation (22), which adds a dummy variable *D75* as an additional regressor (*D75* = 1 for the period 1975–2003, 0 otherwise). Here, the process exhibits clear mean reversion for the whole period, but the effect seems to be small. The size of the ρ coefficient of equation (5.15) implies that ceteris paribus in Austria, an additional federal debt of EUR 100 leads to an increase in the primary surplus in the following year by EUR 9.2. The other variables included by Bohn and in the specifications by Barro (1979, 1986), which are derived from the tax-smoothing theory, have no significant influence. In Haber and Neck 2006, we examine additional (especially political and institutional)

Table 5.7
Bohn's sustainability test for Austria (dependent variable: primary surplus of the federal government budget, ratio to GDP)

	Estimation (22) Coefficient (t-statistic)	Estimation (23) Coefficient (t-statistic)	Estimation (24) Coefficient (t-statistic)	Estimation (25) Coefficient (t-statistic)	Estimation (26) Coefficient (t-statistic)
Constant	−1.2994 (−5.3935**)	−4.5370 (−10.9527**)	−4.8030 (−2.5471*)	−4.5310 (−9.6434**)	−4.3674 (−8.2148**)
d_{t-1}	0.0918 (9.5209**)	0.3703 (9.3436**)	0.3883 (2.4308*)	0.0912 (8.6440**)	0.3408 (6.7717**)
D75 (= 1 for period after 1974)	−3.2555 (−8.3368**)				
$d_{t-1} \cdot D75$		−0.2790 (−8.6395**)			−0.2531 (−6.0876**)
AR(1)					0.8784 (6.0885**)
AR(2)					−0.3915 (−2.6571*)
$\bar{R}^2$	0.6823	0.6964	0.2596	0.7247	0.8438
F-statistic	47.1695	50.3163	5.9088	74.7195	56.3683
Durbin-Watson	0.8077	0.7766	1.5973	0.5924	1.8190
No. of observations	44	44	15	29	42
Period	1960–2003	1960–2003	1960–1974	1975–2003	1962–2003

Source: OLS estimation.
$^{**}p < 0.01$, $^{*}p < 0.05$, $(^{*})p < 0.1$.

variables for explaining the primary surplus; these do not change the order of magnitude of the effects resulting from the estimates given in table 5.7.

Multiplying the dummy variable for the period starting in 1975 with the coefficient for the debt-to-GDP ratio d_t instead of the constant (i.e., splitting the reaction coefficient instead of the constant) adds further explanatory power to the model (est. [23]). This result indicates that the reaction of fiscal policymakers (increasing the primary surplus upon increased public debt) was significantly lower in the second period than in the first. While until 1974, an increase in public debt of EUR 100 led ceteris paribus to an increase in the primary surplus by around EUR 37, this reaction decreased to around EUR 9 on average from 1975 onward. A similar result for the estimates for d_{t-1} can be derived by separately estimating the fiscal policy's reaction for the two periods (est. [24] and [25] in table 5.7).

The estimations (23)–(25) still face problems with autocorrelation of the residuals. Thus, the model was reestimated including two autoregressive terms (Cochrane-Orcutt procedure). Estimation (26) shows that the coefficients of d_{t-1} and $d_{t-1} \cdot D75$ remain roughly the same as before. The sign and size of the coefficients indicate that the process of the development of primary surplus has a clear mean-reverting tendency in the first period (1960–1974); that tendency still exists but is much weaker in the second period (1975–2003).

The coefficient for d_{t-1} (i.e., ρ in equation [5.15]) can be interpreted as follows (cf. Bohn 1998). Assuming stationarity of ps_t, the debt-to-GDP ratio should follow a stationary, mean-reverting process if $\bar{x}(1-\rho) < 1$. $\bar{x}$ is the ratio of the average real interest rate $\bar{r}$ (approximated by the average return on long-term nongovernment bonds) to the growth rate of real GDP, $\bar{y}$. $\bar{x}$ can be approximated by $\bar{x} \approx 1 + \bar{r} - \bar{y}$.[2]

As mentioned before, in the first period (1960–1974), the average real interest rate was 2.82 percent, while real GDP grew by 4.68 percent. Thus, $\bar{x}$ would amount to 0.98. According to the previous condition for stationarity of the public debt-to-GDP ratio, $\bar{x}(1-\rho) < 1$ means $0.65 < 1$; this leads to the conclusion that d_t was stationary in the first period and thus fiscal policy was sustainable. In the second period, $\bar{x} = 1.0149$. Inserting $\bar{x}$ in the above equation and accounting for an estimated ρ of 0.088 for the second period (see est. [26]) leads to $0.93 < 1$. The calculated measure comes closer to the critical value of 1, but does not surpass it. This indicates that in the second period, d_t still followed a mean-reverting process, but the coefficient of mean-reversion was quite small. From this, we can conclude that fiscal policy may still have been sustainable in this period, but the policy reaction to ensure sustainability was much weaker than before the first oil price shock that hit Austria in 1975. A strong conclusion about sustainability in this period cannot be drawn from these calculations because the stationarity of the primary surplus variable ps_t is doubtful in the period 1975–2003.

5.6 Summary and Conclusions

The following conclusions can be drawn from the description of Austrian fiscal policies and the econometric exercises applied to test for the sustainability of public debt in Austria. We identify a significant structural break in the mid-1970s in the development of fiscal policy. From the early 1960s to 1974, the debt-to-GDP ratio was stable at around 10–12 percent, while from 1975 to 2003 it increased at an average annual rate of about 2.5 percentage points, culminating at more than 60 percent in the last few years. Since 1995, the ratio has been rather stable again. It seems that with the first oil price shock, fiscal policymakers changed their paradigm: while in the first period, stabilizing public debt was a major task (which could be more easily achieved owing to high GDP growth rates and low unemployment), the major policy goal in the second period, which was characterized by lower growth and higher (and rising) unemployment, seems to have been lowering the rate of unemployment, at the cost of high federal budget deficits and thus increasing federal government debt.

The paradigm shift in fiscal policy can also be shown econometrically by testing for the stationarity of the discounted public debt and primary surpluses. While there is some evidence for stationarity in the first period (1960–1974), in the second period (1975–2003) discounted public debt has clearly been following some kind of growth process. Although the unit root tests do not conclusively reveal nonstationarity of discounted public debt for the second period in all cases, estimations based on the generalized and restricted Flood-Garber tests show some indications of a nonstationary growing public debt. According to these econometric tests, Austrian fiscal policy may not have been (ad hoc) sustainable in the period from 1975 onward.

Since these econometric tests rest on assumptions about an appropriate discount rate, we also follow an approach to explore the sustainability of Austrian fiscal policy that does not depend on any particular discount rate. Sustainability of fiscal policy is tested by exploring policymakers' reactions to increases in public debt. If policymakers increase the primary surplus sufficiently as a reaction to increased public debt, fiscal policy can be considered sustainable. While there is a clear mean-reverting tendency in the first period until 1974, the policymakers' reaction to growing public debt is much smaller (but still positive) in the second period. After the first oil price shock, unemployment may have played a more significant role as a policy objective in the sense of a countercyclical orientation of Austrokeynesian fiscal policy. Owing to the low number of observations available since Austria's entry into the EU in 1995 or since the start of the center-right coalition government in 2000, it is not yet possible to identify another possible structural break owing to a higher weight being given to public debt sustainability.

Notes

The research presented in this chapter was supported by the Ludwig Boltzmann Institute for Economic Analyses (Vienna) and the Jubiläumsfonds of the Austrian National Bank (project no. 9506). The views expressed are not necessarily those of the Austrian National Bank. We are indebted to Henning Bohn, Gebhard Kirchgässner, Harald Stieber, and other participants of the CESifo-LBI Conference on Sustainability of Public Debt, Tutzing, October 22–23, 2004, and the 3rd Public Economics Workshop, University of Innsbruck, January 20–21, 2005, as well as two anonymous referees for helpful comments and discussions. Any remaining shortcomings are our (joint) responsibility.

1. Hypothesis H_0 of the ADF and PP tests states the opposite of the Flood-Garber test: here, H_0 postulates nonstationarity of the series. If the estimation results in an insignificant estimator of the coefficient, one cannot conclude that the time series is nonstationary (i.e., that H_0 is confirmed).

2. While the econometric tests are not based on assumptions about the "appropriate" discount rate, assessing the sustainability of fiscal policy in such a way again needs some measure of the "appropriate" real interest rate. However, as Bohn (chapter 2) shows, fulfilling $\rho > 0$ in an appropriately specified reaction function (5.15) is sufficient for public debt sustainability irrespective of the preceding interpretation.

References

Barro, R. J. 1979. On the determination of the public debt. *Journal of Political Economy* 87:940–971.

Barro, R. J. 1986. U.S. deficits since World War I. *Scandinavian Journal of Economics* 88:195–222.

Bohn, H. 1998. The behavior of U.S. public debt and deficits. *Quarterly Journal of Economics* 113:949–963.

Breuss, F. 1999. Wozu fiskalische Tragfähigkeit in der Wirtschafts- und Währungsunion der Europäischen Union? In *Was wird aus Euroland? Makroökonomische Herausforderungen und wirtschaftspolitische Antworten*, ed. R. Neck and R. Holzmann, 92–159. Vienna: Manz.

De Grauwe, P. 2005. *Economics of Monetary Union*. 6th ed. Oxford: Oxford University Press.

Flood, R. P., and P. M. Garber. 1980. Market fundamentals versus price level bubbles: The first tests. *Journal of Political Economy* 88:745–770.

Getzner, M., E. Glatzer, and R. Neck. 2001. On the sustainability of Austrian budgetary policies. *Empirica* 28:21–40.

Greiner, A., and W. Semmler. 1999. An inquiry into the sustainability of German fiscal policy: Some time-series tests. *Public Finance Review* 27:220–236.

Gros, D., and N. Thygesen. 1998. *European Monetary Integration*. Harlow: Addison Wesley-Longman.

Haber, G. and R. Neck. 2006. Sustainability of Austrian public debt: A political-economy perspective. *Empirica* 33:141–154.

Hamilton, J. D., and M. A. Flavin. 1986. On the limitations of government borrowing: A framework for empirical testing. *American Economic Review* 76:808–819.

Neck, R. 2005. Staatsverschuldung aus politisch-ökonomischer Sicht: Theorie und österreichische Evidenz. In *Haushaltspolitik und öffentliche Verschuldung*, ed. B. Genser, 95–130. Berlin: Duncker & Humblot.

Seidel, H. 1985. Die Stabilisierungsfunktion der Budgetpolitik: Gestern—Heute—Morgen. *Empirica* 12:87–107.

Smekal, C., and M. Gantner. 1983. Österreich. In *Handbuch der Finanzwissenschaft*, vol. IV, ed. F. Neumark et al., 577–609. 3rd ed. Tübingen: Mohr.

Trehan, B., and C. E. Walsh. 1991. Testing intertemporal budget constraints: theory and applications to U.S. federal budget and current account deficits. *Journal of Money, Credit, and Banking* 23:206–223.

Wilcox, D. W. 1989. The sustainability of government deficits: Implications of the present-value borrowing constraint. *Journal of Money, Credit, and Banking* 21:291–293.

6 The Stability Pact Pains: A Forward-Looking Assessment of the Reform Debate

Marco Buti, Sylvester Eijffinger, and Daniele Franco

6.1 Introduction

The Stability and Growth Pact (SGP) is one of the pillars of the European Economic and Monetary Union (EMU). It is a discipline device aimed at ensuring sound budgetary balances and low public debts. Being widely regarded as a major innovation (Artis 2002), the pact has been the subject of a heated controversy ever since its inception. It has been extensively criticized by academics and opinion makers. Proposals for radical changes have been put forward and even the suppression of the pact has been considered.

This debate accelerated in 2002 under the influence of public finance developments in a number of Euro Area countries that called into question the effectiveness (and wisdom) of the pact. The crisis mainly reflected the lack of improvement in structural budget positions in the late 1990s and early 2000s and the impact of the subsequent downturn. This pushed the deficits of several countries toward or above the 3 percent of GDP deficit ceiling.

The pace of events heightened in the aftermath of the November 2003 decision by the European Council not to follow the European Commission's recommendations concerning the excessive deficit procedures applying to France and Germany, which had had deficits exceeding the 3 percent limit since 2002. Some countries supported the commission's view. This laid open the differences in opinions and interests among European institutions and member states. Following a request by the commission, in July 2004, the European Court of Justice gave its judgment concerning this contrast. The bottom line of the judgment is that EU fiscal rules can work smoothly only if the council and the commission cooperate.

In September 2004 the commission put forward a number of proposed changes to the SGP with the aim of avoiding procyclical policies, better defining the medium-term objective, giving greater prominence to the debt criterion, considering economic circumstances in the implementation of the excessive deficit procedure, and improving governance and enforcement (European Commission 2004b).

After a difficult and at times heated debate, an agreement was reached at the ECOFIN Council in March 2005 in a report that envisaged changes to both the preventive and corrective arms of the pact (ECOFIN Council 2005).

This debate has taken place against the background of unsatisfactory fiscal outcomes. A budgetary behavior inconsistent with the requirements of the SGP occurred especially in large countries. Since 2002 France and Germany have had deficits largely exceeding 3 percent of GDP. Following sizeable statistical revisions, in 2004 it was revealed that Greece had systematically exceeded the limit since 1997; in 2005 it became clear that Italy had exceeded the limit in 2001, 2003, and 2004, though by a small amount. Portugal also breached the deficit ceiling by a wide margin in 2005. Other countries have temporarily exceeded the limit or have budget deficits that are clearly inconsistent with the close-to-balance clause of the SGP. Moreover, some countries have made recourse to one-off measures or to new accounting and financial operations, which, even if formally consistent with EMU rules, do not improve the underlying public finance conditions (European Commission 2004a, 2005).

In a way, these developments are related to the success of EMU rules in curbing deficits in earlier years. When in the late 1980s and early 1990s the public finances of several EU countries appeared to be on an unsustainable path, the benefits of lower deficits were evident. Fiscal discipline was recognized as a precondition to lower interest rates and to use fiscal policy for cyclical stabilization (Buti, Franco, and Ongena 1998). Even an arbitrary target such as the 3 percent of GDP deficit limit was deemed desirable because it forced countries to undertake the inevitable adjustment. As soon as the budgetary situation improved, the issue of the proper balance between fiscal discipline and other targets came to the forefront. The move to the EMU radically changed the structure of incentives faced by EU governments, lowering the relative weight of abiding by common rules compared to other, more domestic objectives (Buti and Giudice 2002).

This chapter evaluates the critical aspects of EMU fiscal rules, considers the main reform proposals, and assesses the changes introduced in the pact in 2005. The outline is as follows. Section 6.2 reviews the critical issues in the implementation of the SGP and the main proposals put forward to replace or radically revise the pact. Section 6.3 outlines some implications of the debate on the SGP in the light of recent literature on fiscal rules. Section 6.4 considers the changes in the SGP agreed in 2005 and their possible impact on its functioning and effectiveness. The final section concludes.

6.2 Revisiting the SGP: Critical Issues and Reform Proposals

According to its critics, the 1997 Stability Pact had several shortcomings: it reduced budgetary flexibility, worked asymmetrically, was too uniform, did not sanction politically motivated fiscal policies, discouraged public investment, disregarded the Euro Area-wide fiscal stance, and ignored long-term sustainability.

In this context several proposals have been put forward for replacing or modifying the pact. In one way or another, all the proposals draw on one or more of the above criticisms. A summary of the main proposals put forward mainly by academics to replace, reform, or improve the SGP is presented in table 6.1.[1]

6.2.1 Reform National Procedures and Institutions

The first-best strategy in ensuring sound fiscal policies would be that of dealing directly with the factors leading to excessive deficits at the national level. This would avoid relying on numerical parameters that are necessarily arbitrary and subject to fudging.[2] Fiscal policy soundness would be ensured either by procedures assuring fiscal responsibility at the national level or by market discipline.[3] This strategy answers to the criticism concerning the lack of budgetary flexibility.

Two sets of proposals come under this heading.

Procedural reforms: Procedural reforms impose changes on the rules concerning the presentation, adoption and execution of government budgets. Hierarchical procedures are more conducive to fiscal discipline than collegial procedures. At the national level, hierarchical rules attribute strong power to treasury ministers to overrule spending ministers during the intra-governmental preparation of the budget and

Table 6.1
Reforming the SGP: Main proposals

Critical issue	Reform proposals	Authors	Institutional implications
Numerical rules do not tackle budgetary misbehavior at source; SGP needs a more credible and nonpartisan enforcement.	Reform national institutions: • change budgetary procedures • create independent FPCs Strengthen financial market discipline.	Buiter and Sibert 2005, Eichengreen 2003, Fatás et al. 2003, Wren-Lewis 2003, Wyplosz 2002, 2005.	Reform the treaty, abolish excessive deficit procedure. Amend Large Exposure Directive. Change rules about collateral in ECB open market operations.
The SGP pays too much attention to the budget deficit, not to the quality of public finances.	Factor in the "quality of public finances": • expenditure rules • golden rule	Blanchard and Giavazzi 2003, Brunila 2002, Fitoussi and Creel 2002, Mills and Quinet 2002.	Institutionalization of the golden rule requires changes in the treaty.
Sustainability depends on the stock of debt and future stream of expenditure and revenue, not on the short-run deficit.	Focus on debt and sustainability: • Debt Sustainability Pact • Permanent Balance Rule • diversified deficit ceiling	Buiter and Grafe 2003, Calmfors and Corsetti 2002, Coeuré and Pisani-Ferry 2003, Gros 2003, Pisani-Ferry 2002.	These proposals require changes in the treaty.
The SGP does not address the issue of the appropriate fiscal stance for the Eurozone as a whole.	Fiscal policy coordination at Eurozone level: • aggregate budget balance target • tradable deficit permits	Bofinger 2004, Casella 2001, Schelkle 2002.	Within a national 3 percent ceiling, not incompatible with the treaty.

limit the ability of parliament to amend the government's budget proposals.

Replacing the numerical limits with procedures ensuring sound budgetary positions would raise two problems. First, there is still a need for transparent and rapid criteria for selecting new entrants to the Euro Area. Second, the adoption of harmonized budgetary procedures would raise problems from the point of view of national sovereignty and might conflict with national institutions and traditions. The alternative solution—country-specific procedures approved at the EU level—would also be cumbersome. The ex ante effectiveness of these procedures would be very difficult to evaluate. Moreover, in case they did not prove effective in constraining deficits, the attribution of responsibility would be difficult as national governments might argue that they had conducted their fiscal policy in compliance with the agreed procedures.

In the end, while effective budgetary procedures are important in ensuring sound fiscal policies at national level,[4] they do not appear at present to be a viable alternative to numerical rules at the EU level. However, some procedural rules (such as common accounting conventions) are called upon to ensure compliance with the budget constraints.

Institutional reforms: Under this heading, the proposal that has attracted most attention is that of creating independent fiscal policy committees (FPC). This idea draws on the experience of central banks running monetary policy. In the strongest versions, such bodies would be given the responsibility for setting the budget balance targets (Wyplosz 2002, 2005) or even be responsible for some specific tax rates (Wren-Lewis 2003).

While intellectually appealing, these proposals run into serious feasibility problems. Fiscal policy is—differently from monetary policy—at the heart of the political decision-making process. The separation between setting a target for the budget balance (to be entrusted to the FPC) and the allocative and distributive functions (to remain in the responsibility of government and parliament) may turn out to be difficult. Decisions about the budget balance affect the composition of expenditure and revenues. Politically, it is hard to conceive that a government would delegate part of fiscal policy authority to an independent agency. In a softer version (Sapir et al. 2004; Annett, Decressin, and Deppler 2005), however, such bodies could be entrusted with the task of monitoring and assessing policy proposals and decisions, thereby improving visibility and transparency.[5] As such, however, they appear more as a complement than as a substitute for numerical rules.

6.2.2 *Factoring in the "Quality" of Public Finances*

The SGP focuses on the yearly budget balance. However, a growing body of literature points out that the composition of public finances matters as well. The focus on quality has been translated into two proposals for reforming the SGP: shifting from a deficit target to an expenditure target/rule or moving to the so-called golden rule of deficit financing.

Expenditure rules: Focus on expenditure has the advantage of controllability because expenditure depends much less than revenue on the business cycle. Expenditure rules can link the annual budgetary process to a multi-annual policy framework. They refer to the budgetary items that governments can control, and they can be easily defined and monitored. Moreover, they allow stabilizers to work on the revenue side and may prevent expenditure relaxation in upturns.

The use of expenditure rules in a supranational context (see section 6.3), however, appears problematic. First, uniform spending rules would de facto impose homogeneous social preferences to politically heterogeneous countries while country-specific rules would be difficult to enforce. Second, spending norms do not refer to the fiscal variables that can produce negative externalities: while a rising deficit or debt level in one country can create area-wide problems, a rising expenditure level as such does not have negative repercussions on other countries. Moreover, expenditure rules cannot prevent deficit and debt increases stemming from tax cuts. Therefore, they would have to be complemented by a deficit or debt rule. Third, since no uniform expenditure-to-GDP ratio can be prescribed, countries would be required to indicate targets for the expenditure ratio consistent with the desired deficit ratio. Finally, the size of the budget typically reflects the political preferences of the government. A new government may want to renegotiate the commitments of its predecessor.

In sum, while expenditure rules may prove useful at the national level, they are more appropriate as complements rather than substitutes of common rules on deficits and debt.

The golden rule: A number of authors have suggested replacing the SGP with some form of golden rule (Blanchard and Giavazzi 2003). The golden rule would allow governments to spread the burden of capital projects over the different generations of taxpayers benefiting from them and would avoid the efficiency loss caused by distortionary taxation if the tax rate fluctuates over time. This would answer some criticisms expressed against the SGP. In fact, maintaining budget positions "close to balance or in surplus" implies that capital expenditure has to be funded from current revenues; that may imply a disincentive to undertake projects producing deferred benefits. The disincentive is stronger during consolidation periods.

However, there are a number of arguments against the introduction of the golden rule (Balassone and Franco 2000a; Buiter 2001). First, the alleged incompatibility between the SGP and a properly defined golden rule is questionable. In order to spread the burden of capital spending over the different generations of taxpayers, the rule would have to refer to net spending. In developed countries in which infrastructures are partly developed by subjects not included in general government, the level of net investment is limited and not necessarily inconsistent with a reasonable interpretation of the close-to-balance rule of the SGP (European Commission 2004a). Second, if applied to gross public investment, the golden rule would be an obstacle to deficit and debt reduction. Given the ratio of public investment as a percentage of GDP, the long-run equilibrium level of government debt could be quite high, especially in an environment of low inflation. Third, singling out public investment from other budget items makes little sense. What is important is overall capital accumulation in both private and public capital. For instance, a well-devised tax reform that, by lowering tax burden and distortions, leads to higher investment may be preferable to public investment. Also, there is no clear evidence in the empirical literature that investment in public infrastructure always leads to significant positive growth effects. Some studies suggest that government investment may be subject to rapidly decreasing returns (see, e.g., de la Fuente 1997). Moreover, a golden rule may distort expenditure decisions in favor of physical assets and against spending on intangibles that can make a relevant contribution to economic growth, for example those increasing human capital. Fourth, the golden rule would make the multilateral surveillance process more complex, by providing leeway for opportunistic behavior since governments would have an incentive to classify current expenditure as capital spending. Finally, there are problems of cross-country comparability of the data concerning amortization.

On top of that, there is no guarantee that government investment would increase as a result of introducing the golden rule. This occurs only if public investment is kept under the desired level because of the ceiling of the overall deficit, while the same does not occur for current expenditure. It may be the case that by introducing a golden rule the additional room for deficits is used to increase current expenditure (or cut taxes) without an impact on investment (see Turrini 2004).

6.2.3 *Focus on Debt Level and Sustainability*

The Maastricht Treaty rules do not focus on the issue of sustainability, and they disregard the fact that countries are different. This criticism has different nuances. First, the SGP focuses almost exclusively on short-term objectives for the budget deficit. As such, it provides incentives for creative accounting and one-off measures that blur the transparency of public accounts. Second, the stock of public debt does not enter the SGP, nor does the stock of implicit liabilities of public pension systems. Hence, the pact treats as equals countries with different medium and long-term prospects and different debt levels. Third, the pact may prevent countries from implementing policies—such as pension reforms—which improve long-term sustainability at the price of a short-term worsening in the deficit.[6]

Two solutions have been put forward in the literature: the first is to compute a medium-term target that factors directly in country-specific sustainability concerns; the second is to give more weight to the public debt in the common rules.

From the Maastricht parameters to tax smoothing: It has been argued that the SGP is over-restrictive and too crude to deliver the appropriate fiscal stance at national level (Allsopp and Artis 2003). The pact is particularly unfit in the case of catching-up countries that are characterized by higher potential growth and higher inflation, and hence can afford to have higher deficits without endangering the long-term sustainability of public finances. Given the higher public investment needs of less mature economies, a rigid application of the close-to-balance cum 3 percent ceiling could allegedly harm the catching-up process.

Buiter and Grafe (2003) propose a permanent balance rule that would ensure sustainability and fiscal prudence while taking into account country differences. Their rule is a strong form of tax smoothing: it requires the inflation- and real-growth-adjusted permanent government budget to be in balance or surplus. The permanent budget balance is given by the difference between the constant long-run average future values of tax revenue and government spending.

While the rule is theoretically appealing, requiring governments to take into account future social and political preferences and make assumptions on future growth rates for the calculation of the permanent value of taxes and expenditures, its practical applicability appears doubtful (Pench 2003). Moreover, considering the need to ensure creditworthiness and strong macrofinancial stability to attract foreign direct investment (FDI), the argument that catching up would necessarily be fostered by allowing higher deficits is debatable (European Commission 2005).

More weight on the public debt: A way to overcome the uniformity of the pact is to attribute more importance to public debt. Calmfors and Corsetti (2002) suggest making the deficit ceiling dependent on the stock of debt: the deficit ceiling of 3 percent of GDP should be binding only for countries with a debt ratio in excess of 55 percent of GDP, while a higher ceiling would apply to countries with lower debt. This proposal respects the requirement of simplicity while improving incentives and country differentiation. It would be "enlargement friendly" since most of the newcomers have a fairly low stock of debt. However, it would require a change in the treaty.

Tackling the issue head on, Pisani-Ferry (2002) and Coeuré and Pisani-Ferry (2003) suggest giving countries with debt ratios below 50 percent of GDP the choice of opting out of the excessive deficit procedure and embracing a so-called debt sustainability pact. These countries would be required to submit a medium-term program indicating a five-year target for the debt ratio and presenting a complete account of implicit liabilities, which would represent the benchmark for assessing their results. They would have greater flexibility in the short term. The focus of EU monitoring would shift from the year-by-year monitoring of the deficit to a medium-term perspective based on long-term fiscal sustainability.

This proposal, however, is also somewhat problematic. First, it is built on the assumption that deficits do not matter in the EMU if debt levels are under control. This, however, is doubtful, especially from a policy mix standpoint. Second, while greater reference to the debt ratio does not raise measurement problems, reference to implicit liabilities is more problematic. Estimates are subject to considerable uncertainty related to the macroeconomic, demographic, and behavioral scenarios (see section 6.4).

Nonetheless, disregard of the issue of public debt is a clear limitation of the original SGP.

6.2.4 *Fiscal Policy Coordination at the Euro Area Level*

This category of reform proposals envisages fiscal coordination at the Euro Area level. In a currency union, only the aggregate fiscal stance is relevant for the policy mix at Euro Area level and, as such, enters the reaction function of the central bank. Hence it is suggested to set a target for the Euro Area as a whole and then share it between member countries.

These solutions answer the allegation that the SGP disregards the aggregate fiscal stance. Under the pact, each country is responsible for national fiscal policies and the aggregation of nationally determined fiscal policies may not result in an optimal fiscal stance at the Euro Area level.

Fiscal coordination can be achieved via either community-level decisions indicating the desirable budget balance of each country or a market-based allocation of national deficit shares of the total Euro Area deficit.

Community allocation of deficit shares: A proposal for a coordination mechanism in the budgetary domain was submitted by French Finance Minister Dominique Strauss-Kahn, at the informal ECOFIN Council in April 1999. The proposal stressed that the aggregate policy stance at EMU level must be examined on the basis of an aggregate stability program. It pointed out that the objective to achieve an adequate policy stance for the EMU as a whole should be taken into account when examining the national stability programs.[7]

A natural implication of this is that the 3 percent of GDP deficit criterion would apply only to the average deficit for the Euro Area. Member states would be permitted to overshoot the deficit ceiling if there were other countries with deficits below that value. Since the amplitude of cyclical fluctuations is much smaller for the Eurozone as a whole, the targets needed to prevent an overshooting of the aggregate deficit ceiling would be less stringent than those necessary for each member state individually.

However, in the present institutional setup of the EMU, the deficit criterion applies to each member state individually. The Maastricht budgetary rules would thus have to be renegotiated in order to allow this interpretation to be implemented. Moreover, bureaucratic allocation of deficit shares would be highly controversial.

Market allocation of deficit permits: Casella (2001) proposes using market mechanisms in the allocation of "deficit shares" in the EMU. Having chosen an aggregate target for the European Union and an initial distribution of tradable deficit permits, EMU countries could be allowed to trade rights to deficit creation. While this system keeps the aggregate area-wide deficit unchanged, it allows individual member states to deviate from the initial allowances in case of idiosyncratic shocks.

The mechanism would minimize the aggregate cost of compliance with the aggregate targets and provide rewards for countries running surpluses in favorable cyclical conditions, thereby tackling the issue of the asymmetric working of the pact. It would also reduce the room for political manipulation.

This scheme is, however, subject to three main difficulties. First, the market solution would be efficient only if the deficits of the various governments generate the same externality; namely, they are perfect substitutes. But the risk of triggering a financial crisis is not uniform across governments. Second, the efficiency of the market in permits depends on how competitive it is. This makes the mechanism ill suited to situations in which the number of governments is small. Finally, there is no easy solution to the problem of determining the initial allotment of permits. The possible criteria (GDP, population, etc.) would produce greatly differing allocations.

6.3 Lessons from the Debate

Each of the proposals examined previously draws the attention to one or more potentially serious problems with the design and implementation of the SGP. The suggestion to implement institutional and procedural reform highlights the need for an independent enforcer. The idea to move to a golden rule stresses the need to preserve the growth aspect of the SGP. A number of proposals highlight the excessive uniformity of the current rules. Taking into account the different levels of public debt points to the need to insert the sustainability dimension into the core of the SGP. The proposal of establishing a market for deficit permits tackles the problem of the procyclical bias in good times.

However, none of the proposals represents a "Pareto improvement": while appropriate to tackling some of the problems highlighted in the debate, none of them solves all problems and some problems may even be aggravated. Certain reform proposals present the same element of inflexibility as the current regime (golden rule); others require estimates that may turn out to be problematic in a multinational context (debt sustainability pact, permanent balance rule); others again require a decisive leap forward in the integration of fiscal policy (procedural reforms, budgetary target for Euro Area).

In evaluating the SGP, one should also consider the indications provided by the literature concerning the role and design of fiscal rules. The role of fiscal institutions and procedures in shaping budgetary outcomes has increasingly been recognized. While "good rules" do not necessarily entail "good policies," inadequate budgetary institutions and procedures may contribute to a lack of fiscal discipline.

In previous papers (Buti, Eijffinger, and Franco 2003a, b), we have analyzed the "quality" of EU fiscal rules in terms of the criteria identified by Kopits and Symansky (1998) and Inman (1996) for the design, implementation, and enforcement of a fiscal rule. A good fiscal rule should be well designed (clearly defined, simple, transparent, consistent and flexible), allow effective implementation (by entailing ex ante and ex post compliance and efficient monitoring), and be enforceable (in terms of decision, amendment, and sanctions).

Our conclusion was that the SGP has strong points—in particular, with regard to simplicity and monitoring—and weak points—namely, enforcement. Lack of effective enforcement de facto shifts the pact into the realm of "soft law" (Schuknecht 2004). However, in order to pass a judgment on the "quality" of the SGP as a fiscal rule, one has to consider that the criteria discussed in the literature were devised for assessing the quality of domestic fiscal rules. With the EMU, fiscal rules had to be devised in a supranational context for the first time.

EMU fiscal rules reflect the interaction between the multinational nature of EMU and the lack of a political authority of federal rank (Balassone and Franco 2001). This has important implications. First, national sovereignty and subsidiarity concerns have to be respected. This implies that rules are to be as neutral as possible vis-à-vis the countries' social preferences, which are quite heterogeneous in the EU. This prevented, for instance, the adoption of rules that entail a choice of the role and size of the public sector in the economy.

Second, in a supranational context, ex post compliance is important, given the higher risks of moral hazard and the higher difficulty in monitoring ex ante policy announcements.

Third, the supranational character influences the trade-offs between the various criteria in complex ways. Take the trade-off between simplicity and flexibility. On the one hand, there may be a preference for simplicity over flexibility to allow for peer pressure, allow for central monitoring, and prevent moral hazard. On the other hand, a multiplicity of countries increases heterogeneity and dispersion of preferences with the consequence that a one-size-fits-all fiscal rule is likely to be suboptimal.[8]

Finally, since imposing formal sanctions on sovereign countries raises political difficulties, one should strengthen the role of reputational effects, such as those of "early warnings" and excessive deficit positions, also via increased fiscal transparency, and limit the recourse to sanctions to cases of serious misbehavior.

While no proposal appears adequate as a ready-made alternative to the SGP, the debate has pointed to a number of key areas where improvement to the original pact could be made. In our view (Buti, Eijffinger, and Franco 2003a, b), key aspects are (1) overcoming excessive uniformity of the rules by allowing a certain country-specificity with respect to structural and cyclical economic factors; this would increase the economic foundations of the rules; (2) improving transparency in current and perspective fiscal accounts, which would ensure the credibility of the rules and strengthen market and political mechanisms of deficit control; (3) correcting procyclicality by rebalancing incentive schemes with a view to avoiding misbehavior especially in good times; and (4) strengthening enforcement by moving toward a nonpartisan application of the rules.[9]

In the following section, after briefly outlining its main features, we assess how the SGP reform agreed in 2005 fares vis-à-vis such objectives.

6.4 Revisiting the SGP: Enter the Policymakers

6.4.1 *The New SGP*

While the debate in academic circles showed the depth of the divisions among economists, a certain consensus gradually emerged in the course of 2004 among the main policy players as to what changes were needed to the EMU fiscal framework. It was recognized that EMU needed numerical fiscal rules (since financial market discipline and national procedures were not deemed sufficient to ensure budgetary discipline) and that any radical changes to the rules introduced in 1992 (Maastricht Treaty) and 1997 (SGP) would be highly problematic. "Internal adjustment" of the existing framework rather than a radical overhaul of the rules came to be regarded as the only feasible way forward. It was also acknowledged that complementary measures at national level (such as better budgetary procedures and independent fiscal councils) would be highly desirable. The common menu of internal reforms included action to improve fiscal policy in good times, more consideration of public debt and long-term sustainability in assessing member states' budgetary positions, a greater focus on cyclical developments, and more transparency in fiscal data. Other aspects were more controversial: these included changes to the excessive deficit procedure and a stronger role for the European Commission as an enforcing agency.

The risks involved in embarking on a reform process under the pressure of unfavorable fiscal developments were also highlighted in the debate: the credibility of the framework itself could be endangered, and the reform process could prove very long and uncertain. It was also noted that if the problem was primarily one of adherence to the rules, the priority should be to ensure rigorous implementation of the existing rules rather than to change them. At the same time, it was widely recognized that simply attempting to apply the existing rules after the watershed of November 2003 was not a viable option. Reestablishing a sense of ownership of the fiscal rules by all parties would be the precondition for their effective enforcement.

At the request of the European Council, in September 2004 the commission issued a communication suggesting a number of changes to the pact that, while preserving its overall architecture, aimed at avoiding pro-cyclical policies, especially in good times; better defined the medium-term objective by taking into account country-specific circumstances and reforms; gave greater prominence to the debt criterion; modified the implementation of the excessive deficit procedure, in particular by allowing more time to correct an excessive deficit under certain circumstances; and improved governance and enforcement (European Commission 2004b).

After a difficult and at times heated debate, an agreement was reached at the ECOFIN Council in March 2005. The guidelines of the reform were set out in a report which envisaged changes to both the preventive and corrective arms of the pact (ECOFIN Council 2005).[10]

On the preventive side (i.e., the medium-term targets and the adjustment path toward them), medium-term budgetary objectives are now to be somewhat differentiated from one country to another on the basis of debt ratios and potential growth rates. Targets will be specified in structural terms—that is, cyclically adjusted and net of the effects of temporary measures—and will range between a deficit of 1 percent of GDP and a small surplus. The latter would apply to high-debt, slow-growth countries. Implicit liabilities will also be taken into account in the future, once further technical analysis allows the council to agree on criteria and methodological aspects. Major structural reforms with long-term fiscal benefits will be taken into consideration both when defining the adjustment path toward the medium-term objective and when considering temporary deviations from the target. A more articulated set of provisions also concerned the path toward the medium-term objectives, though a minimum annual adjustment of 0.5 percent of GDP had to be ensured.

On the corrective side (i.e., the application of the excessive deficit procedure), a modification was introduced in the definition of the "exceptional cyclical circumstances" that may have justified the reference value for the deficit being exceeded: a breach of the threshold would now be considered exceptional if it resulted from a negative growth rate or an accumulated loss of output during a protracted period of very low growth relative to potential growth. When evaluating deficits exceeding the 3 percent limit, the commission would take into account a number of factors ranging from cyclical conditions to the implementation of the Lisbon agenda and policies to foster R&D and innovation, from debt sustainability to the overall quality of public finances, from financial contributions to international solidarity to fiscal burdens related to European unification. However, any excess over the 3 percent deficit threshold should remain limited and temporary. The implementation of pension reforms establishing a compulsory funded pillar would also be taken into consideration, especially when assessing whether an excessive deficit has been corrected.[11]

While confirming that, as a rule, the deadline for the correction of an excessive deficit would remain the year after it is identified, the council decided that the initial deadline could be set one year later if there were special circumstances, and could be revised at a later stage if unexpected adverse economic events with major unfavorable budgetary effects occurred.

The council called for giving a stronger weight to public debt, but was not able to agree on quantifying the minimum debt reduction for countries with very high debt ratios, as suggested by the commission.

The council also outlined a number of steps to improve the governance of EU rules. It suggested closer cooperation among member states, the commission, and the council in the implementation of the pact. It indicated the need to develop national budgetary rules and ensure that national parliaments are closely involved in the process. Finally, it called for reliable macroeconomic forecasts and budgetary statistics.

6.4.2 *An Evaluation of the Reform*

These changes had a mixed reception. Some commentators argued that, given the host of exceptions to the 3 percent rule, the pact was de facto dead. Others considered the proposals to be an important step forward in achieving a better balance in the pact between fiscal discipline and flexibility. The same divisions that animated the debate on the original SGP surfaced again in the reactions to its reform.

The review of the debate on the SGP has highlighted the critical issues that any effective reform of the pact should tackle. As argued earlier, any reform of the rules should aim at (1) overcoming excessive uniformity, (2) improving transparency, (3) correcting procyclicality, and (4) strengthening enforcement.

Table 6.2 provides a qualitative assessment of the main changes introduced by the council in the governance of the new rules, the pre-

Table 6.2
Desirable improvements to the SGP "Mark I"

2005 SGP Reform	Overcoming excessive uniformity	Improving transparency	Correcting procyclicality	Strengthening enforcement
Governance				
Stability program for the legislature		(+)		
Involvement of national parliament				(+)
Reliable forecasts		(+)		(+)
Better statistical governance		+		+
Preventive arm				
Medium-term objectives	++	–		
Adjustment path	+		+	
Structural reforms	+	–		–
Corrective arm				
Exceptional circumstances	+		+	
"All other relevant factors"	+	––		––
Systemic pension reforms	+			–
Debt and sustainability	+	–	+	
Repeatability of steps	+	–	+	–
Overall assessment	+	–/+	+	–/+

++ strong improvement, + improvement, – deterioration, –– strong deterioration. (+) improvement if effectively implemented at national level.

ventive and the corrective arm of the SGP.[12] In the rest of this section, we provide a first assessment of the 2005 reform and give some indications of where further progress is needed to ensure the effectiveness of the new rules.

6.4.2.1 Overcoming Excessive Uniformity

The new SGP has introduced some elements of country specificity in both the preventive and the corrective arms of the pact. The close-to-balance rule of the original SGP, interpreted as broadly balanced budgets in cyclically adjusted terms, treated equally countries with different levels of public debt, implicit and contingent liabilities, and public investment needs.

In the early years of EMU, the only dimension along which countries were differentiated was the variability of the cyclical component of the budget balance: economies subject to higher business cycle volatility and having larger automatic stabilizers require a larger cyclical safety margin in order to avoid breaching the 3 percent of GDP deficit ceiling under normal cyclical circumstances (Artis and Buti 2000). In the new pact, the articulation of the medium-term budgetary targets was extended to other dimensions, such as the financial fragility of the country embodied in stock of public debt and—in the future—the threat to long-term sustainability given by the implicit liabilities of pension systems, as well as the capacity of countries to "grow out of their debt," by taking into account their potential growth.

The council took a cautious approach by stipulating that, in order to safeguard the 3 percent deficit ceiling, the medium-term target should never exceed a deficit 1 percent of GDP.[13] This implies that countries with a relatively low stock of debt and estimated implicit liabilities would be allowed to have cyclically adjusted budget deficits up to 1 percent of GDP. This solution is consistent, in most cases, with a prudent version of the golden rule.[14] The debt ratios in high-debt countries and in countries with expected rising expenditure levels would decline fast, thereby contributing to offset the burden of aging in the future, while in the other countries deficit levels would ensure the maintenance of a small public debt. The solution would strengthen the political incentives to reduce the current and implicit debt at a faster pace.

In order to avoid moral hazard, commonly agreed estimates of implicit liabilities in EU countries would have to be computed, following the experience of the Economic Policy Committee's estimates (2003) of age-related public spending. The use of long-term projections in the EU fiscal framework should be conditional on progress concerning the comparability, transparency, and independence of the projections. A variety of sustainability indicators could be used: tax gaps, government net worth, and generational accounting. Since each indicator requires some arbitrary choices, it would be necessary to predefine the relevant assumptions and parameters and agree on a common set of indicators.[15]

The new SGP has also introduced elements of country specificity also in the corrective arm of the pact. As argued later, while such changes may reduce excessive uniformity of the rules, they may in some instances increase the complexity of the rule, with negative implications for transparency and enforcement.

6.4.2.2 Improving Transparency

Transparency has several dimensions: it includes accounting conventions, forecasting exercises and reporting practices (Kopits and Symansky 1998). Two aspects are particularly important: (1) Fiscal indicators providing a comprehensive view concerning current and perspective fiscal accounts and compliance with the rules should be available to monitoring institutions, the general public, and financial markets. (2) The design of the rules should allow for an unambiguous assessment of compliance. This asks for simple and well-defined rules.

As for the first aspect, the EU fiscal framework has been widely criticized for a lack of transparency.[16] This issue has different facets. First, the deficit indicator as defined by ESA-95 does not provide a full picture of countries' public finance imbalances. Second, the debt indicator (gross financial debt at face value) allows targets to be achieved via operations that do not improve fiscal sustainability and tends to underestimate overall outstanding liabilities. Third, under the current system of national accounts, monitoring is hampered by delays in data provision and allows some manipulation of statistics with the implication that the whistle is often blown far too late or only when the true data eventually surface. Finally, the forecasts underlying stability programs have frequently turned out to be optimistically biased.

The new SGP includes potentially important provisions leading to improved transparency but also elements that work in the opposite direction.

In recent years, in order to meet the short-term targets, countries have frequently adopted one-off, cash-raising measures instead of making the necessary structural adjustments. The decision that compliance with the medium-term target as well as with the minimum annual adjustment of 0.5 percent of GDP is to be assessed in *structural* terms, by netting out the estimated effect of the cycle and one-off measures, will lead to improved transparency.[17] In order to implement this, an agreed definition of one-off measures could complement the existing agreement on how to compute cyclically adjusted balances.[18] However, given the current legislation and accounting conventions, the 3 percent rule has not been modified. Hence, in practice, one-off measures can still be used at the margin to avoid an excessive deficit. As to the abrogation of an excessive deficit, it will be important to focus on the *durability* of the adjustment, thereby reducing the incentives to use one-off measures to temporarily bring the deficit below the reference value without correcting the underlying imbalances.

As for public debt, the application of the fiscal rules will continue to focus on its definition in *gross* terms. However, this overlooks the fact that government assets can be sold to repay the debt and that there are nonfinancial liabilities. Relying on both a gross and a net debt definition is preferable. The former is more precise, timely available, and more relevant over the short term; the latter is more complete and relevant from a longer time perspective. On the basis of an agreed and transparent framework, governments could be required to provide estimates of off-budget liabilities, of their net asset position and of long-term budgetary trends.[19] Estimates should be revised every year and changes extensively explained.

The availability of high quality statistics and timely fiscal indicators still remains an issue. The problem of early detection of deviations from targets was vividly exposed in the case of Portugal in 2001. Even more serious was the case of Greece, which in 2004 turned out to have had a deficit in excess of 3 percent of GDP since 1997. In this, but also in other countries, the yearly increase in public debt has frequently exceeded the deficit level as below-the-line operations have systematically contributed to debt growth.

The new pact acknowledges the importance of quality, timeliness and reliability of fiscal statistics and pledges to ensure the independence, integrity and accountability of both national statistical offices and Eurostat.[20] The availability of better statistics should be complemented by a more comprehensive surveillance of fiscal variables. A way forward is to resurrect, in parallel with national accounts definitions, regular monitoring of cash flows. National authorities could be required to indicate ex ante cash figures broadly consistent with the

ESA95 balance. In parallel, changes in the debt level (net of the effects of exchange rate changes and privatization proceeds) could be closely monitored:[21] if a significant departure from target is detected in financial flows, it would be up to national authorities to explain the difference.[22]

Overly optimistic forecasts that are common in some member states[23] can translate into higher than projected deficits, since government revenues quickly respond to changes in potential output whereas adjustments on the expenditure side normally require a lengthy process of political decision making. The new pact indicates that budgetary projections should be based on realistic and cautious macroeconomic forecasts. The European Commission (2004b) proposed that stability programs should be based on macroeconomic assumptions provided by the commission. The council decided that countries are still free to use their own assumptions, but they should explain in detail divergences with respect to the commission's forecasts.[24]

While these changes move closer to improving the quality and availability of fiscal indicators, others are likely to negatively affect the second aspect of transparency mentioned earlier—that is, the possibility to easily assess compliance with the rules.

As for the corrective part of the pact, the most notable amendment is the specification of so-called other relevant factors in the assessment of whether a deficit in excess of 3 percent of GDP can be considered "excessive" in the sense of the treaty. Such factors—ranging from the implementation of the Lisbon agenda and policies to foster R&D and innovation to the overall quality of public finances, from financial contributions to international solidarity to fiscal burdens related to European unification—may give countries easy escape roads in the case of deficits in excess of the reference value. While there is an important safeguard in the provision that any excess over the 3 percent deficit threshold should remain limited and temporary, encompassing such a long list of factors risks blurring the assessment.

The preventive part of the SGP has also become more complex. The medium-term objectives are no longer defined ex ante but as objectives that countries set themselves in their programs on the basis of commonly agreed criteria that might evolve over time.

6.4.2.3 Correcting Procyclicality

It is widely recognized that the original SGP did not provide sufficient incentives for countries to run prudent fiscal policies in good times, which resulted in having their room to maneuver curtailed in bad times. The new agreement explicitly aims to correct procyclicality by emphasizing the importance of reliable macroeconomic forecasts, and the commitment to step up consolidation in good times—relaxing the "exceptionality clause," making the timing for the correction of the excessive deficit a function of the prevailing cyclical conditions, and foreseeing the guarded possibility to repeat steps of the procedure in case of adverse shocks.

While these changes go in the right direction, one may ask whether they go far enough in terms of sticks and carrots.

In order to step up peer pressure, a possible solution could be that of using the early warning procedure of the SGP not only in bad times when the deficit approaches the 3 percent ceiling, but also in good times when a significant divergence from structural targets is detected. The idea of an early warning procedure independent of the immediate danger of an excessive deficit is considered in European Commission (2004b). However, the new SGP, while foreseeing the possibility of the commission issuing "policy advice" in this regard, did not accept this proposal.

Buti, Eijffinger, and Franco (2003a, b) and Sapir et al. (2004) have argued that the introduction of rainy-day funds may improve the incentives for prudent fiscal behavior in good times. These funds, which would be used in times of recession and replenished in upturns, might increase the incentive for governments not to waste the surpluses in good times and increase the room for maneuver in bad times. However, their establishment would imply a review of the current ESA accounting rules for computing budgetary statistics, so although interesting, such a move is not unproblematic.[25]

6.4.2.4 Strengthening Enforcement

A strong criticism of the Maastricht Treaty and the old SGP is that enforcement is partisan: national authorities are supposed to apply the rules themselves, thereby having strong incentives for collusion and horse trading.

As indicated in table 6.2, similarly to the case of transparency, the new pact includes provisions that will strengthen enforcement and others that are likely to weaken it further.

As pointed out in Buti, Eijffinger, and Franco (2003a, b), enforcement is particularly problematic in the case of supranational fiscal rules applying to sovereign countries. A step forward would be to enhance the national ownership of the rules so that there is a better chance that they become self-enforcing.[26] In parallel, one should strengthen the role of the commission in the enforcement of the SGP.

On the first count (national ownership), the new provisions concerning governance—notably the involvement of national parliaments—go in the right direction but are modest overall. In particular, the suggestion to establish independent monitoring bodies at the national level (see table 6.1), which was mentioned in the initial proposals by the commission (European Commission 2004b), was not accepted. On the second count (stronger role of the commission), the new pact does not introduce any significant change in the voting or procedural arrangements. Evidently, the council was not prepared to strengthen the authority of the commission in the interest of the credibility of EU fiscal rules. On the contrary, provisions such as the considerations of "other relevant factors," by reducing transparency and increasing the possibility of collusion in the council, risk working against an effective enforcement of the rules.

6.4.2.5 An Overall View

All in all, can the reform be considered an improvement on the original pact? We can answer this either by comparing the new with the old provisions, or by also considering the process that has led to the new framework. In the first case, one can conclude that some elements of the reform improve the quality of the EU budgetary framework, while others worsen it.

Some innovations allow greater flexibility in dealing with special circumstances and country-specific problems, while retaining a prudent approach to fiscal behavior as flexibility will remain bounded by the provision that any excess over 3 percent of GDP has to remain temporary and limited and no category of spending is excluded from the definition of the deficit. The steps being considered to improve fiscal transparency, enhance the quality of statistics, and strengthen national budgetary institutions can reinforce the rules. The emphasis on long-term sustainability makes the fiscal rules less myopic, a criticism often leveled at the old pact. The revision of the exceptionality clause is positive in that it removes an excessively restrictive condition.

On the other hand, some changes may be more problematic. This is the case for the extended deadlines for correcting deficits that may risk becoming a moving target. The greater complexity of the new framework may lower the visibility of the fiscal targets and make monitoring less effective. As the literature stresses, complex and less clearly defined rules are more difficult to enforce. There are also a number of controversial technical issues that remain to be addressed, such as how sustainability is to be measured, how temporary measures are to be defined, how the quality of public finances is to be assessed, and how to account for the cost of European integration. Finally, few changes have been introduced in the key provisions affecting the enforceability of the rules.

In other areas, further progress is warranted. This applies to the provisions concerning governance (reliable forecasts, role of national parliaments, continuity over the legislature), to the definition of the satisfactory pace of debt reduction, and to the development and implementation of a broader set of fiscal indicators. In due course, to increase coherence and visibility, one could resurrect the initial suggestion by the commission to establish a "European semester," where the broad orientations for fiscal policy are agreed, followed by a "national semester" where such general orientations are translated into concrete policy actions.

If we take the second approach to assess the reform, the process that has led to the reform gives rise to certain unease, since the changes may be interpreted as having been designed to accommodate the specific fiscal difficulties of well-identified countries. Clearly, the ideal would be to set or reform rules under a "veil of ignorance," without knowing in advance who the winners and losers would be. However, the vacuum created by the de facto suspension of the rules following the ECOFIN decision of November 2003 demanded a policy response from the European institutions.

6.5 Conclusions

This chapter has taken the view that the current EU fiscal framework should be examined in the light of the theoretical and empirical work on fiscal rules, but encompassing its supranational nature. The framework aims at balancing fiscal discipline and fiscal stabilization in a context in which countries ultimately remain responsible for national fiscal policy.

Clearly, the Stability Pact "mark I" had a number of drawbacks—particularly in terms of asymmetric incentives and lack of a long-term view. The reformed pact goes a long way toward correcting such problems while retaining the original architecture. But, in the end, the major weakness of the old rules was poor enforcement mechanisms. Will the new rules be more effectively enforced? The fact is that in the new pact there is a greater margin for discretion, but no independent enforcer may increase the incentives for collusion by the council in subverting the implementation of the rules. If so, lack of enforcement would persist or even be aggravated. However, as the new pact encompasses better economic rationale and may improve national ownership and fiscal transparency, there may be a better chance that it becomes self-enforcing.

Whatever judgment is ultimately made regarding the revision of the SGP, it would be wrong to assume that the pact will become irrelevant. First, the reasons for adopting fiscal rules in a monetary union of many sovereign countries in the first place are still valid. The future enlargement of the Euro Area to Central and Eastern European countries actually strengthens the need for a common fiscal framework. Second, as shown by the debate on the reform of the pact, no viable alternative to a credible supranational rule emerged, since all the other potential solutions came up against serious criticism of one kind or another. Third, many countries need sound fiscal policies leading to a reduction in debt levels also for purely domestic reasons, particularly the demographic shock that lies around the corner: an external anchor may continue to be useful. Finally, it is likely that, as soon as serious imbalances emerge in some countries, threatening the stability of the Euro Area, the other Euro Area members will step up the pressure for rigorous implementation of the rules.

Therefore, in our view, the SGP will not become "yet another EU coordination process" that, after a burst of attention, fades away and de facto is forgotten. On the contrary, since rules are necessary in a monetary union but as such put a constraint on national choices, it can safely be predicted that the revised pact will remain at the core of policy debate in Europe. And there will be no shortage of proposals for a "reform of the reform."

Notes

The views expressed in this chapter are those of the authors and should not be attributed to the institutions with which they are affiliated. The authors thank Alessandro Turrini and Max Watson for their suggestions and two anonymous referees for valuable comments to a previous draft of the chapter.

1. Adapted and updated from Buti, Eijffinger, and Franco 2003a. See also Begg and Schelkle 2004.

2. Strong evidence of the widespread use of one-off measures and creative accounting in the early years of EMU is found by Koen and van den Noord (2005). See also von Hagen and Wolff 2005.

3. The possibility of relying on market mechanisms to provide effective incentives to fiscal discipline was assessed in depth in the late 1980s when the EMU was designed. It was widely considered that the constraints imposed by market forces are either too slow and weak or too sudden and disruptive. More recent work confirms that market mechanisms cannot be relied upon for replacing fiscal rules. However, greater transparency in fiscal accounts can allow markets to usefully complement rules. See Balassone, Franco, and Giordano 2004. For a survey of the proposals aiming at strengthening financial market discipline, see Buti, Eijffinger, and Franco 2003a. The issue has been recently raised again by Buiter and Sibert (2005).

4. Actually, the treaty protocol on the excessive deficit procedure calls upon member states to ensure the consistency of national procedures and institutions with the provisions of the treaty.

5. While most proposals suggest introducing FPCs at the national level, Fatás et al. (2003) propose creating such a body at the EU level.

6. For a theoretical model, see Razin and Sadka 2002.

7. Similar proposals have been put forward lately by Bofinger (2004) and Schelkle (2002).

8. This trade off will be sharpened by the enlargement of the Euro Area to new member states. For a discussion, see Orbán and Szapáry 2004.

9. As emphasized in the debate on fiscal rules, there are trade offs and complementarities between the desired features of a "good" rule. For instance enhancing country specificity is likely to lead to less transparency, while improving the latter is likely to lead to more effective enforcement. For a discussion, with particular reference to supra-national rules, see Buti, Eijffinger, and Franco 2003a.

10. These changes were subsequently translated into legislative amendments of the SGP regulations in July 2005. For a detailed presentation of the new pact, see European Commission 2005.

11. See Schuknecht and Tanzi (2005), who suggest that country circumstances and reform design matter.

12. For earlier assessments of the reform, see the postscript in Buti and Franco 2005, Eijffinger 2005, and European Commission 2005.

13. According to the European Commission estimates, these margins would be adequate for the larger countries. See European Commission 2002.

14. As pointed out earlier, in the case of public investment, the right concept is that of *net* investment (hence taking amortization into account).

15. See Balassone and Franco 2000b and the other essays in Banca d'Italia 2000.

16. See Balassone, Franco, and Zotteri 2006, Koen and van den Noord 2005, and von Hagen and Wolff 2004.

17. This will extend the experience of 2000–2001 with the universal mobile telecommunications system (UMTS) proceeds to all temporary measures.

18. The estimation of cyclically adjusted figures and one-off measures raises technical problems and requires some decisions concerning methodological solutions. Moreover, cyclically adjusted balances can be revised ex post on the basis of new information concerning the macroeconomic outlook. Public spending normally reflects several measures and events with temporary expansionary or restrictive effects. It may probably be useful to consider only the measures having transitory effects on public revenues (e.g., sales of assets, anticipation of tax payments, tax amnesties). Guidelines concerning the definition of one-off measures would have to be agreed in advance. For a tentative taxonomy of one-off measures, see European Commission 2004a.

19. See Balassone, Franco, and Zotteri 2006. A first step in this direction is represented by introducing long-term expenditure projections in the stability programs.

20. On the importance of a reliable statistical framework for the application of EU fiscal rules, see Balassone, Franco, and Zotteri 2003.

21. See Balassone, Franco, and Zotteri 2006 and European Commission 2005.

22. As proposed by the commission, in the cases of application of the excessive deficit procedure to Greece, Portugal, and Italy in 2005, the recommendation issued by the council included a mention of avoiding reliance on below-the-line operations.

23. As shown in Buti and van den Noord 2004, producing overly optimistic forecasts is particularly tempting in electoral periods as a way to increase the room for maneuver of discretionary fiscal policy. See Strauch, Hallerberg, and von Hagen 2004 and Larch and Salto 2005 for a more detailed discussion of this topic.

24. The case for independent forecasts is advocated by Jonung and Larch (2004).

25. Alternatively, the treaty protocol could be revised, mentioning that the 3 percent reference value refers to budget balances net of accumulation of assets in the rainy-day fund. However, an issue arises when the fund is depleted after protracted deficits: the budget balance figure used in the SGP would quickly worsen, leading to difficulties in the implementation of the SGP.

26. As argued in Buti and Pench 2004 and as shown by the experience of the early years of the EMU, this is particularly important in the case of large Euro Area countries where the threat of external sanctions is less effective.

References

Allsopp, C., and M. Artis. 2003. The assessment: EMU four years on. *Oxford Review of Economic Policy* 19 (1): 1–29.

Annett, A., J. Decressin, and M. Deppler. 2005. Reforming the Stability and Growth Pact. IMF Policy Discussion Paper PDP/05/2.

Artis, M. J. 2002. The Stability and Growth Pact: Fiscal policy in the EMU. In *Institutional, Legal and Economic Aspects of the EMU*, ed. F. Breuss, G. Fink, and S. Griller, 101–115. Vienna-New York: Springer.

Artis, M. J., and M. Buti. 2000. Close to balance or in surplus—A policy maker's guide to the implementation of the Stability and Growth Pact. *Journal of Common Market Studies* 38:563–592. Edited version in Buti and Franco (2005).

Balassone, F., and D. Franco. 2000a. Public investment, the Stability Pact and the golden rule. *Fiscal Studies* 21:207–229.

Balassone, F., and D. Franco. 2000b. Assessing fiscal sustainability: A review of methods with a view to EMU. In *Fiscal Sustainability*, ed. Banca d'Italia, 22–60. Rome: Banca d'Italia.

Balassone, F., and D. Franco. 2001. EMU fiscal rules: A new answer to an old question? In *Fiscal Rules*, ed. Banca d'Italia, 33–58. Rome: Banca d'Italia.

Balassone, F., D. Franco, and R. Giordano. 2004. Market induced fiscal discipline: Is there a fall-back solution for rule-failure? In *Public Debt*, ed. Banca d'Italia, 389–426. Rome: Bank of Italy.

Balassone, F., D. Franco, and S. Zotteri. 2003. Fiscal rules: Indicators and underlying statistical frameworks. Paper presented at the IIPF Congress, Prague.

Balassone, F., D. Franco, and S. Zotteri. 2006. EMU fiscal indicators: A misleading compass? *Empirica* 33:63–87.

Banca d'Italia. 2000. *Fiscal Sustainability*. Rome: Banca d'Italia.

Begg, I., and W. Schelkle. 2004. The pact is dead: Long live the pact. *National Institute Review* 189:86–98.

Blanchard, O. J., and F. Giavazzi. 2003. Reforms that can be done: Improving the SGP through a proper accounting of public investment. Mimeo., February.

Bofinger, P. 2004. Should the Stability and Growth Pact be reformed? Briefing paper for the Committee on Economic and Monetary Affairs of the European Parliament, February.

Brunila, A. 2002. Fiscal policy: Coordination, discipline and stabilization. Paper prepared for the Group of Economic Analysis of the European Commission, April.

Brunila, A., M. Buti, and D. Franco, eds. 2001. *The Stability and Growth Pact—The Architecture of Fiscal Policy in EMU*. Basingstoke: Palgrave.

Buiter, W. H. 2001. Notes on a "code for fiscal stability." *Oxford Economic Papers* 53:1–19.

Buiter, W. H., and C. Grafe. 2003. Reforming EMU's fiscal policy rules: some suggestions for enhancing fiscal sustainability and macroeconomic stability in an enlarged European Union. In *Monetary and Fiscal Policies in EMU: Interactions and Coordination*, ed. M. Buti, 92–145. Cambridge: Cambridge University Press.

Buiter, W. H., and A. C. Sibert. 2005. How the ECB's open market operations weaken fiscal discipline in the Eurozone (and what to do about it). Paper presented at the conference on Fiscal Policy and the Road to the Euro, National Bank of Poland, June 30–July 1.

Buti, M., S. Eijffinger, and D. Franco. 2003a. Revisiting the Stability and Growth Pact: Grand design or internal adjustment? CEPR Discussion Paper no. 3692.

Buti, M., S. Eijffinger, and D. Franco. 2003b. Revisiting the Stability and Growth Pact: A pragmatic way forward. *Oxford Review of Economic Policy* 19:100–111.

Buti, M., and D. Franco. 2005. *Fiscal Policy in EMU—Theory, Evidence and Institutions*. Cheltenham, UK: Edward Elgar.

Buti, M., D. Franco, and H. Ongena. 1998. Fiscal discipline and flexibility in EMU: the implementation of the Stability and Growth Pact. *Oxford Review of Economic Policy* 14 (3): 81–97.

Buti, M., and G. Giudice. 2002. Maastricht's fiscal rules at ten: an assessment. *Journal of Common Market Studies* 40:823–847.

Buti, M., and L. R. Pench. 2004. Why do large countries flout the Stability Pact? And what can be done about it? *Journal of Common Market Studies* 42:1025–1035.

Buti, M., and P. van den Noord. 2004. Fiscal discretion and elections in the early years of EMU. *Journal of Common Market Studies* 39:737–756.

Buti, M., J. von Hagen, and C. Martinez-Mongay, eds. 2002. *The Behaviour of Fiscal Authorities—Stabilisation, Growth and Institutions.* Cheltenham: Edward Elgar.

Calmfors, L., and G. Corsetti. 2002. How to reform Europe's fiscal policy framework. *World Economics* 4 (1): 109–116.

Casella, A. 2001. Tradable deficit permits. In *The Stability and Growth Pact—The Architecture of Fiscal Policy in EMU,* ed. A. Brunila, M. Buti, and D. Franco, 394–413. Basingstoke: Palgrave.

Coeuré, B., and J. Pisani-Ferry. 2003. A sustainability pact for the Eurozone. Mimeo., Ecole Polytechnique.

De la Fuente, A. 1997. Fiscal policy and growth in the OECD. CEPR Discussion Paper no. 1755.

ECOFIN Council. 2005. Improving the implementation of the Stability and Growth Pact. 7423/05, March.

Economic Policy Committee (EPC). 2003. The impact of ageing populations on public finances: Overview of analysis carried out at EU level and proposals for a future work programme. Brussels.

Eichengreen, B. 2003. Institutions for fiscal stability. Institute for European Studies Working Paper PEIF 14.

Eijffinger, S. C. W. 2005. On a reformed Stability and Growth Pact. *Intereconomics* 40 (3): 141–147.

European Commission. 2002. Public finances in EMU—2002. *European Economy* 3.

European Commission. 2004a. Public finances in EMU—2004. *European Economy* 3.

European Commission. 2004b. Strengthening economic governance and clarifying the implementation of the Stability and Growth Pact. COM 581, September.

European Commission. 2005. Public finances in EMU—2005. *European Economy* 3.

Fatás, A., J. von Hagen, A. Hughes Hallett, R. Strauch, and A. Sibert. 2003. *Stability and Growth in Europe: Towards a Better Pact.* CEPR MEI 13.

Fitoussi, J.-P., and J. Creel. 2002. *How to Reform the European Central Bank.* Centre for European Reform.

Gros, D. 2003. Stability pact for public debt. CEPS Brief no. 30. Brussels: Centre for European Policy Studies.

Inman, R. P. 1996. Do balanced budget rules work? U.S. experience and possible lessons for the EMU. NBER Working Paper no. 5838. National Bureau of Economic Research, Washington, DC.

Jonung, L., and M. Larch. 2004. Improving fiscal policy in the EU: The case for independent forecasts. *European Economy Economic Papers* no. 210.

Koen, V., and P. van den Noord. 2005. Fiscal gimmickry in Europe: One-off measures and creative accounting. OECD Economics Department Working Paper no. 417.

Kopits, G., and S. Symansky. 1998. Fiscal policy rules. IMF Occasional Paper no. 162.

Larch, M., and M. Salto. 2005. Fiscal rules, inertia and discretionary fiscal policy. *Applied Economics* 37:1135–1146.

Mills, P., and A. Quinet. 2002. How to allow the automatic stabilisers to play fully? A policy-maker's guide for EMU countries. In *The Behaviour of Fiscal Authorities—Stabilisation, Growth and Institutions*, ed. M. Buti, J. von Hagen, and C. Martinez-Mongay, 115–129. Cheltenham: Edward Elgar.

Orbán, G., and G. Szapáry. 2004. The Stability and Growth Pact from the perspective of the new member states. *Journal of Policy Modeling* 26:839–864.

Pench, L. R. 2003. Comment on Buiter and Grafe. In *Monetary and Fiscal Policies in EMU: Interactions and Coordination*, ed. M. Buti, 146–153. Cambridge: Cambridge University Press.

Pisani-Ferry, J. 2002. Fiscal discipline and policy coordination in the Eurozone: Assessment and proposals. Paper prepared for the Group of Economic Analysis of the European Commission, April.

Razin, A., and E. Sadka. 2002. The Stability and Growth Pact as an impediment to privatizing social security. CEPR Discussion Paper no. 3621.

Sapir, A., et al. 2004. *An Agenda for a Growing Europe.* Oxford: Oxford University Press.

Schelkle, W. 2002. Disciplining device or insurance arrangement? Two approaches to the political economy of EMU policy coordination. LSE European Institute Working Paper no. 1/02.

Schuknecht, L. 2004. EU fiscal rules: issues and lessons from political economy. ECB Working Paper no. 421. European Central Bank, Frankfurt.

Schuknecht, L., and V. Tanzi. 2005. Reforming public expenditure in industrialised countries: Are there trade-offs? ECB Working Paper no. 435. European Central Bank, Frankfurt.

Strauch, R., M. Hallerberg, and J. von Hagen. 2004. Budgetary forecasts in Europe—The track record of Stability and Convergence Programmes. ECB Working Paper no. 307. European Central Bank, Frankfurt.

Turrini, A. 2004. Public investment and the EU fiscal framework. European Commission Economic Papers no. 202.

von Hagen, J., and G. B. Wolff. 2004. What do deficits tell us about debt? Empirical evidence on creative accounting with fiscal rules in the EU. Deutsche Bundesbank Discussion Paper no. 38.

Wren-Lewis, S. 2003. Fiscal policy, inflation and stabilisation in EMU. In *Monetary and Fiscal Policies in EMU: Interactions and Coordination*, ed. M. Buti, 65–87. Cambridge: Cambridge University Press.

Wyplosz, C. 2002. Fiscal policy: rules or institutions? Paper prepared for the Group of Economic Analysis of the European Commission, April.

Wyplosz, C. 2005. Fiscal policy: institutions versus rules. *National Institute Economic Review* 191:64–78.

7 The Welfare State and Strategies toward Fiscal Sustainability in Denmark

Torben M. Andersen, Svend E. Hougaard Jensen, and Lars Haagen Pedersen

7.1 Introduction

Denmark has a large public sector that offers a wide range of welfare services and income replacement schemes to the population. The Danish welfare model builds on universality; that is, individuals have basic rights to welfare arrangements like health care, old-age care, and pension benefits independently of their ability to pay, labor market history, and so forth.[1] These welfare arrangements are tax financed, and since the level of welfare services is high and income replacement schemes are extensive, this implies that the tax burden is high (about 50 percent of GDP). It is an implication of this system that there is a strong pay-as-you-go (PAYG) element in the sense that individuals on average are net recipients as young and old, while they are net contributors when active in the labor market. Consequently, changes in the age composition of the population can have dramatic consequences for public finances. Under a balanced budget requirement, this would translate into substantial changes in either taxes or welfare services. To the extent that neither of these options is politically acceptable, the issue arises as to how to maintain the same welfare opportunities for different generations without causing substantial intergenerational redistribution, yet ensuring that the system is fiscally sustainable.

The outset for considering this challenge is rather favorable. Unemployment is down to 6 percent of the labor force, prices are fairly stable, there has been a surplus on the current account each year since the late 1980s, and a high degree of fiscal discipline has been demonstrated by governments of different colors over the last couple of decades. In fact, the gross public debt-to-GDP ratio has been gradually brought down, from 81 percent in 1993 to 46 percent in 2003.[2] However, even though demographic changes in Denmark are not dramatic by international standards, the implications for public finances may be substantial owing to the extended form of the welfare state.

To cope with this challenge, a medium-term strategy—the "DK 2010" plan—has been launched. The plan includes an intermediate target of a reduction in the debt-to-GDP ratio to 25 percent by the year 2010. The basic idea of DK 2010 is to consolidate public finances so as to be able to finance an unchanged supply of welfare arrangements with constant taxes. Constant taxes are consistent with both tax-smoothing arguments and concerns for intergenerational distribution.

The aim of this chapter is to provide an assessment of the consolidation strategy implied by DK 2010. Since substantial uncertainty surrounds key variables over the time span in which the demographic changes unfold, it is essential to assess the robustness of the strategy to such uncertainty. Uncertainty is inherent in demographic projections, and experience has shown that they may be prone to radical changes, even within relatively short periods of time.[3] There is also uncertainty concerning other key variables, including the interest rate and the productivity growth rate. In the presence of uncertainty, it is also important to assess the implications of a given strategy for risk sharing across time and generations. Moreover, issues of political implementability and the implications for intergenerational distribution have to be taken into account.

The main findings of the chapter are that maintaining the current welfare arrangements leaves a substantial problem of fiscal sustainability. Just to illustrate the order of magnitude of the fiscal imbalance, putting fiscal policy back on a sustainable path would require a permanent increase in income taxation of approximately 4 percent of GDP. If this was achieved by adjusting the base direct income tax rate, an increase of about 9 percentage points would be necessary. Interestingly, the fiscal position is fairly robust to a number of demographic changes, with the important exception of changes in longevity. An expected increase in longevity is thus one of the important reasons for the fiscal sustainability problem. Moreover, the fiscal position is relatively sensitive to changes in the interest rate and the productivity growth rate. The fact that increases in life expectancy and uncertainty play such a substantial role raises a fundamental question as to whether a prefunding strategy is appropriate. This applies in relation to its implications not only for intergenerational distribution but also for the ability to cope with the inherent uncertainty.

The chapter is organized as follows. Section 7.2 offers a brief account of the public-sector activities and fiscal policy in Denmark, including details of the medium-term strategy DK 2010. Section 7.3 presents a demographic projection, an outline of our analytical framework, and an analysis of whether current fiscal policies are sustainable. We define sustainability in terms of consistency with the intertemporal budget constraint (see also chapter 2) in a fully specified overlapping generations model capturing welfare arrangements in Denmark. Given the sustainability problems associated with current policies, section 7.4 studies how sustainability can be achieved through prefunding. Finally, section 7.5 suggests an alternative strategy based on introducing a stronger link between old-age pension rules and changes in life expectancy.

7.2 Trends in Fiscal Performance and Design

In this section we first portray some aggregate patterns in the recent behavior of public finances in Denmark. We then try to identify some fiscal strategies followed since 1960, emphasizing the expansion of the welfare state in the 1960s and 1970s and the reform programs since the early 1980s.

7.2.1 Public Expenditures, Revenues, and Debt

In most industrialized countries, the magnitude of government involvement has increased significantly over the last century (Masson and Mussa 1995; Tanzi and Schuknecht 2000). In Denmark, the growth in public expenditures was particularly extensive over the period 1960–1980; see table 7.1. In fact, prior to that period, the share of public expenditures to GDP in Denmark was below the average share in other OECD countries, but during the 1960s and 1970s the public expenditure share grew by nearly twice as much as in those countries.

One noteworthy point is that the growth in public expenditures up to the mid-1970s was driven by increasing public consumption, whereas increases in transfer incomes have been the major driving force thereafter. This is, of course, partly a reflection of the increase in unemployment, which took place in the mid-1970s and which brought unemployment up to a persistently higher level. The fall in unemployment during the 1990s has lowered transfer payments, but not to the

Table 7.1
Public expenditures and revenues: 1971–2001

	1971	1976	1981	1986	1991	1996	2001
	Percentage of GDP						
Total expenditures	41.9	44.8	52.7	45.1	50.1	52.9	50.2
Transfer payments	11.0	13.1	17.2	15.1	18.4	19.8	17.3
Consumption	22.2	24.7	28.4	24.6	25.7	25.9	25.9
Other expenditures	8.7	7.0	7.1	5.4	6.0	7.2	7.0
Total revenues	46.9	44.1	48.5	53.5	51.6	54.7	54.5
Surplus	5.1	−0.7	−4.1	8.4	1.5	1.8	4.3
Net interest payments	0.0	−0.9	1.8	5.1	3.9	2.8	1.4
Gross debt	12.6	11.1	48.4	66.7	62.5	65.1	45.4

Source: Statistics Denmark.
Note: The old definition of gross debt according to the Stability and Growth Pact.

same extent that unemployment has been reduced. The reason for this is that the fall in unemployment figures is partly because of the introduction of various paid leave schemes in the early 1990s, which have reduced the labor supply.

The total tax revenue as a share of GDP has risen steadily since 1960, constituting 53.5 percent in 2003. Because the expenditure share has fallen since the early 1990s, the rise in the revenue share over the last decade shows that a fiscal consolidation program is being followed.

The Danish tax structure differs in several respects from the structure in other OECD countries in that (1) a relatively large share of the (high) tax revenue stems from personal income taxation, unlike other European countries which rely more heavily on social security contributions; (2) consumption taxes are used to a larger extent in Denmark than in other OECD countries; and (3) wealth, property, and corporate taxes are used on a relatively smaller scale in Denmark than in other OECD countries.

Of particular interest are the relatively high marginal tax rates faced by medium- to high-income earners. A recurrent theme in policy debates is the effects of such high marginal tax rates on labor supply decisions both at the intensive and the extensive margins (working hours and labor force participation). Moreover, the combination of the taxation system with the social assistance system implies that the economic incentive to work is low for some groups. A further important aspect is the robustness of the current tax system to further globalization.

It is important for the current debate that Denmark experienced a debt crisis in the early 1980s. Public debt was growing rapidly on account of both persistent budget deficits reaching 10 percent of GDP and very high interest rates. There was a growing recognition that the development was not sustainable, and a major policy shift took place in the early 1980s. This policy shift had many ingredients, including a fixed exchange rate policy, abolition of wage indexation, and fiscal consolidation via both expenditure control and tax increases (mainly on pension funds). This policy shift had important short-run implications, including a dramatic fall in inflation and interest rates, higher activity and lower unemployment, but also increasing current account deficits. Moreover, public finances improved dramatically. The primary budget thus changed from a deficit of about 6 percent in 1982 to a surplus of 8 percent in 1986. This shift was partly due to discretionary policy changes and partly due to automatic budgetary reactions following from booming activity.

7.2.2 *Welfare Policies and Reforms*

It is beyond the scope of this chapter to give a detailed account of the mechanisms that led to the development and expansion of the Danish welfare model. For our purpose here it suffices to note that the aim of ensuring a social balance and egalitarian outcome has very broad support in the Danish population. Moreover, the model has a particular blend of state intervention and liberal policy. There has always been a concern for ensuring a competitive private sector, since Denmark is, after all, a small and open economy. An illustrative example of this is the flexibility of the Danish labor market with very flexible hiring and firing rules. The flip side of this is the relatively generous unemployment insurance scheme that is largely tax-financed—that is, the welfare state plays a key role in diversifying risk. In assessing welfare arrangements, it is important to keep an eye on both the incentive and the insurance effects.

During the 1980s and 1990s a number of important changes were made in the taxation system. Against the background of persistent current account deficits and the implied "savings deficit," a motivation for reforms has been to improve savings incentives. In fact, the incentives to save have been improved through substantive cuts in the tax value of the right to deduct interest expenses. Whereas interest rates in the early 1990s could be deducted at a maximal rate of 73 percent, as a result of a sequence of reforms it has now been reduced to about 30 percent. Moreover, the implication of high marginal tax rates for the labor market is a recurrent policy theme, and several changes to the tax system have been implemented since 1985. The marginal tax rates on personal income have been reduced, by broadening the tax base and switching to green taxes. For example, the highest marginal tax rate on income has been brought down from 69 to 63 percent. The tax system has also been modified in view of the increased international mobility of capital, by bringing down the nominal corporate tax rate from 50 percent in 1990 to its current level of 30 percent, thereby making the tax system more robust with respect to profit shifting by international firms.

An important initiative in the labor market has had crucial effects on pension saving—namely, the gradual expansion of the negotiated but mandatory labor market pension scheme. These schemes had existed previously, but they became much more widespread from the late 1980s and early 1990s onward. While the schemes can be said to break with the universality principle, they solve a problem in relation to income support for pensioners. The schemes are fully funded, defined-contribution pension schemes. The contribution rate of blue-collar workers is now being increased to typically 10.8 percent of the wage income, but for white-collar workers and public employees, rates remain 12–15 percent. The contributions amount to 6.8 percent of GDP in 2004. At present, the total wealth of private pension funds is about 100 percent of GDP, but it is expected to reach a level of almost 200 percent of GDP in 2050. From a fiscal point of view, it is important to note that the contributions to pension funds are deductible from income tax, whereas payments from the funds are taxed. Thus, since contributions are still high compared to what is being paid out, the tax base is increasing over time as the pension funds mature. This automatic increase in the tax base is a feature that is unique to Denmark and the Netherlands in the European Union (European Commission 2000).

The 1990s also witnessed several welfare reforms, including important changes in the labor market and social policy. A very important change was the so-called activation policy. This essentially means that passive claiming of unemployment benefits and social assistance has become more difficult, since entitlement can only be maintained if the recipient is involved in work or education programs. Moreover, the entitlement period for claiming unemployment benefits has been reduced. Previously, it was effectively open-ended—participation in labor market programs counted as fulfillment of the work requirement—but now there is a maximum of four years. Without changing the level of compensation in unemployment benefits or social assistance, the incentive structure has thus been changed substantially. For young persons the compensation level has also been reduced since "normal" compensation can only be claimed for six months, and thereafter it is reduced by 50 percent.

With the aim of increasing the labor supply, initiatives to postpone the retirement decision have been taken. For example, the early retirement benefit scheme allowing people to retire at the age of sixty was reformed in 1998. This reform makes retirement before the age of sixty-two less attractive, by offering a premium to people who abstain from using the scheme. Since this reform, there has been no major reform initiative.

7.2.3 DK 2010: A Medium- to Long-Term Strategy

Fiscal policy in Denmark is conducted according to the DK 2010 plan that was originally formulated in 2001 by a center-left government led by the Social Democrats. The current center-right government adopted the plan when it took office at the end of 2001, so the plan is therefore effectively accepted across a broad political spectrum in Denmark. The plan defines a benchmark for assessing the government's performance on economic policy.

The overall objective of this medium- to long-term strategy is to prepare for meeting the pressure on public finances caused by population aging, and thus to avoid dramatic policy changes when the expected increases in the demographic dependency burden unfold. Specifically, in order to smooth the fiscal adjustments, explicit targets of debt reduction were formulated, involving a reduction in the gross public debt-to-GDP ratio to 35 percent in 2005 and 20–25 percent in 2010. The original plan included intermediate fiscal targets of annual surpluses on the public budget of 2–3 percent of GDP over a period of ten years and a limit of 1 percent on the annual real growth rate of public services from 2002 to 2005 and 0.5 percent in subsequent years. The plan also contained intermediate targets in the form of an increase in employment of 3.5 percent of the labor force; an increase in the labor force of 2.8 percent; and a reduction in the rate of unemployment to

4.5 percent of the labor force. However, the plan did not originally—and has also subsequently failed to—provide details of the structural reforms needed to reach these targets.[4] The current government has added a so-called tax freeze to the plan, meaning that no current tax rate is allowed to increase. Moreover, some tax reductions have been implemented, which has strengthened the requirements to the growth targets for government consumption.[5]

Fiscal consolidation via debt reduction is the main priority in the plan, and this has to be achieved either through structural reforms to expand the labor supply, or through tight control of public spending. In the absence of structural reforms, the necessary fiscal adjustments must be implemented through tight targets on expenditures for public services, since public expenditures to transfers are more or less given by commitments not to reduce welfare benefit rates (transfer payments per recipient) and by guarantees that these rates will grow in line with the growth in real wages. In fact, the underlying indexation scheme has been defined by law since 1990 (statutory provision).

While much attention has been drawn to the government's ability to fulfill the medium-term targets of the plan, much less attention has been paid to the connection between the medium-term targets and fiscal sustainability. The basic premise for the plan is that if the medium-term targets are fulfilled by 2010, then a fiscal policy where the same supply of welfare arrangements is available to both future generations and current generations will be consistent with fiscal sustainability. In this sense the fiscal policy adjustment is "front-loaded," as the adjustment takes place in the period until 2010.

While acknowledging the positive impact on fiscal discipline of DK 2010, this chapter provides a broader economic assessment of this plan, including (1) whether it is robust with respect to uncertainty in key demographic and economic variables; (2) the implications for intergenerational distribution and risk sharing; and (3) whether the plan is credible in a political economy sense. Before turning to these questions, we examine whether current fiscal policy is sustainable.

7.3 Assessing Fiscal Sustainability

This section examines whether the promise to provide future generations with the same benefit and contribution rules as current generations is consistent with fiscal sustainability. We first present some details of the underlying demographic projection, then we briefly describe the essential elements of our analytical framework, and finally we offer a more fundamental macroeconomic evaluation of current fiscal policy, including the existing welfare arrangements.

7.3.1 The Demographic Projection

Demographic projections are based on assumptions concerning future fertility, mortality, and migration. The uncertainty associated with the projection of each of these determinants is significant, and the evolution of the total population becomes highly uncertain in longer-run projections. However, what really matters in relation to fiscal sustainability is the robustness of the demographic dependency ratio with respect to changes in the underlying population flows. In what follows, we discuss the effect of permanent changes in each of the three population flows on the dependency ratio. The analysis is based on the demographic forecast of the Welfare Commission (2004).[6]

The projection of future fertility is based on estimation of age-dependent fertility rates for different population groups based on the origin of the individuals (immigrants from less developed countries, immigrants from more developed countries, descendants of these two groups of immigrants, and individuals of Danish origin). This leads to a projection of the total fertility of the whole population that is almost constant at the current level of 1.7. The assumptions underlying the projection of net immigration imply a fairly constant level corresponding to 0.13 percent of the population. For example, we have assumed—in line with Boeri and Brücker (2001)—that immigration from new EU countries accumulates to a level of 1 percent of the population.

Because changes in mortality are by far the most important determinant of changes in the demographic dependency burden, we need to be more detailed here. Life expectancy in Denmark was among the highest in the world in 1960, but this picture has changed dramatically. Indeed, with an average annual growth rate of life expectancy of 0.1 years in Denmark, only Slovakia and Hungary (for men) among the OECD countries have experienced slower growth in life expectancy than Denmark over the past four decades (OECD 2003). The slow growth implies that life expectancy for men in Denmark in 2000 was in the lower half of OECD countries ranked by life expectancy, and for women it was in the lowest third. However, according to more recent Danish statistics, the current annual growth rates are approximately 0.2 years, which is closer to the European average.

Using the methods suggested by Lee and Carter (1992), Haldrup (2004) estimates age- and gender-specific mortality rates for Denmark using data from 1900–2002. These estimates imply that the average annual future growth rates in life expectancy are in the range from 0.08 to 0.09 years for both men and women. However, even these new estimates imply that the growth rate in life expectancy remains approximately 50 percent below the average growth rate for western Europe over the next fifty years (United Nations 2004). In any case, this suggests that uncertainty with respect to life expectancy may be significant.

The projection shows a fall in the size of the population (from 5.4 million today to 5.0 million in 2070), and the number of working-age persons (15–64) is reduced by 10 percent from 2002 to 2040 and by 16 percent from 2002 to 2080. Over the same two periods, the number of elderly citizens (65+) increases by 52 percent and 47 percent, respectively. Consequently, the demographic dependency ratio increases by 27 percent from 2002 to 2040 and by 28 percent from 2002 to 2080. This indicates that the increase in the dependency ratio during the next thirty-five years is not an isolated phenomenon owing to the echo effects of the large postwar generations. Rather, it is a permanent shift to a higher level.

Compared to previous yet very recent demographic forecasts, the shift in the dependency ratio is qualitatively different. Figure 7.1 compares the current dependency ratio to the dependency ratio based on the 2001 demographic forecast (the year DK 2010 was launched). In the 2001 forecast, the dependency ratio has a global peak around 2040, but the ratio is then reduced to a level that is between the current level and the peak in 2040. This suggests that the demographic aging problem has both a temporary and a permanent component. The current demographic projection implies that the aging problem is almost entirely a permanent phenomenon.

Since this change in the characteristics of the demographic projection may have serious implications for the design of fiscal policy, it is important to consider the robustness of the dependency ratio with respect to changes in fertility, migration, and mortality. We therefore examine how the dependency ratio responds to a permanent change to each of these factors. The shocks are quantified such that the long-run effects on the total population are similar. The accumulated increase in the total population is in the range of 4–5 percent after seventy-five years for all three analyses. Figure 7.2 shows the dependency ratio in the

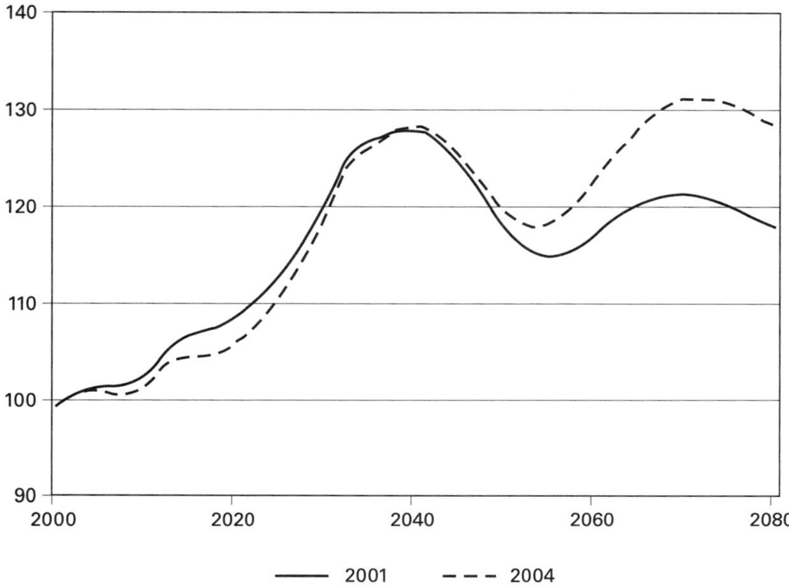

Figure 7.1
Dependency ratio: 2001 vs. 2004 projection
Source: The Danish Welfare Commission and DREAM.

baseline and given the three different permanent changes. The result is very clear: the dependency ratio is robust with respect to changes in fertility and immigration, whereas the change in life expectancy has a major impact.

The reason increases in future life expectancy have qualitatively different effects from increases in fertility and migration is that the latter two affect individuals in all phases of life, whereas increases in life expectancy only tend to increase the number of individuals aged sixty and over, the majority of whom have retired in any case. This also explains why fertility and immigration only have minor effects on the demographic dependency ratio: these changes tend to affect both the numerator and the denominator of the ratio, whereas increased life expectancy tends to affect only the numerator.

7.3.2 *The Analytical Framework*

The analysis is conducted using a large-scale dynamic CGE model called DREAM that was developed with the purpose of evaluating

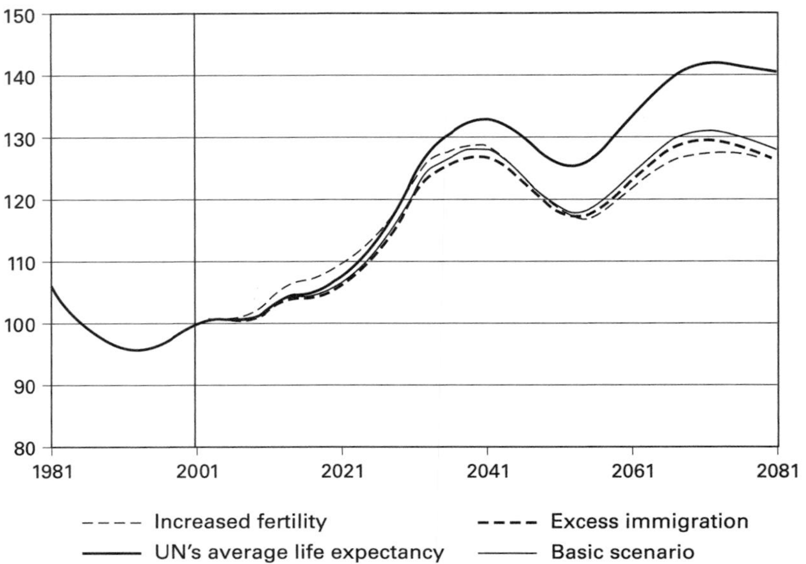

Figure 7.2
Effects on the dependency ratio of permanent shocks to population flows
Source: The Danish Welfare Commission, DREAM, and United Nations 2004.

medium- to long-term effects of fiscal policy in Denmark.[7] This model is thus quite appropriate for assessing issues of fiscal sustainability and evaluating the sensitivity to changes in key variables.

The model is based on an overlapping generation structure and the focus is demographic development and the Danish public sector. DREAM represents a small open economy with a fixed exchange rate regime, perfect mobility of capital and residence-based capital taxation, so that the nominal interest rate is given by the international capital market. Danish and foreign products are considered imperfect substitutes in both production functions and consumption, and foreign trade is modeled using the Armington approach. Prices and wages are therefore influenced by internal Danish economic developments.

The core of DREAM is the household structure. The model uses the detailed projection of the Danish population presented in section 7.3.1. The adult population is divided into seventeen generations, each consisting of cohorts in a five-year interval, starting with people who are seventeen to twenty-one years of age. For each generation a representative household is constructed. Children are distributed among the households according to the age-specific fertility rates of the demographic forecast.

Each representative household optimizes its labor supply, consumption, and savings decisions in each period given perfect foresight. Savings take place in owner-occupied dwellings, financial assets (stocks and bonds), and labor market (second pillar) and private (third pillar) pension schemes. The labor market is characterized by unionized behavior giving rise to structural unemployment.

There are two private production sectors: a construction sector and a sector producing other goods and services. Firms optimize intertemporally and use labor, capital, and materials in the production process. Investments are subject to convex costs of installation, giving rise to gradual capital adjustments. Like the labor market, product markets are characterized by imperfect competition. An exogenous Harrod-neutral, labor-augmenting productivity growth rate of 2 percent annually and an exogenous foreign inflation rate of 2 percent are assumed.

The public sector produces goods that are used mainly for public consumption. In addition it levies taxes and pays transfers and subsidies to households and firms. These are modeled to replicate actual budget conditions as closely as possible. The most important taxes in terms of revenue are local- and central-government income taxes, VAT, excise duties, corporate taxes, property taxes, and a tax on the yield of pension funds. Tax rates are assumed to remain constant in the forecast period. On the expenditure side twenty-three different transfers are distinguished and paid out to individuals of each respective age, gender, and origin group following the actual distribution in 2001. In the same way expenditures for individual public consumption (mainly educational, health, and social expenditures) are distributed to individuals. These individual expenses (per age, gender, and origin group) are forecast to increase with the rate of inflation and the exogenous productivity growth. The remaining collective public consumption is assumed to grow at the same rate as domestic GDP.

The government's intertemporal budget constraint is respected, and the sustainability of fiscal policy may be ensured in various ways. The exact way in which sustainability is enforced is central to, among other things, the intertemporal distribution of taxes and transfers. In this chapter we use a permanent increase in the base income tax rate that is phased in from 2011 to 2021 to measure the necessary adjustment to fulfill the intertemporal budget constraint.

7.3.3 *Is Current Fiscal Policy Sustainable?*

The DK 2010 plan builds on the objective that all generations should enjoy the same supply of welfare arrangements. This may be interpreted as aiming at having both a defined-benefit and a defined-contribution scheme in the sense that benefit and contribution rules should be the same across various generations. It is also assumed that the gains from expected future productivity growth accrue to future generations. This corresponds to extrapolating the fact that current generations benefit from the historical growth in productivity.

The Danish welfare state provides transfers and public services financed almost exclusively by general taxes. The PAYG nature of the Danish welfare state is reflected in the distribution of age-specific net contributions per individual to the public sector, as shown in figure 7.3. The figure displays that children and elderly citizens are net re-

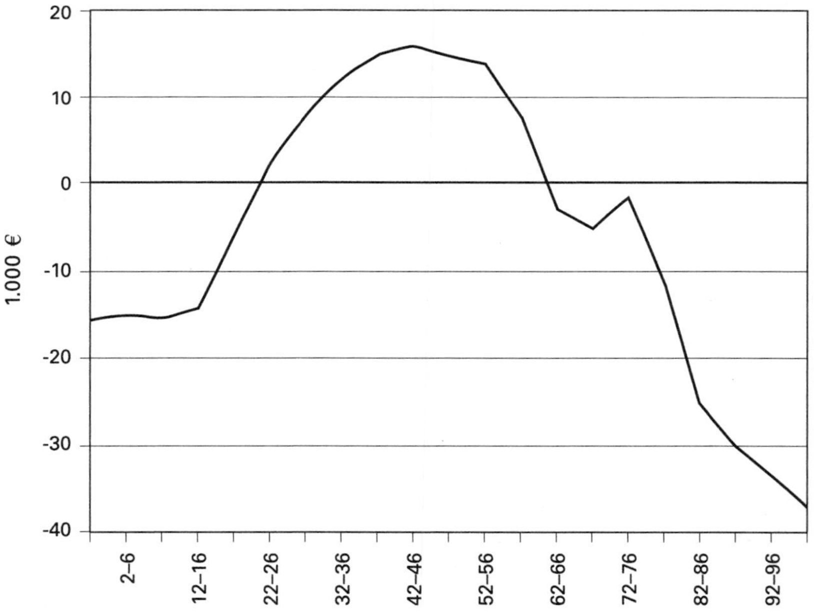

Figure 7.3
Net contributions to the public sector for different age groups, 2001
Source: Our own calculations on DREAM.
Note: The average net contributions by persons aged 67–76 are larger than the surrounding age groups due to technical assumptions in DREAM regarding tax on funded capital pensions and tax on bequests.

ceivers of public expenditures, whereas working-age people are net contributors to the public sector.[8]

Population aging implies that the density of the age distribution of the population moves from the net contributors of working age to the elderly net recipients. This creates an upward pressure on public expenditures relative to public revenues and therefore a potential problem of fiscal sustainability.

Using the CGE-OLG model DREAM, the macroeconomic consequences of "an unreformed welfare system" have been analyzed; see table 7.2. The development in GDP is driven by exogenous technological progress and developments in the labor force.[9] Technological progress is assumed to be 2 percent per year, which corresponds to historical experience. The labor force is reduced by 12 percent from 2002 to 2041 and by 19 percent from 2002 to 2081. This reduction is, by assumption, only due to the change in the demographic composition of the population. As a benchmark it is assumed that labor market participation rates and average annual working hours for a given age, gender, and origin group remain constant at the current level. Therefore, the three major determinants of the reduction in the labor force are the reduction in the number of working-age individuals, a relative increase in the number of immigrants (with a lower labor market

Table 7.2
Unreformed welfare state: Macroeconomic projection, 2001–2061

	2001	2006	2011	2021	2041	2061
	Index in constant prices, 2001 = 100					
Private consumption	100.0	116.3	126.5	150.8	206.4	287.8
Real GDP	100.0	109.8	119.3	138.4	183.2	254.6
Unemployment rate	5.2	5.1	4.7	4.8	4.9	5.1
Employment	100.0	100.2	98.6	95.6	86.9	82.5
Private sector	100.0	97.1	95.6	91.2	79.1	74.2
Construction sector	100.0	115.2	106.2	99.6	90.7	87.0
Public sector	100.0	102.5	102.8	103.6	102.4	98.8
Capital stock						
Private sector	100.0	111.2	121.4	141.3	182.7	251.7
Construction sector	100.0	131.2	140.1	160.1	217.3	307.0
Public sector	100.0	99.1	98.4	97.9	140.5	198.7
Foreign assets**	−17.7	−13.8	−5.6	6.6	−12.9	−54.8

Source: Our own calculations on DREAM.
*Levels are in percentages; **index is foreign assets as a percentage of nominal GDP at factor prices.

participation rate), and a tendency toward a higher average age in the labor force.

The GDP effect of a falling labor force is more than offset by the increase in productivity, implying that real GDP (at factor prices) grows by 83 percent from 2001 to 2041. Similarly, real private consumption is more than doubled over that period, so private consumption per capita is increased even more because of the reduction in the total population. So if the effects of population aging are assessed in terms of (changes in) the absolute level of wealth available to the entire economy, the phenomenon cannot be said to pose a problem, at least not if the historical record of technological progress continues. Rather, the problem is about the intergenerational distribution of wealth.

Most important, we find that population aging implies that current fiscal policy is unsustainable. Formally, this means that the government does not run primary surpluses that are large enough (in present value terms) to offset its initial debt; that is, the government's intertemporal budget constraint is not fulfilled. As table 7.3 shows, total primary public expenditures increase gradually from the current level of around 50 percent of GDP to around 60 percent of GDP in 2061. Until around 2041, the increase in expenditures is distributed equally between public transfers and public services. After 2040, the additional increase is mainly a result of increases in expenditures on public services. This reflects the fact that not only does the share of retirees increase, but so does the share of the very old within the group of retirees. This "double aging" phenomenon is intensified after 2040

Table 7.3
Unreformed welfare state: Public finances, 2001–2061

	2001	2006	2011	2021	2041	2061
	Percentage of GDP					
Total expenditures	50.2	49.9	51.3	53.8	58.7	59.4
Transfer payments	17.3	17.1	17.9	19.6	21.4	21.5
Individual public consumption	18.3	18.3	19.0	20.0	22.8	23.4
Collective public consumption	7.6	7.7	7.7	7.7	7.7	7.7
Other expenditures	7.0	6.8	6.7	6.5	6.8	6.8
Total revenues	54.5	53.1	52.6	53.1	55.2	55.5
Surplus	4.3	3.2	1.3	−0.7	−3.5	−3.8
Net interest payments	1.4	0.3	−0.6	−1.2	0.1	2.7
Net debt	6.5	−9.4	−17.4	−19.6	30.0	97.1

Source: Our own calculations on DREAM.

owing to the assumed growth in life expectancy. The higher proportion of the very old within the group of retirees means an increase in average expenditures on health care per retiree.[10]

One would expect that the assumption of constant tax rates would imply that the public revenue-to-GDP ratio is fairly constant. However, we find that there is a gradual reduction until 2011 which is mainly due to the current tax cut and the assumed duration of the current "tax freeze." The latter reduces the revenue from property taxes and some specific indirect taxes. The gradual increase in the following years is due to the (taxable) pension payments from the funded pension schemes. The development in the expenditures and revenues implies that the current fairly large primary surplus is gradually eroded and turned into a deficit in around 2020. After that, the aging of the population is intensified, which tends to boost the primary deficit. From around 2030, the total deficit exceeds the 3 percent SGP limit.

The fact that the primary deficit is increasing despite the temporary peak in the dependency ratio in 2040 (cf. figure 7.1) reflects that the demographic aging problem is not a temporary phenomenon. The current public surplus obviously reduces public debt and, interestingly, the public sector in Denmark is currently being turned into the position of net creditor.[11] However, the large public deficits after 2025 rapidly change this picture, and around 2060 the net public debt will have accumulated to the same level as the annual GDP.

In sum, a fiscal policy that promises the same supply of welfare arrangements across generations regardless of what generation the individual belongs to is found to suffer from a serious problem of fiscal sustainability. This clearly raises the question of how to change economic policy to ensure the long run solvency of the public sector.

From here the chapter focuses on a policy analysis of achieving fiscal sustainability. As a starting point, it is useful to consider the benchmark case where the budget is balanced in each period. This case with PAYG financing of welfare arrangements clearly captures the so-called intergenerational (or social) contract, whereby young and middle-aged persons finance expenditures allocated to older members in society, expecting that future generations will do the same for them. Focusing on the generational aspect, one can in very broad terms say that the benefits accruing from this include income transfers, health care, and so forth, and the contributions are made in the form of tax payments when young or middle-aged.[12] This is reflected in the age distribution of the net contribution profile shown in figure 7.3.

Under a balanced budget any change in, for example, age distribution would have to be absorbed by either current young or old generations, and it is well known from the literature that defined-benefit and defined-contribution schemes imply different distribution and risk profiles (see, e.g., Bohn 2001). Under a defined-benefit scheme, variations in the age distribution will be borne by young and middle-aged generations, while with defined-contribution schemes the old generations will face the consequences.[13]

An implication of a PAYG system is thus that various generations may end up being treated differently. From an efficiency point of view, it is also a question as to whether all possibilities for risk diversification across generations have been fully exploited. The implied intergenerational distribution profile may also be politically unacceptable. This can be circumvented by using the public budget as a buffer, since accumulation (or decumulation) of public debt can be used to change both the intergenerational distribution and risk-sharing profile (Gordon and Varian 1988). Obviously, the intertemporal budget constraint for the public sector is still a constraint on these possibilities.

Against that, we next study the requirements to realize a combined defined-benefit and defined-contribution scheme by using the public budget as a shock absorber. We also look at the efficiency and distributional consequences of such a policy.

7.4 Achieving Fiscal Sustainability through Prefunding

The strategy considered in this section is also one of front-loading the fiscal adjustment. In the extreme case, one may consider an initial once-and-for-all change in benefits or contribution rules to ensure fiscal sustainability. Such permanent adjustments guarantee that benefit and contribution rules can be maintained for all future generations. The adjustment may run via tax increases, cuts in public consumption or a smaller share of the population receiving income transfers (either fewer recipients or lower transfers). Here we consider an adjustment involving a permanent increase in the base income tax rate that is gradually phased in during the decade from 2011 to 2021.

7.4.1 Budgetary Effects

To obtain fiscal sustainability it is necessary to increase the base income tax rate by no less than 8.7 percentage points.[14] This large adjustment implies that the tax revenue-to-GDP ratio increases by 5.6 percentage points from 2011 to 2021. This should be compared to the 0.5 percentage point increase in the previous case of constant tax rates. Expenditures also rise relative to GDP owing to a contractionary effect on GDP from reduced labor supply as a consequence of the increase in the marginal tax rate. However, the resulting positive effect on the primary budget is significant as shown in figure 7.4. In 2021 the primary budget increases from a deficit of 0.7 percent of GDP in the absence of a tax increase to a surplus of 3.3 percent of GDP in the presence of a tax increase. Even in 2040, when the dependency ratio has a local maximum, a primary surplus of 0.3 percent of GDP prevails. After 2040, expenditures grow relative to GDP owing to the mentioned effect of double aging, whereas the growth rate of revenues relative to GDP is gradually reduced. This turns the primary public budget into a deficit, which is maintained throughout the time horizon of the analysis.

The long period of primary surpluses that lasts until around 2060 generates an accumulation of public wealth. By 2061, the net public wealth amounts to 115 percent of GDP, and it is almost stabilized at that level.

The demographic change implies an increasing expenditure profile relative to GDP, whereas revenues as a share of GDP are relatively

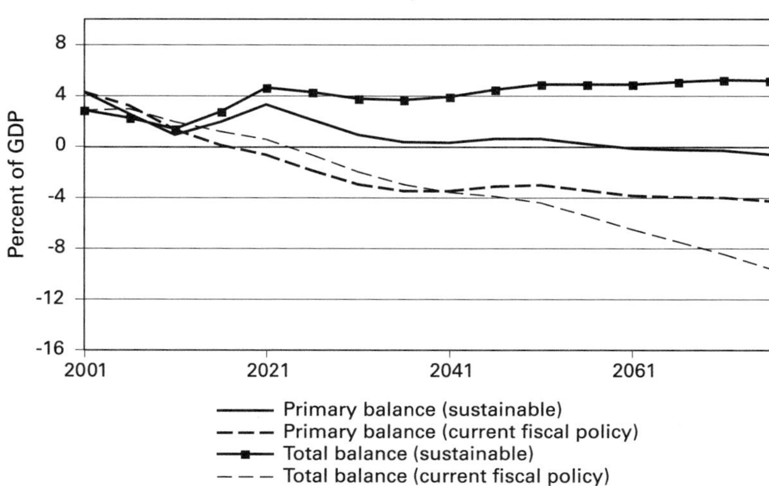

Figure 7.4
Public-sector balances: 2001–2081
Source: Our own calculations on DREAM.

constant. Hence, since the change is permanent it follows that the wealth accumulation during the initial period has to be significant to generate sufficient interest income to permanently finance the gap between revenue and expenditures. The extent to which such prefunding makes sense depends on both the demographic changes and their cause. If the demographic change is "temporary," the funding creates a buffer fund by ensuring some consolidation prior to the demographic change, and allowing for some debt accumulation afterward. Thereby the burden of the demographic changes is shared between current and future generations.

However, if—as in the present case—the change is of a more permanent kind, the needed consolidation is not only larger, but it also implies that current generations to a large extent contribute to the financing of future welfare arrangements. The latter raises important equity issues. Since the major reason for a change in the demographic composition of the Danish population and hence the fiscal sustainability problem is an increase in life expectancy, it is not clear from an equity point of view whether the pursuit of a savings strategy is particularly wise. This is so since it essentially implies that current generations are going to contribute to the financing of the longer lives of future generations. In any case, it is worth stressing that a permanent tax increase of 8.7 percentage points should *not* be interpreted as a policy suggestion but only as a way of illustrating the magnitude of the current fiscal imbalance under baseline assumptions.

7.4.2 *Robustness*

A prefunding strategy is based on forecasts of future expenditures and revenues that, by nature, are highly uncertain. This section discusses the robustness of the strategy with respect to variation in some essential demographic and economic variables; see table 7.4.

7.4.2.1 Demographic Variables

We have seen that changes in life expectancy tend to generate significant effects on the dependency ratio, whereas changes in fertility and migration have less significant effects. This is also expected to be the case with respect to the necessary adjustment in the base tax rate to ensure fiscal sustainability. The results in table 7.4 are consistent with these findings.

Table 7.4
Robustness of the necessary fiscal adjustment

	Tax increase in percentage points
Baseline scenario	8.7
Problem reduced	
Life expectancy as in DK 2010	1.6
Increase in real interest rate (+1)	5.0
Problem unchanged	
Increase in fertility rate (+0.1)	8.9
Increase in net immigration from more developed countries (+5,000 persons)	8.6
Problem worse	
UN life expectancy	16.0
Higher productivity growth rate (+0.5)	12.8
Fall in labor supply, reduction in working time (0.15 percent per year)	15.1

Source: Our own calculations on DREAM.

The needed increase in the base tax rate becomes 16.0 percentage points if the annual increase in life expectancy is doubled from 0.1 years annually to 0.2 years, that is, if it is assumed that the future growth rate in life expectancy in Denmark corresponds to the average growth rate for western Europe (as projected by the United Nations 2004).

The large effect of an increase in life expectancy on fiscal sustainability appears because the dependency ratio increases by 10 percent in the long run compared to the baseline (cf. figure 7.2). This implies that the expenditure-to-GDP ratio also gradually grows to a higher level. The necessary prefunding therefore increases significantly. Compared to the baseline, the stock of public wealth needs to be increased by 100 percent of GDP in 2060. This implies that public wealth is twice as large as GDP in this scenario.

If, on the other hand, no increases in life expectancy are assumed, then Danish fiscal policy is almost sustainable. In this case, the necessary increase in the base tax rate is as low as 1.6 percentage points. Similarly, prefunding becomes very low and almost no increase in the stock of public wealth is required. Thus, a policy based on prefunding is highly sensitive to the growth in life expectancy.

Increases in the total fertility and immigration rate, respectively, were found to have only marginal effects on the dependency ratio. This is reflected in the economic results where fiscal sustainability is found to be rather insensitive to these changes. Increasing total fertility by 0.1 implies that the increase in the base tax rate necessary to ensure fiscal sustainability is 8.9 percentage points, which is only 0.2 percentage points higher than in the baseline. Thus, an increase in the birth rate does not appear attractive from the perspective of fiscal sustainability.

Increased immigration from more developed countries is often seen as a possible solution to the fiscal sustainability problem. However, an increase in this type of immigration by 33 percent is almost neutral to the Danish sustainability problem. The necessary increase in the base tax rate to ensure fiscal sustainability is 8.6 percent in this case, which is 0.1 percentage points less than in the baseline case. The improvement is less than one would expect from the impact on the dependency ratio. This is mainly due to the fact that the labor market participation rate for female immigrants from more developed countries is significantly lower than for females of Danish origin. Therefore the net contribution from an average immigrant from a more developed country is lower than for an individual of Danish origin.[15]

7.4.2.2 Economic Variables

The prefunding strategy combined with the permanent nature of the aging problem implies, as shown earlier, that a public stock of wealth is accumulated such that the interest payments partly finance future expenses. Therefore, fiscal sustainability becomes highly sensitive to changes in the interest rate.[16] A permanently higher interest rate implies that interest payments on the public stock of wealth increase, and, furthermore, the same is true for the interest payments on the accumulated stock of pension savings in private pension funds. Since pension payments from the funds are taxable, approximately half of the accumulated wealth in the funds is deferred taxes. So both future public revenues and future public interest income are increased in case of a higher rate of interest. In addition to these direct effects, the traditional indirect effects of an increased rate of interest on economic activity appear. It reduces the capital-labor ratio and also the wage rate in the economy. This reduces both public revenue and public expenditures (through indexation to the wage rate). These parallel changes in revenues and expenditures imply that the indirect effects on the public budget are minor compared to the direct effects of the higher interest rate. If the interest rate is increased by 1.0 percentage points, the necessary increase in the base tax rate to ensure fiscal sustainability is reduced to 5.0 percentage points, which is a reduction of 3.7 percentage points compared to the baseline. Thus, sustainability is highly sensitive to the rate of interest. This is, however, only partly due to the prefunding. Another, and more important, reason is that a significant part of the accumulated assets in private pension funds is deferred taxes.

Similarly, fiscal sustainability is highly sensitive to changes in the growth rate of productivity. At the outset, this sensitivity is reduced by the fact that public expenditures are indexed to the wage rate.[17] Therefore, an increase in productivity tends to increase both expenditures and revenues. Two effects of the change in productivity growth remain. First, a higher productivity growth rate reduces the growth-adjusted real rate of interest, and, other things being equal, the sustainability problem thus increases in present-value terms when the productivity growth rate increases. Second, since aging implies a future reduction in the labor force (and therefore a fall in future tax revenues) and an increase in the number of pensioners (and therefore a rise in expenditures), there is a "double loss" for the public sector when the population is aging and there is an increase in productivity growth. Both the "discounting effect" and the "aging effect" associated with productivity shocks work in the same direction. Indeed, the sensitivity of fiscal sustainability with respect to growth is considerable—and even higher than with respect to the interest rate. An increase in productivity growth of 0.5 percent implies that the necessary increase in the base tax rate to obtain fiscal sustainability becomes 12.8 percentage points. This is 4.1 percentage points higher than in the baseline.

Fiscal sustainability is also highly sensitive to the assumption concerning the future annual number of working hours. The baseline of this analysis is based on the combined assumption of constant age, gender, and origin distributed labor market participation rates and of constant annual working time per average employed individual distributed across the same groups. Contrary to this assumption, average annual working time has been reduced by 0.3 percent annually over the last twenty-five years. Assuming that annual working hours are reduced by 0.15 percent each year for the next hundred years implies that the necessary increase in the base tax rate to ensure fiscal sustainability becomes 15.1 percentage points, compared to the 8.7 percentage points in the baseline case. This significant increase in the necessary adjustment is because the growth in the public provision of services is not reduced when the number of working hours, and therefore the tax base, is reduced. Public benefits, on the other hand, are indexed to annual salary, and the growth rate in these expenditures is therefore reduced along with the number of working hours.

In sum, no substantial fiscal sustainability problem exists if life expectancy remains constant. Pursuing a prefunding strategy becomes increasingly difficult with increasing growth in life expectancy, since the aging problem has not only a temporary component but also a permanent effect on the dependency ratio. This implies that the accumulated fund has to finance expenditures in excess of revenue throughout the time horizon. Fiscal sustainability is also highly sensitive to the interest rate and to productivity growth. In both cases, pursuing a prefunding strategy increases the sensitivity of fiscal sustainability. Finally, if productivity growth and the associated increase in wealth lead to a reduction in the labor supply, this increases the sensitivity of fiscal sustainability with respect to productivity growth. This additional sensitivity is not affected by a prefunding strategy.

7.4.3 Risk Sharing

The preceding sensitivity analysis shows that uncertainty about some key variables has fundamental implications for fiscal sustainability. This risk has to be taken seriously since any strategy would have implications for diversification of risk across generations. It is therefore necessary to evaluate how different possible developments would affect different generations as well as the scope for risk diversification across generations. Since we have identified longevity as one of the most crucial variables for the sustainability issue, and since there is an inherent uncertainty about life expectancy for future generations, we consider the risk associated with longevity in some detail in this section.

To discuss this issue, we must distinguish between the trend and the risk in, for example, demographic projections. How to cope with the trend change in, say, lifetime is basically a question of intergenerational distribution. As for risk, the question is how to exploit the scope via the public budget of diversifying risk across various generations.

A key problem for the savings strategy is assessing the needed consolidation, since the strategy aims to make it possible for future generations to have the same benefit and contribution rules.[18] It is obvious from the previous subsection that both demographic projections and calculations of fiscal sustainability are highly uncertain. To determine the needed consolidation it is necessary to base policy on a particular projection. This raises various problems.

First, if, for example, demographic projections changed frequently, there would be frequent changes in benefits and/or contribution rules, but this runs counter to the main objective of this strategy, namely, to keep these rules stable across different generations. The importance of this point is substantial, as seen by the large change in the demographic projections from the beginning of the century compared to the latest population forecast, namely, since the formulation of DK 2010. The need for prefunding is thus much larger today than was perceived just a few years ago.

Second, it is necessary to determine the needed consolidation or prefunding. If the needed consolidation is calculated on a certainty equivalence basis, it means that all risk is transferred to future generations. The only way current generations can participate in risk sharing with future generations is through precautionary savings—that is, by creating a buffer fund. Auerbach and Hassett (2001) show that the sharing of productivity risks calls for precautionary savings when utility displays constant relative risk aversion. However, for the various types of risks involved, it is not clear whether an argument for precautionary savings is, in general, supported. The literature on precautionary savings leaves few unambiguous results (Lippman and McCall 1981).[19]

Finally, policy changes are irreversible in the sense that the effects on past generations cannot be undone. With an analogy to the investments literature, it is thus possible to argue that there is a value in waiting to accumulate further information before policy changes are undertaken. Auerbach and Hassett (2002a, b) consider a situation where there are political impediments to frequent policy change. They show that this leads to inertia in policy and may imply that policy changes are "delayed."

7.4.4 *Credibility*

The savings strategy implies that public finances have to be tightly controlled; that is, public consumption growth should be kept low (to avoid increases in welfare levels, and thus even larger future burdens) and the budget should be kept in surplus for decades. Accordingly, the public accumulates wealth at the same time that politicians work to convince the electorate that there is no financial room for welfare improvements. This is not an easy task and there is thus a fundamental credibility problem: will sufficient savings be accumulated, or will it induce expenditure increases? This problem can partly be solved if the savings take place in a special fund with clearly defined rules for how the funds can be used.

7.5 Directions for an Alternative Strategy

The Danish medium- to long-term fiscal strategy DK 2010 has been very important and successful in obtaining fiscal discipline by formulating medium-term goals for fiscal and structural adjustment. On the other hand, the formulation of the plan implies a front-loading of fiscal adjustment that may not be optimal for several reasons. First, even if current fiscal policy is not far from the medium-term goals, we have found that a significant fiscal adjustment is necessary to obtain fiscal sustainability by a front-loading strategy. In fact, under baseline assumptions a permanent increase in the base tax rate of 8.7 percentage points is required. Second, this result is sensitive to changes in key demographic and economic variables, especially with respect to changes in life expectancy, the interest rate, and the rate of productivity growth. This lack of robustness implies that there may be frequent changes in benefits and/or contribution rules. However, this runs counter to the main objective of this strategy, namely, to keep these rules stable across different generations. Third, intergenerational distribution is affected by the prefunding strategy, since current generations produce very large public surpluses that are accumulated to build up a stock of public wealth that generates interest income that is distributed to all future generations. And is it credible to accumulate a large stock of public wealth while maintaining a tight fiscal policy in order to reduce future welfare increases?

A premise for the front-loading or savings strategy is that the same benefit and contribution rules should be maintained across generations. However, it is not obvious that this leads to an acceptable distributional profile, and it may not ensure an efficient diversification of risk.

An important question is thus which contingencies should be built into the benefit and contribution rule. Present rules include contingencies via income dependence (for the contribution side via tax payments and the benefit side via means testing of various pension supplements), which play a role in insuring against both idiosyncratic and aggregate risks (Andersen and Dogonowski 2002). More generally there are contingencies in the sense that the benefit side also includes needs testing that is related to basic social insurance functions provided by the welfare arrangements.

One potential contingency would be to let benefits and contributions depend on changes in life expectancy. This is motivated by the issue that has already been raised—namely, that the major problem is the increased life expectancy of future generations and that it is questionable to what extent current generations should contribute to the financing thereof. Under the reasonable assumption that a longer life is considered welfare enhancing, the argument may go the other way. One way to separate distributional issues from risk diversification would be to let the pension entitlement be a fixed sum, for example, which is converted to an annual benefit depending on lifetime (possibly merged with an insurance arrangement); namely, in present-value terms everybody gets the same pension regardless of life length. This type of adjustment is found in private pension contracts. However, this implies that all risk associated with the lifetime of the generation is carried by the generation itself, and this scheme therefore has unfortunate implications for risk sharing.

Moreover, if one takes the broader perspective of an extended welfare state like the Danish one, it is important that the problem be confined not only to the benefit side but also to the contributions made over lifetime via tax payments. With existing rules, longer lifetime will imply an increase in the proportion of life for which the individual is a net recipient of welfare arrangements, primarily because there are fixed age limits for eligibility to early retirement and pensions. It is possible to make both benefits and contributions contingent on expected life length by letting the age limits for retirement and pension (the early retirement scheme has an age limit of 60 years, and the public pension scheme of 65) follow expected lifetime. Since current demographic projections imply that future generations can expect longer lifetimes, it follows that such a scheme effectively means that age limits become systematically linked to the generation to which an individual belongs (higher for younger generations). If so, generations expecting to live longer would be net contributors for a larger share of their life, since they will be active in the labor market longer, postponing the time when they are entitled to pension benefits. Thereby, a better balance is ensured between the number of years the person contributes to the system and the number of years the person benefits from the system. Without such a regulation, the share of life for which one is a net contributor will fall as life expectancy increases.

Such a scheme still leaves risk diversification of unanticipated changes in lifetime, since the age limits are made dependent on expected lifetime and therefore unanticipated changes will be absorbed by the public budget. Part of the risk will also be resolved over time, and it is therefore possible to consider appropriate adjustments at intervals—say, every ten years. When adjustments to changes in projections of expected lifetime are made well in advance of the pension age, it follows that the risk arising from unanticipated changes is smoothed over current and future generations.

Such an indexation scheme will reduce but not eliminate the fiscal sustainability problem arising on account of increasing longevity. A simple scheme making eligibility ages for early retirement and the public pension dependent on expected lifetime (essentially meaning that the age limits are increased by one month per year) reduces the sustainability problem by about one-third, implying a needed permanent tax increase of 5.9 rather than 8.7 percentage points. Figure 7.5

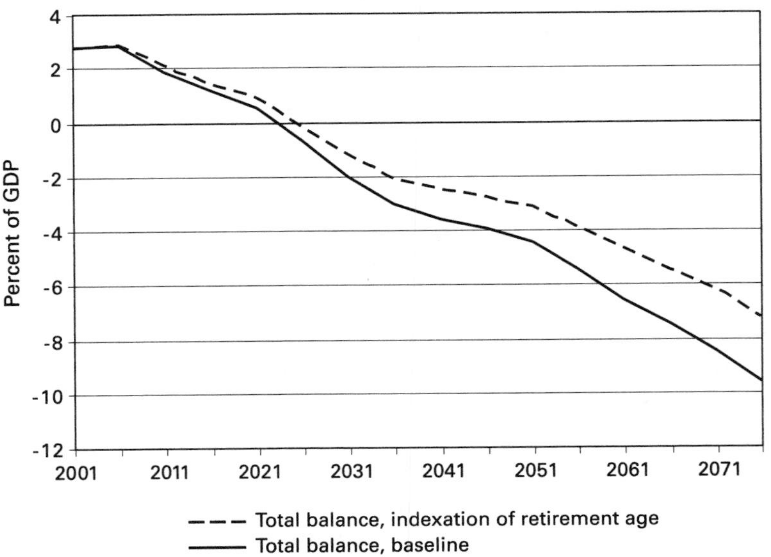

Figure 7.5
Fiscal effects of introducing retirement age indexation
Source: Our own calculations on DREAM.

illustrates the magnitude of the improvement in the total budget balance that would result from introducing such an indexation scheme.

There are some basic reasons this simple indexation scheme does not ensure fiscal neutrality of changes in longevity. Inducing later retirement from the labor market would, of course, increase the tax contribution from a given cohort. However, not everybody in the cohort is active in the labor market, and one must expect that more would qualify for a disability pension if formal retirement ages were increased. In addition, the cohort would benefit from various public-sector activities for a longer period, and this effect is more than proportional to longevity. This is due to the double aging effect arising from an increasing proportion of "very old" people in the population, and this group draws more extensively on publicly provided services like health care.

Despite the fact that such an indexation scheme does not fully solve the sustainability problem, it has some nice properties and it should therefore be part of a reform package. Indexing benefits and contributions to expected lifetime is an example of a gradual adjustment strategy in the sense that it does not require substantial prefunding, but rather aims at adjustment over time of net expenditures of the welfare state so as not to produce a tendency toward systematic budget deficits in line with aging and longer lifetime. As such, this strategy does not raise the same problems as the savings strategy. However, it is essential that the adjustment mechanisms like the indexation scheme be introduced immediately to avoid sudden changes in welfare arrangements and to make clear how sustainable finances are ensured.

Finally, it should be pointed out that a policy announcement on subjecting the age limits for retirement and pension benefits to changes in longevity may also suffer from a credibility problem. In fact, this political economy aspect is bound to play a significant role in any discussion of welfare reform.

Notes

We appreciate helpful comments from three anonymous referees, Fabio Padovano, Nick Draper, Peter Lindert, and participants at the CESifo-LBI conference on Sustainability of Public Debt in Munich, October 2004.

1. See Esping-Andersen 1990. Note that although there are strong elements of universality in the Danish welfare model, there are also substantial deviations from this principle: e.g., entitlement to unemployment benefits and early retirement benefits requires that contributions have been paid in advance, though not fully financing these schemes.

2. Debt figures are defined according to the Stability and Growth Pact (SGP). The definition has been changed recently, implying that the new figures are approximately 3 percentage points higher than those based on the previous definition. The debt target is set according to the previous definition.

3. See, e.g., Alho and Spencer 1985 and Lee and Tuljapurkar 2001.

4. The Danish government has recently estimated that the remaining necessary increase in employment corresponds to approximately 1.9 percent of the labor force, meaning that more than half of the original target remains to be achieved (Ministry of Finance 2004).

5. The real growth in public services in 2004 is reduced to 0.7 percent, while the average annual growth rate in the remaining period until 2010 is targeted at 0.5 percent.

6. The Danish Welfare Commission is an independent advisory body to the Danish government. The task of the commission is to consider reforms to the Danish welfare state that ensure fiscal sustainability and fair inter- and intragenerational distribution.

7. DREAM is an acronym for Danish Rational Economic Agents Model. Details of the model are available in Knudsen et al. 1998, 1999, and in Pedersen, Stephensen, and Trier 1999. General information on DREAM can be found at http://www.dreammodel.dk.

8. It is worth pointing out that while the public PAYG pension benefit is in principle offered on a flat-rate basis, an element of means testing is built into the system in the sense that supplementary benefits to some extent depend on the pensioner's annual income and personal wealth.

9. A fixed exchange rate, perfect capital markets, and a constant international rate of interest tend to generate a fixed ratio between capital and labor measured in productivity units. The relationship is modified by sluggish capital adjustment and changes in the real exchange rate, for example.

10. The assumption that health care expenditures increase with age is not uncontroversial. If increased life expectancy is mainly associated with increased health, then health care expenditures may be related to expected-time-to-death instead of age. On the other hand, if increased life expectancy mainly reflects technological progress in medical treatment, then age dependency of health care expenditures may underestimate the growth in these expenditures.

11. The net public debt in table 7.2 follows current definitions of Danish National Accounts and is therefore not comparable to the SGP debt measure. This figure includes the ATP pension fund, which is a compulsory fully financed labor market pension fund. Due to a change in legislation regulating the ATP fund, the accumulated wealth in the fund will be registered as private wealth from 2005. This also affects the primary surplus since net contributions to the ATP fund are currently included in the surplus.

12. The Danish welfare state also involves the "reverse" generational contract with respect to the financing of child care and education.

13. Alho et al. (2005) propose an indexation scheme where benefits are indexed to the wage bill rather than the wage rate to ensure that risks associated with population changes are shared between young and old generations.

14. If fiscal sustainability is to be achieved by a reduction in public spending that is phased in during the same ten-year period, the necessary permanent reduction amounts to 3.7 percent of GDP.

15. A similar, but less pronounced, reduction in the labor market participation rate is found for female descendants of immigrants from more developed countries.

16. The relevant measure here is the growth-adjusted real rate of interest. This rate is 0.9 percent in the projection. This is based on an average over the period 1924–1999 (Nielsen and Risager 2001). In addition, a real risk premium of 3.0 percent on share is used. The growth-adjusted yield after tax of a pension fund with 40 percent of the wealth in shares is 1.2 percent.

17. More precisely, public transfer payments (pension benefits, unemployment benefits, cash benefits, etc.) are indexed to changes in real wages. This scheme is regulated by law (*satsreguleringsloven*). In addition, the salaries of public employees grow in line with the salaries of employees in the private sector.

18. Note that this would preserve the option for future generations' possibilities of making a choice. If they choose something different, it must be because they prefer that to maintaining the existing system.

19. Other literature focuses on precautionary saving arising in a situation with capital market perfections and risk (Aiyagari 1994). A buffer stock motive for saving can also arise from the risk of facing a very low (eventually zero) income (Carroll 2001). Consumers wanting to smooth consumption will in this case have an "aversion" to borrowing too much. In terms of fiscal policy, this provides an argument for debt or deficit limits.

References

Aiyagari, S. 1994. Uninsured idiosyncratic risk and aggregate saving. *Quarterly Journal of Economics* 109:659–684.

Alho, J., S. E. H. Jensen, J. Lassila, and T. Valkonen. 2005. Controlling the effects of demographic risks: The role of pension indexation schemes. *Journal of Pension Economics and Finance* 4:139–153.

Alho, J., and B. Spencer. 1985. Uncertain population forecasting. *Journal of the American Statistical Association* 80:306–314.

Andersen, T. M., and R. Dogonowski. 2002. Social insurance and the public budget. *Economica* 69:415–432.

Auerbach, A. J., and K. Hassett. 2001. Uncertainty and the design of long-run fiscal policy. In *Demographic Change and Fiscal Policy*, ed. A. J. Auerbach and R. D. Lee, 73–92. Cambridge, UK: Cambridge University Press.

Auerbach, A., and K. Hassett. 2002a. Fiscal policy and uncertainty. *International Finance* 5:229–242.

Auerbach, A., and K. Hassett. 2002b. Optimal long-run fiscal policy: Constraints, preferences and the resolution of uncertainty. NBER Working Paper no. 7036. National Bureau of Economic Research, Washington, DC.

Boeri, T., and H. Brücker. 2001. Eastern enlargement and the EU-labour markets: Perceptions, challenges and opportunities. *World Economics* 2 (1): 49–68.

Bohn, H. 2001. Social security and demographic uncertainty: The risk-sharing properties of alternative policies. In *Risk Aspects of Investment Based Social Security Reform*, ed. J. Campbell and M. Feldstein, 203–241. Chicago: University of Chicago Press.

Carroll, Christopher D. 2001. Precautionary saving and the marginal propensity to consume out of permanent income. NBER Working Paper no. 8233. National Bureau of Economic Research, Washington, DC.

Esping-Andersen, G. 1990. *The Three Worlds of Welfare Capitalism*. Cambridge, UK: Policy Press.

European Commission. 2000. The impact of ageing populations on public pension systems. Progress report to the ECOFIN Council. Brussels: EU Commission.

Gordon, R., and H. Varian. 1988. Intergenerational risk sharing. *Journal of Public Economics* 37:185–202.

Haldrup, N. 2004. Estimation af middellevetider for mnd og kvinder i Danmark, 2002–2010, baseret på Lee-Carter metoden. Arbejdsrapport 2004:3, Velfærdskommissionen.

Knudsen, M. B., L. H. Pedersen, T. W. Petersen, P. Stephensen, and P. Trier. 1998. Danish Rational Economic Agents Model—DREAM Ver. 1.2. Working paper. DREAM, Copenhagen. Available at www.dreammodel.dk.

Knudsen, M. B., L. H. Pedersen, T. W. Petersen, P. Stephensen, and P. Trier. 1999. Dynamic calibration of a CGE-model with a demographic application. Working paper. DREAM, Copenhagen. Available at www. dreammodel.dk.

Lee, R., and L. Carter. 1992. Modeling and forecasting the time series of U.S. mortality. *Journal of the American Statistical Association* 87:659–671.

Lee, R., and S. Tuljapurkar. 2001. Population forecasting for fiscal planning: issues and innovations. In *Demographic Change and Fiscal Policy*, ed. A. Auerbach and R. Lee, 7–57. Cambridge, UK: Cambridge University Press.

Lippman, S., and J. McCall. 1981. The economics of uncertainty: Selected topics and probabilistic methods. In *Handbook of Mathematical Economics*, ed. K. J. Arrow and M. D. Intriligator, 211–284. Amsterdam: North-Holland.

Masson, P., and M. Mussa. 1995. Long-term tendencies in budget deficits and debt. In *Budget Deficits and Debt: Issues and Options*, ed. T. Hoenig, 5–55. Kansas City, MO: Federal Reserve Bank of Kansas City.

Ministry of Finance. 2004. *Finansredegorelse* (Medium Term Survey). Copenhagen.

Nielsen, S., and O. Risager. 2001. Stock returns and bond yields in Denmark 1922–1999. *Scandinavian Economic History Review* 49 (1): 63–82.

Pedersen, L., P. Stephensen, and P. Trier. 1999. A CGE analysis of the Danish ageing problem. Working paper. DREAM, Copenhagen. Available at www.dreammodel.dk.

Tanzi, V., and L. Schuknecht. 2000. *Public Spending in the 20th Century—A Global Perspective*. Cambridge, UK: Cambridge University Press.

United Nations. 2004. *World Population in 2300*. New York: United Nations.

Welfare Commission. 2004. *Fremtidens velfærd kommer ikke af sig selv*. Copenhagen: Velfærdskommisionen.

8 Post-Thatcher Fiscal Strategies in the United Kingdom: An Interpretation

Andrew Hughes Hallett

8.1 Introduction: British Fiscal Policy to 2004

British fiscal policy has changed radically since the days when it tried to micromanage all of aggregate demand with an accommodating monetary policy in the 1960s and 1970s; and again from the 1980s when it was passive but set out to strengthen the economy's supply-side responses, while monetary policies actively pursued low inflation and stable growth.

The 1990s saw a return to more activist fiscal policies—but policies designed strictly in combination with an equally active monetary policy based on inflation targeting and an independent Bank of England. They are set, in the main, to gain a series of medium- to long-term objectives—low debt, the provision of public services and investment, social equality, and economic efficiency. The income stabilizing aspects of fiscal policy have therefore been left passive, to act through the automatic stabilizers that are part of any fiscal system, while the discretionary part (the bulk of the policy measures) is set to achieve those longer-term objectives—including balancing the budget, barring public investment projects, over the cycle. Monetary policy, meanwhile, is left to take care of any short-run stabilization around the cycle, that is, beyond what, predictably, would be done by the automatic stabilizers.[1]

To draw a sharp distinction between actively managed long-run policies, and short-run stabilization efforts restricted to the automatic stabilizers is of course the strategic policy prescription of Taylor (2000). Marrying that with an activist monetary policy directed at cyclical stabilization, but based on an independent Bank of England and a monetary policy committee with instrument (but not target) independence, appears to have been the distinctive U.K. feature. It implies a leadership role for fiscal policy that allows fiscal and monetary policies to be better coordinated—but without either losing their ability to act independently.[2]

In short, Britain appears to have adopted a Stackelberg solution that lies somewhere between the discretionary (but Pareto-superior) cooperative solution and the fully independent (but noncooperative) solution. Nonetheless, by forcing the focus onto long-run objectives, to the exclusion of the short term, this setup has imposed a degree of precommitment (and potential for electoral punishment) on fiscal policy because governments naturally wish to lead. But the regime remains noncooperative so that there is no incentive to renege on earlier plans in the absence of changes in information. Thus the policies and their intended outcomes will be sustained by the government of the day.[3]

In any event, British fiscal policy has been relatively successful under this regime. It has been more successful than that in the country's European partners, as table 8.1 shows, and arguably at least as successful as in the United States, Canadian, or Australian economies. So it is not that fiscal policy was not used. On the contrary, the evidence suggests

Table 8.1
The United Kingdom's fiscal performance relative to the EU-12

	HICP inflation (%)	Output growth (%)	Deficit ratio (%)	Debt ratio (%)	Unemployment (%)
1999					
UK	1.3	3.6	+1.1	45.1	5.9
EU-12	1.1	2.8	−1.3	72.5	9.4
2000					
UK	1.0	3.5	+2.7	42.1	5.3
EU-12	2.1	3.5	+0.2	70.1	8.5
2001					
UK	0.8	2.3	+0.9	38.9	5.2
EU-12	2.3	1.6	−1.7	69.5	8.0
2002					
UK	1.2	1.8	−1.6	38.5	5.1
EU-12	2.3	0.9	−2.4	69.4	8.4
2003					
UK	1.3	2.2	−3.2	39.8	5.0
EU-12	2.1	0.5	−2.7	70.7	8.9
2004					
UK	1.3	3.5	−2.9	39.8	4.7
EU-12	2.3	2.0	−2.8	70.6	9.0

that it has been used more effectively to produce lower debt, more stable incomes, and employment, but without any additional inflation.

8.2 The Hypothesis in This Chapter

The hypothesis in this chapter is that the United Kingdom's improved performance is due to the fact that fiscal policy leads an independent monetary policy. This leadership derives from the fact that fiscal policies typically have long-run targets (sustainability, low debt), are not easily reversible (public services, social equality), and do not stabilize well if efficiency is to be maintained. Nevertheless, there are also automatic stabilizers in any fiscal policy framework, implying that monetary policy must condition itself on the fiscal stance at each point. That automatically puts the latter in a follower's role. This is all to the good, however, because it allows the economy to secure the benefits of an independent monetary policy *but also* to enjoy a certain measure of coordination between the two sets of policymakers—discretionary/automatic fiscal policies on one side, and active monetary policies on the other. The extra coordination arises in this case because the constraints on, and responses to, an agreed leadership role reduce the externalities of self-interested behavior that independent agents would otherwise impose on one another. That allows a Pareto improvement over the conventional noncooperative (full independence) solution, without reducing the central bank's ability to act independently.[4] It is important to realize that the coordination here is implicit (rule-based), not discretionary.

To show that U.K. fiscal policy does lead monetary policy in this sense, and that that is the reason for the Pareto-improved results in table 8.1, I produce evidence in three parts:

- *Institutional evidence*: taken from the U.K. Treasury's own account of how its decision making works, what goals it needs to achieve, and how the monetary stance may affect it or vice versa;
- *Empirical evidence*: the extent to which monetary policy is affected by fiscal policy, but fiscal with its longer objectives does not depend on monetary policies;
- *Theoretical evidence*: shows how, with different goals for governments and central banks, Pareto-improving results can be expected from fiscal leadership. The United Kingdom has therefore had the incentive, and capacity, to operate in this way.

8.3 Institutional Evidence: The Treasury's Mandate

8.3.1 History

British fiscal policy has changed a great deal over the past thirty years. It is no exaggeration to say that fiscal policy was the principle instrument of economic policy in the 1960s and 1970s and was focused almost exclusively on demand management. Monetary policy and the provision of public services (subject to a lower bound) were essentially accommodating factors since the main constraint was perceived to be the financing of persistent current account trade deficits. The result of this was a short-term view, in which the conflicts between the desire for growth (employment) and the recurring evidence of overheating (trade deficits) led to an unavoidable sequence of "stop-go" policies. There were many[5] who argued that the real problem was a lack of long-run goals for fiscal policy and that the lags inherent in recognizing the need for a policy change, and in implementing it through Parliament until it took hold in the markets, had produced a system that was actually destabilizing rather than stabilizing. But there would have been conflicts anyway because there were two or more competing goals, but effectively only one instrument to reach them.

Such a system could not provide the longer-run goal of public services, public investment, and social equity. It certainly proved too difficult to turn fiscal policy on and off as fast and frequently as required, and to precommit to certain expenditure and taxation plans at the same time. The point here is that if you cannot precommit fiscal policy to certain goals, you won't be able to precommit monetary policy either. That means the "stable growth with low inflation" objective will be lost. Attempts to avoid this problem by imposing longer-run goals and greater coherence on the Treasury's policymaking through the Department of Economic Affairs (1960s), and again with the Social Contract in the 1970s, or by introducing an additional instrument (prices and incomes policies) when the supply side began to slide into "stagflation," all failed because they did nothing to redress the balance between the short run (demand management) and the long run (services, social equity, competitiveness), or between the growth objective and the no-overheating objective. Indeed it would have been difficult to do so with the breakdown of the Phillips curve trade-off between those two objectives.

In the 1980s, the strategy changed when a new regime took office with the aim of reducing the size and role of the government in the economy. The demand management role of fiscal policy was phased out. That role passed over to inflation control and monetary management—with limited success in the earlier phases of monetary and exchange rate targeting, but with rather more success when it was formalized as an inflation targeting regime under an independent Bank of England and monetary policy committee. In this period, therefore, the role of fiscal policy was to provide the "conditioning information" within which monetary management had to work. It was split into two distinct parts. Short-term stabilization of output and employment was left to the automatic stabilizers inherent in the prevailing tax and expenditures rules. Discretionary adjustments would be used only in exceptional circumstances, if at all.[6] The rest of fiscal policy, being the larger part, could then be directed at longer-term objectives: in this instance, changes to free up the supply side (and enhance competitiveness) on the premise that greater microeconomic flexibility would both reduce the need for stabilizing interventions (relative wage and price adjustments would do the job better) and provide the conditions for stronger employment and growth (HM Treasury 2003). Given that, the longer-run goals of better public services, efficiency, and social equity could then be attained. In addition, as the market flexibility changes were made, this part of fiscal policy could be increasingly focused on providing the longer-run goals directly.[7]

8.3.2 *The Present Position*

According to the HM Treasury's own assessment (HM Treasury 2003), U.K. fiscal policy now leads monetary policy in two senses. First, fiscal policy is decided in advance of monetary or other policies (pp. 5, 63, 64, 74),[8] *and* with a longer time horizon (pp. 5, 42, 48, 61). Second, monetary policy is charged with controlling inflation and stabilizing output around the cycle—rather than steering the economy as such (pp. 61–63). Fiscal policy therefore sets the conditions within which monetary has to respond and achieve its own objectives (pp. 9, 15, 67–68). The short-term fiscal interventions, now less than half the total and declining (p. 48, box 5.3, section 6), are restricted to the automatic stabilizers—with effects that are known and predictable. The short-run discretionary components are negligible (p. 59, table 5.5), and the long-run objectives of policy will always take precedence in cases of conflict (pp. 61, 63–68). Fiscal policy would therefore not be used for fine-tuning (pp. 11, 63) or for stabilization (pp. 1, 14). That burden will be carried by interest rates, *given* the fiscal stance and its forward plans (pp. 1, 7, 11, 37).

Third, given the evidence that consumers and firms often do not look forward efficiently and may be credit-constrained, and also that the impacts of fiscal policy are uncertain and have variable lags (pp. 19, 26, 48; Taylor 2000), it makes sense for fiscal policy to be used consistently and sparingly and in a way that is clearly identified with the long term objectives. The United Kingdom has determined what those objectives are (pp. 11–13, 39–41, 61–63, 81–82):

- The achievement of sustainable public finances in the long term, low debt (40 percent of GDP), and symmetric stabilization over the cycle.
- A sustainable and improving delivery of public services (health and education), improving competitiveness/supply side efficiency in the long term, and the preservation of social (and intergenerational) equity and alleviation of poverty.
- Recognition that the achievement of these objectives is often contractual and cannot easily be reversed once committed. The long lead times needed to build up these programs mean that the necessary commitments must be made well in advance. Frequent changes would conflict with the government's medium-term sustainability objectives and cannot be made. Similarly, changes in direct taxes will affect equity and efficiency and should seldom be made.
- The formulation of clear numerical objectives consistent with these goals, a transparent set of institutional rules to achieve them, and a commitment to a clear separation of these goals from economic stabilization around the cycle.[9]
- To ensure fiscal policy can operate along these lines, public expenditures are planned with fixed three-year Departmental Expenditure Limits[10] that, when combined with decision and implementation lags of up to two years, means that the bulk of fiscal policy has to be planned with a horizon of up to five years—versus a maximum of two years in the inflation targeting rules operated by the Bank of England. Moreover, these spending limits are constraints defined in nominal terms, so they will be met. In addition the Treasury operates a tax smoothing approach—having rejected "formulaic rules" that might

have adjusted taxes or expenditures, or the various tax regulators or credit taxes that could have stabilized the economy in the short term. The bulk of fiscal policy will remain focused therefore on the medium to long term.

In summary, the institutional structure itself has introduced fiscal leadership. And, since the discretionary elements are smaller than elsewhere—and smaller than the automatic stabilizers (tables 5.1–5.3) and declining (box 5.3)—something else (monetary policy) must have taken up the burden of short-run stabilization. This arrangement is therefore best modeled as a Stackelberg game, with institutional parameters for goals, independence, priorities, and so forth. We will argue that this has had the very desirable result of increasing the degree of coordination between policymakers without compromising their formal or institutional independence—or indeed their credibility for delivering stability and low inflation, free of political pressures for short-term results; constrained independence, in other words, designed to reduce the externalities that each party might otherwise impose on the other.

8.4 Empirical Evidence

The next step is to establish whether the U.K. authorities have followed the leadership model described previously. The fact that they say that they follow such a strategy does not mean that they do so. The difficulty here is that, although the asymmetry in ex ante (anticipated) responses between follower and leader is clear enough in the theoretical model—the follower expects no further changes from the leader after the follower chooses his reaction function, whereas the leader takes that reaction function into account—such an asymmetry and zero restriction will not appear in the ex post (observed) responses that emerge in the final solution.[11] Since we have no data on anticipations, this makes it difficult to test for leadership directly. But we can use indirect tests based on the degree of competition, or complementarity, between instruments.

8.4.1 Monetary Responses

For monetary policy, it is widely argued that the authorities' decisions can best be modeled by a Taylor rule (1993b):[12]

$$r_t = \rho r_{t-1} + \alpha E_t \pi_{t+k} + \beta gap_{t+h} \quad \alpha, \beta, \rho \geq 0, \tag{8.1}$$

where k, h represent the authorities' forecast horizon[13] and may be positive or negative. Normally $\alpha > 1$ will be required to avoid indeterminacy: that is, arbitrary variations in output or inflation as a result of unanchored expectations in the private sector (Woodford 2003). The relative size of α and β then reveals the strength of the authorities' attempts to control inflation vs. income stabilization, and ρ their preference for gradualism. We set $h = 0$ in (8.1), since monetary policy appears not to depend on expected output gaps (Dieppe, Kuster, and McAdam 2004).

In order to obtain an idea of the influence of fiscal policies on monetary policy, I include some Taylor rule estimates—with and without fiscal variables—in table 8.2a. They show such rules for the United Kingdom and the Eurozone since 1997 and 1999 respectively, the dates

Table 8.2a
Generalized Taylor rules in the United Kingdom and EU-12 (dependent variable: central bank lending rate, r_t)

For the United Kingdom, monthly data from 1997.01–2004.01

	const	r_{t-1}	$\pi^e_{j,k}$	j, k	*gap*	*pd*	*debt*
1)	−1.72 (2.16)	0.711 (5.88)	1.394 (2.66)	+6, +18	0.540 (2.06)	—	—
$\bar{R}^2 = 0.91$		$F_{3,21} = 82.47$	$N = 29$				
2)	−2.57 (2.59)	0.598 (4.38)	1.289 (0.66)	+9, +21	1.10 (1.53)	−0.67 (0.83)	0.43 (0.50)
$\bar{R}^2 = 0.90$		$F_{5,19} = 44.1$	$N = 25$				

For the Eurozone (EU-12), monthly data from 1999.01–2004.01

	const	r_{t-1}	$\pi^e_{j,k}$	j, k	*gap*	*pd*	*debt*
1)	−0.996 (0.76)	0.274 (1.04)	1.714 (3.89)	+9, +21	0.610 (1.77)	—	—
$\bar{R}^2 = 0.82$		$F_{3,11} = 22.2$	$N = 15$				
2)	−13.67 (0.59)	0.274 (1.04)	1.110 (1.19)	−6, +6	0.341 (1.22)	0.463 (2.89)	0.191 (0.63)
$\bar{R}^2 = 0.87$		$F_{5,13} = 24.7$	$N = 19$				

Notes: j, k give the bank's inflation forecast interval; $\pi^e_{j,k}$ represents the average inflation rate expected over the interval $t + j$ to $t + k$: $E\pi_{t+j,t+k}$; gap = GDP − trend GDP; pd = primary deficit/surplus as a percentage of GDP (a surplus > 0); $debt$ = debt/GDP ratio.

Estimation: instrumented 2SLS; t-ratios in parentheses; j, k determined by search; and the output gap is obtained from a conventional HP filter to determine trend output.

when new policy regimes were introduced. The Eurozone has been included to emphasize the potential contrast between fiscal leadership in the United Kingdom, and the lack of it in Europe.

8.4.2 *Different Types of Leadership*

Conventional wisdom would suggest that Europe has either monetary leadership or independent policies, and hence policies that are either jointly dependent in the usual way, or complementary and mutually supporting. The latter implies that monetary policy tends to expand/contract whenever fiscal policy needs to expand or contract—but not necessarily vice versa when money is expanding or contracting and is sufficient to control inflation on its own. That is a weak form of monetary leadership in which fiscal policies are an additional instrument for use in cases of particular difficulty, rather than policies in a Nash game with conflicting aims that need to be reconciled.

More generally, leadership implies complementarity between policy instruments in the leader's reaction function but conflicts (competition) between them in the follower's responses. A weak form of leadership also allows for independence between instruments in the leader's policy rules. Thus monetary leadership would imply some complementarity (or independence) in the Taylor rule, but conflicts in the fiscal responses. And fiscal leadership would mean complementarity or independence in the fiscal rule, but conflicts in the monetary responses. Evidently, from section 8.3, we might expect Stackelberg leadership (with fiscal policy leading) in the United Kingdom but the opposite in the Eurozone.

8.4.3 *Observed Behavior*

The upper equations in each panel of table 8.2a yield the standard results for monetary behavior in both the United Kingdom and Eurozone. Both monetary authorities have targeted expected inflation more than the output gap since the late 1990s—and with horizons of eighteen to twenty-one months ahead. The ECB has been more aggressive in this respect. But, contrary to conventional wisdom, it was also more sensitive to the output gap and had a longer horizon and less policy inertia.

However, if we allow monetary policies to react to changes in fiscal stance, we get different results (the lower equations). Here we see that

U.K. monetary decisions may take fiscal policy into account, but the effect is *not* significant or well defined. However this model of monetary behavior does imply more activist policies, a longer forecast horizon (up to two years as the Bank of England claims), and greater attention to the output gap—the symmetry in the United Kingdom's policy rule. And to the extent that fiscal policy does have an influence, it would be as a substitute (or competitor) for monetary policy—fiscal deficits lead to higher interest rates. This is potentially consistent with fiscal leadership, since that form of leadership can allow independence or complementarity between instruments in the leader's rule. We need to check the fiscal reaction functions directly. The lack of significance for the debt ratio is easily understood, however. Since that is a declared long-run objective of fiscal policy, it would not be necessary for monetary policy to take it into account. So far the evidence could imply a Stackelberg follower role or independence for monetary policy, easing the competition (externalities) between policy instruments.

The ECB results look quite different. Once fiscal effects are included, the concentration on inflation control is much reduced (it comes close to indeterminacy and may not even be significant) and the forecast horizon shrinks to six months. Moreover, a feedback element, to correct past mistakes, comes in. At the same time, output stabilization becomes less important, which implies symmetric targeting goes out. Instead monetary policy now appears to react to fiscal policy, but with the "wrong" sign: the larger the primary deficit, the looser the monetary policy. In this case, therefore, the policies are acting as complements—circumstances that call for a primary deficit will also call for a relaxation of monetary policy. Thus we have evidence of monetary leadership, where fiscal policy is used as an additional policy instrument.

8.4.4 Fiscal Reaction Functions in the United Kingdom and Eurozone

Many analysts have hypothesized that fiscal policy responses can best be modeled by means of a "fiscal Taylor rule":

$$d_t = a_t + \gamma gap_t + sd, \quad \gamma > 0, \tag{8.2}$$

where sd = the structural deficit ratio, d_t is the actual deficit ratio ($d > 0$ denotes a surplus),[14] and a_t represents all the other factors such as the influence of monetary policy, existing or anticipated inflation, the debt burden, or discretionary fiscal interventions. The coefficient γ then gives a measure of an economy's automatic stabilizers. The European Commission (2002), for example, estimates $\gamma \approx \frac{1}{2}$ for Europe—a little more in countries with an extensive social security system, a little less elsewhere. And a similar relationship is thought to underlie U.K. fiscal policy (see HM Treasury 2003, boxes 5.2 and 6.2).

The expected signs of any remaining factors are not so clear. The debt burden should increase current deficits, unless there is a systematic debt reduction program underway. Inflation should have a positive impact on the deficit ratio if fiscal policy is used for stabilization purposes, but no effect otherwise. Finally, the output gap should also have a positive impact on the deficit ratio if the latter is being used for stabilization purposes—in which case interest rates should be negatively correlated with the size of the deficit because monetary policies focused on inflation and fiscal policies focused on short-run stabilization would conflict. Conversely, a negative association with the output gap, but a positive one with interest rates, would imply no automatic stabilizer effects but mutually supporting policies: namely, higher interest rates go with tighter fiscal policies. That implies complementary policies.

Table 8.2b contains our estimates of the fiscal policy reaction functions for the United Kingdom and the Eurozone. Higher debt increases the surplus ratio in the United Kingdom but has no effect in the Euro Area. So, while the United Kingdom evidently has had a systematic

Table 8.2b
Fiscal policy reaction functions

For the United Kingdom, sample period 1997q3–2004q2

$$\underset{}{d_t} = \underset{(0.37)}{-0.444} + \underset{(7.64)}{0.845 debt_t} + \underset{(0.30)}{0.0685 r_t} + \underset{(1.72)}{1.076 gap_t}$$

$\bar{R}^2 = 0.78,\ F_{3,24} = 33.23$

For the Eurozone, sample period 1999q1–2004q2

$$d_t = \underset{(2.96)}{3.36} + \underset{(9.66)}{1.477 d_{t-1}} - \underset{(2.21)}{0.740 \pi^e_{+9,21}} - \underset{(1.16)}{0.207 r_t} - \underset{(2.18)}{0.337 gap_t}$$

$\bar{R}^2 = 0.95,\ F_{4,11} = 54.55$

Notes: At current debt, interest rates, and inflation targets, these estimates imply a structural deficit of about 0.1 percent for the United Kingdom and 2.6 percent for the Eurozone. d_t = gross deficit/GDP (%), where $d < 0$ denotes a deficit; $debt_t$ = debt/GDP (%); r_t is the central bank lending rate; $\pi^e_{j,k}$ and gap_t as in table 2a.

Estimation method, instrumented 2SLS; linear interpolation for quarterly deficit figures; and t-ratios in parentheses.

debt reduction program, no such efforts have been made in Europe. Inflation, on the other hand, has had no effect on the U.K. deficit, but a negative one in Europe. Similarly the output gap produces a negative reaction in Europe, but a positive one in the United Kingdom. These two variables therefore indicate that fiscal policy has been used for output stabilization in the United Kingdom—consistent with allowing automatic stabilizers to do the job—but for purposes other than that in the Eurozone. This result fits in neatly with Europe's evident inability to save for a rainy day in the upturn *and* inability to stabilize in the downturn because of the Stability Pact.[15]

Consequently, the United Kingdom appears to use fiscal policy for stabilization in a minor way as claimed, while the Euro Area economies seem not to use fiscal policy that way at all. Confirmation of this comes from the responses to interest rate changes, which are positive but very small and statistically insignificant in the United Kingdom, and negative and near significant in Europe. That implies British fiscal policies are chosen independent of monetary policy, as suggested by our weak leadership model. But if there is any association at all, then fiscal and monetary policies would be complementary and weakly coordinated.

The U.K. results are therefore inconclusive. They are consistent with independent policies, or fiscal leadership—the latter, despite the insignificance of the direct fiscal-monetary linkage, because of the significant output gap term in the fiscal equation that, given the same effect, is not found in the monetary policy reactions, suggests fiscal leadership may in fact have been operating. In any event, there is no suggestion of monetary leadership; if anything, the results imply independence or fiscal leadership.

In the Eurozone, the results are quite different. Here the significant result is the conflict between instruments in monetary policy (and essentially the same conflict in the fiscal policy reactions). Hence the policies are competitive, which suggests they form a Nash equilibrium, or possibly monetary leadership since the coefficient on fiscal policy in the Taylor rule is small and there is no output gap smoothing. That suggests weak monetary leadership, or a simple noncooperative game.

8.5 Theoretical Evidence: A Model of Fiscal Leadership

Restricted sample sizes, and the fact that the new monetary regimes have had a limited time to establish themselves, mean that any statistical tests are of necessity rather weak. We therefore turn to a theoretical test to show that policymakers have a clear incentive to follow the fiscal leadership model. That allows us to calculate how much fiscal leadership could be expected to improve on noncooperative policy-making in any particular case. We find that this provides results that match the United Kingdom's experience rather closely. That provides rather stronger evidence in favor of our fiscal leadership model.

8.5.1 *The Economic Model and Policy Constraints*

The remaining question is, would governments actually want to pursue fiscal leadership? The model set out by Hughes Hallett and Weymark (2004a, b, 2005, 2007) can be used to analyze that question. For exposition purposes, we suppress the possible spillovers between countries and focus on the following three equations to represent the economic structure of any country:

$$\pi_t = \pi_t^e + \alpha y_t + u_t, \tag{8.3}$$

$$y_t = \beta(m_t - \pi_t) + \gamma g_t + \varepsilon_t, \tag{8.4}$$

$$g_t = m_t + s(b y_t - \tau_t), \tag{8.5}$$

where π_t is the inflation rate in period t, y_t is output growth in period t, and π_t^e represents the rate of inflation that rational agents expect will prevail in period t conditional on the information available at the time expectations are formed. The policy instruments m_t, g_t, and τ_t represent the growth in the money supply, government expenditures, and tax revenues in period t; and u_t and ε_t are random disturbances distributed independently with zero mean and constant variance. *All* variables are defined as deviations from their long-run equilibrium growth paths, and we treat the trend budget variables as precommitted and balanced. The coefficients α, β, γ, s, and b are all positive by assumption. The assumption that γ is positive is sometimes controversial.[16] However, the short-run impact multipliers derived from Taylor's (1993a) multicountry estimation provide empirical support for this assumption. More important in this context, the U.K. Treasury also works on the assumption that these multipliers are positive (HM Treasury 2003).

According to (8.3), inflation is increasing in the rate of inflation predicted by private agents and in output growth. Equation (8.4) indicates that both monetary and fiscal policies have an impact on the output gap. The microfoundations of the aggregate supply equation (8.3), originally derived by Lucas (1972, 1973), are well known. McCallum (1989) shows that aggregate demand equations like (8.4) can be derived from a standard, multiperiod utility maximization problem.

Equation (8.5) describes the government's budget constraint. In the interests of simplicity, we allow *discretionary* tax revenues to be used for redistributive purposes only, but we allow *discretionary* expenditures for enhancing output. We further assume that there are two types of agents, rich and poor, and that only the rich use their savings to buy government bonds. In (5), b is the proportion of pretax income (output) that goes to the rich and s is the proportion of after-tax income that the rich allocate to saving. Tax revenues, τ_t, are used by the government to redistribute income from the rich to the poor (a declared policy objective in the United Kingdom), either directly or via public services. Thus, the fiscal structure we describe has output-enhancing expenditures g_t and transfers τ_t. Both are financed by aggregate tax revenues—that is, from discretionary and trend revenues. Expenditures above those revenues must be financed by the sale of bonds.

Using (8.3) and (8.4) to solve for π_t^e, π_t, and y_t yields the following reduced forms:

$$\pi_t(g_t, m_t) = (1 + \alpha\beta)^{-1}\left[\alpha\beta m_t + \alpha\gamma g_t + m_t^e + \frac{\gamma}{\beta} g_t^e + \alpha\varepsilon_t + u_t\right], \tag{8.6}$$

$$y_t(g_t, m_t) = (1 + \alpha\beta)^{-1}[\beta m_t + \gamma g_t - \beta m_t^e - \gamma g_t^e + \varepsilon_t - \beta u_t]. \tag{8.7}$$

Solving for τ_t using (8.5) and (8.7), then yields

$$\tau_t(g_t, m_t) = [s(1 + \alpha\beta)]^{-1}[(1 + \alpha\beta + sb\beta)m_t - (1 + \alpha\beta - sb\gamma)g_t - sb\beta m_t^e - sb\gamma g_t^e + sb(\varepsilon_t - \beta u_t)]. \tag{8.8}$$

8.5.2 *Government and Central Bank Objectives*

In our setup, we allow for the possibility that the government and an independent central bank may differ in their objectives in some significant way. In particular, we assume that the government cares about inflation stabilization, output growth, and the provision of public services (income redistribution); whereas the central bank, if left to itself, would be concerned only with the first two objectives, and possibly only the first one. We also assume that the government has been elected by majority vote, so that the government's loss function reflects society's preferences to a significant extent.

Formally, the government's loss function is given by

$$L_t^g = \frac{1}{2}(\pi_t - \hat{\pi})^2 - \lambda_1^g y_t + \frac{\lambda_2^g}{2}[(b - \theta)y_t - \tau_t]^2, \tag{8.9}$$

where $\hat{\pi}$ is the government's inflation target, λ_1^g is the relative weight or importance the government assigns to output growth,[17] and λ_2^g is the relative weight it assigns to income redistribution. The parameter θ represents the proportion of output that the government would ideally like to allocate to the rich. All other variables are as previously defined.

The objectives of the central bank, however, may be quite different from those of the government. We model that as follows:

$$L_t^{cb} = \frac{1}{2}(\pi - \hat{\pi})^2 - (1 - \delta)\lambda^{cb} y_t - \delta\lambda_1^g y_t + \frac{\delta\lambda_2^g}{2}[(b - \theta)y_t - \tau_t]^2, \tag{8.10}$$

where $0 \leq \delta \leq 1$, and λ^{cb} is the weight that the central bank assigns to output growth. The parameter δ measures the degree to which the central bank is forced to take the government's objectives into account when formulating monetary policy. The closer δ is to 0, the greater is the independence of the central bank in making its choices. And the lower λ^{cb}, the greater is the degree of conservatism in those choices.

In (8.9) we defined the government's inflation target as $\hat{\pi}$. The fact that the same inflation target appears in (8.10) reflects the situation at the Bank of England, where the bank has instrument independence but not target independence. However, it is easy to relax that assumption and allow the central bank to choose its own target (as the ECB does). But, as we show in Hughes Hallett and Weymark 2004a, there is no advantage in doing so since the government would simply adjust its parameters to compensate. Hence, only if the bank is free to choose the value of λ^{cb} as well do we get an extra advantage.[18] Yet even that will not be enough to outweigh the advantages to be gained from fiscal leadership—as we note at the end of this section. Nevertheless, our formulation is the correct one for the United Kingdom. The current monetary policy regulations require the Bank of England to achieve a 2 percent inflation target—a target set by the government—and also to write an open letter, to the government, explaining the reasons for any deviations larger than ± 1 percent around that target and specifying the actions the bank deems necessary to recover it.

The second feature important for British policy is that (8.9) and (8.10) specify symmetric inflation targets around $\hat{\pi}$. Symmetric inflation targets are particularly emphasized as being required of both the Monetary Policy Committee and of the fiscal authorities (HM Treasury 2003). Symmetric output gap targets are also emphasized in the context of fiscal policy, but the U.K. Treasury's careful rejection of "formulaic" decision rules for fiscal policy on practical grounds leads us to rely on symmetry in inflation targets to capture this point.

8.5.3 *The Policy Outcomes*

We characterize the strategic interaction between the government and the central bank as a two-stage noncooperative game in which the structure of the model and the objective functions are common knowledge. In the first stage, the government chooses the institutional parameters δ and λ^{cb}. The second stage is a Stackelberg game in which fiscal policy takes on a leadership role. In this stage, the government and the monetary authority set their policy instruments, given the δ and λ^{cb} values determined at the previous stage. Private agents understand the game and form rational expectations for future prices in the second stage. Formally, the policy game runs as follows:

Stage 1
The government solves the problem:

$$\min_{\delta, \lambda^{cb}} EL^g(g_t, m_t, \delta, \lambda^{cb}) = E\left\{\frac{1}{2}[\pi_t(g_t, m_t) - \hat{\pi}]^2 - \lambda_1^2[y_t(g_t, m_t)]\right\}$$

$$+\frac{\lambda_2^g}{2}E[(b-\theta)y_t(g_t, m_t) - \tau_t(g_t, m_t)]^2, \tag{8.11}$$

where $L^g(g_t, m_t, \delta, \lambda^{cb})$ is (8.9) evaluated at $(g_t, m_t, \delta, \lambda^{cb})$, and E denotes expectations.

Stage 2

1. Private agents form rational expectations about future prices π_t^e before the shocks u_t and ε_t are realized.

2. The shocks u_t and ε_t are realized and observed by the government and by the central bank.

3. The government chooses g_t, before m_t is chosen by the central bank, to minimize $L^g(g_t, m_t, \bar{\delta}, \bar{\lambda}^{cb})$, where $\bar{\delta}$ and $\bar{\lambda}^{cb}$ are at the values determined at stage 1.
4. The central bank then chooses m_t, taking g_t as given, to minimize

$$L^{cb}(g_t, m_t, \bar{\delta}, \bar{\lambda}^{cb}) = \frac{(1-\bar{\delta})}{2}[\pi_t(g_t, m_t) - \hat{\pi}]^2 - (1-\bar{\delta})\bar{\lambda}^{cb}[y_t(g_t, m_t)] + \bar{\delta}L^g(g_t, m_t, \bar{\delta}, \bar{\lambda}^{cb}). \tag{8.12}$$

We solve this game by solving the second stage (for the policy choices) first; and then substituting the results back into (8.11) to determine the optimal operating parameters δ and λ^{cb}. From stage 2, we get

$$\pi_t(\delta, \lambda^{cb}) = \hat{\pi} + \frac{(1-\delta)\beta(\phi - \eta\Lambda)\lambda^{cb} + \delta(\beta\phi + \gamma\Lambda)\lambda_1^g}{\alpha[\beta(\phi - \eta\Lambda) + \delta\Lambda(\beta\eta + \gamma)]}, \tag{8.13}$$

$$y_t(\delta, \lambda^{cb}) = -u_t/\alpha, \tag{8.14}$$

$$\tau_t(\delta, \lambda^{cb}) = \frac{(1-\delta)\beta s(\beta\eta + \gamma)(\lambda^{cb} - \lambda_1^g)}{[\beta(\phi - \eta\Lambda) + \delta\Lambda(\beta\eta + \gamma)]\lambda_2^g} - \frac{(b-\theta)u_t}{\alpha}, \tag{8.15}$$

where

$$\eta = \frac{\partial m_t}{\partial g_t} = \frac{-\alpha^2\gamma\beta s^2 + \delta\phi\Lambda\lambda_2^g}{(\alpha\beta s)^2 + \delta\Lambda^2\lambda_2^g}, \tag{8.16}$$

$$\phi = 1 + \alpha\beta - \gamma\theta s, \tag{8.17}$$

and

$$\Lambda = 1 + \alpha\beta + \beta\theta s. \tag{8.18}$$

Substituting (8.13)–(8.15) back into (8.11) implies we can now get the stage 1 solution from

$$\min_{\delta, \lambda^{cb}} EL^g(\delta, \lambda^{cb}) = \frac{1}{2}\left\{\frac{(1-\delta)\beta(\phi - \eta\Lambda)\lambda^{cb} + \delta(\beta\phi + \gamma\Lambda)\lambda_1^g}{\alpha[\beta(\phi - \eta\Lambda) + \delta\Lambda(\beta\eta + \gamma)]}\right\}^2 + \frac{\lambda_2^g}{2}\left\{\frac{(1-\delta)\beta s(\beta\eta + \gamma)(\lambda^{cb} - \lambda_1^g)}{[\beta(\phi - \eta\Lambda) + \delta\Lambda(\beta\eta + \gamma)]\lambda_2^g}\right\}^2. \tag{8.19}$$

This part of the problem has first-order conditions

$$(1-\delta)(\phi-\eta\Lambda)\lambda_2^g\{(1-\delta)\beta(\phi-\eta\Lambda)\lambda^{cb}+\delta(\beta\phi+\gamma\Lambda)\lambda_1^g\}$$

$$-(1-\delta)^2(\beta\eta+\gamma)^2\alpha^2s^2\beta(\lambda_1^g-\lambda^{cb})=0 \quad (8.20)$$

and

$$\{(1-\delta)\beta(\phi-\eta\Lambda)\lambda^{cb}+\delta(\beta\phi+\gamma\Lambda)\lambda_1^g\}(\lambda_1^g-\lambda^{cb})$$

$$\times\{\delta(1-\delta)\Lambda\Omega+(\phi-\eta\Lambda)\}\lambda_2^g-(1-\delta)(\beta\eta+\gamma)\alpha^2s^2\beta$$

$$\times\{(\beta\eta+\gamma)-(1-\delta)\beta\Omega\}(\lambda_1^g-\lambda^{cb})^2=0, \quad (8.21)$$

where $\Omega=\partial\eta/\partial\delta$. There are two real-valued solutions that satisfy this pair of first-order conditions.[19] Evidently both are satisfied when $\delta=1$ and $\lambda^{cb}=\lambda_1^g$. That solution describes a fully dependent central bank, which is not appropriate in the U.K. case, and, in any event, it is inferior to the solution that follows. The second solution is $\delta=\lambda^{cb}=0$. In this solution, the central bank is fully independent and exclusively concerned with the economy's inflation performance.

Of these two possibilities, the solution that yields the lowest welfare loss, as measured by the government's (or society's) loss function, can be identified by comparing (8.19) to the expected loss that would be suffered under the alternative institutional arrangement. Substituting $\delta=1$ and $\lambda^{cb}=\lambda_1^g$ into (8.19) results in

$$EL^g=\frac{(\lambda_1^g)^2}{2\alpha^2}. \quad (8.22)$$

But substituting $\delta=\lambda^{cb}=0$ into the right-hand side of (8.19) yields

$$EL^g=0. \quad (8.23)$$

Consequently, our results show that, when there is fiscal leadership, society's welfare loss (as measured by [8.19]) is minimized[20] when the government appoints independent central bankers who are concerned only with the achievement of a mandated inflation target and completely disregard the impact their policies may have on output.

However, our results also indicate that an independent central bank with fiscal leadership will be beneficial under more general conditions.

When $\delta = 0$, $\beta\eta + \gamma = 0$; the externalities between policymakers are neutralized. As a result, (8.19) will become

$$EL^g = \frac{1}{2}\left\{\frac{\lambda^{cb}}{\alpha}\right\}^2 \tag{8.24}$$

for any value of λ^{cb}. Hence an independent central bank will always produce better results than a dependent one as long as it is more conservative than the government ($\lambda^{cb} < \lambda_1^g$), and irrespective of the latter's commitment to social equality (λ_2^g). A conservative central bank will therefore be best, but any bank more conservative than the government will do.

A more interesting question is whether fiscal leadership with an independent central bank also produces better outcomes, from society's perspective, than those obtained in a simultaneous move game without leadership. In the simultaneous move game, the solution to the government's stage 1 minimization problem is

$$\delta = \frac{\beta\phi^2\lambda^{cb}\lambda_2^g + \alpha^2\gamma^2 s^2\beta(\lambda^{cb} - \lambda_1^g)}{\beta\phi^2\lambda^{cb}\lambda_2^g + \alpha^2\gamma^2\beta(\lambda^{cb} - \lambda_1^g) - \phi(\beta\phi + \gamma\Lambda)\lambda_1^g\lambda_2^g}, \tag{8.25}$$

and society's welfare loss will then be[21]

$$EL^g = \frac{1}{2}\left\{\frac{\lambda_1^g}{\alpha}\right\}\left\{\frac{(\alpha\gamma s)^2}{(\alpha\gamma s)^2 + \phi^2\lambda_2^2}\right\}. \tag{8.26}$$

That is always smaller than the loss incurred when fiscal leadership is combined with a *dependent* central bank. However, the optimal degree of conservatism for an *independent* central bank, in this case, is obtained by setting $\delta = 0$ in (8.25) to yield

$$\lambda^{cb*} = \frac{(\alpha\gamma s)^2\lambda_1^g}{(\alpha\gamma s)^2 + \phi^2\lambda_2^g}. \tag{8.27}$$

It is straightforward to show that (8.24) is always less than (8.26) as long as

$$\lambda^{cb} < [\lambda_1^g\lambda^{cb*}]^{1/2}. \tag{8.28}$$

It is also evident that $\lambda^{cb*} \leq \lambda_1^g$ for any value $\lambda_2^g \geq 0$. Consequently, fiscal leadership with *any* $\lambda^{cb} < \lambda^{cb*}$ will always produce better outcomes, from society's point of view, than any simultaneous move game between central bank and government. This is an important observation because many inflation targeting regimes, such as those operated by the Bank of England, the Swedish Riksbank, and the Reserve Bank of New Zealand, operate with fiscal leadership; while several others, notably the European Central Bank and the U.S. Federal Reserve System do not. They are better characterized as being engaged in simultaneous move game with their governments.

8.5.4 The Gains from Fiscal Leadership

Finally, where do these leadership gains come from? Substituting $\delta = 0$ and $\lambda^{cb} = 0$ into (8.13)–(8.15) yields

$$\pi_t = \hat{\pi}, \quad y_t = -u_t/\alpha, \quad \text{and} \quad \tau_t = -(b-\theta)u_t/\alpha \tag{8.29}$$

as final outcomes. By contrast, the outcomes for the simultaneous move policy game are

$$\pi_t^* = \hat{\pi} + \frac{\alpha(\gamma s)^2}{[(\alpha\gamma s)^2 + \phi^2\lambda_2^g]}, \tag{8.30}$$

$$y_t^* = -u_t/\alpha, \tag{8.31}$$

$$\tau_t^* = \frac{\gamma s(\lambda^{cb*} - \lambda_1^g)}{\phi\lambda_2^g} - \frac{(b-\theta)u_t}{\alpha}. \tag{8.32}$$

Comparing the two sets of outcomes, we can see that fiscal leadership eliminates an inflationary bias and results in lower inflation. Fiscal leadership also yields higher taxes and more income redistribution.[22] Moreover, these two improvements are achieved with no losses in expected output or in output volatility. The question is, why?

8.5.5 The Coordination Effect

One of the central issues in the coordination literature is whether there are institutional arrangements that yield Pareto improvements over the standard noncooperative outcomes.[23] When such institutions exist, they may be viewed as a coordination device. In our model, the central bank is independent, without further institutional restraints that would necessarily lead to noncooperative outcomes. But if the government is committed to long-term leadership in the manner we have described, without reducing the bank's independence, the policy game will become an example of *rule-based* coordination in which performance gains are available for both parties. Given the structure of a Stackelberg game, there will be no incentive to reoptimize for either party—as long as the government remains committed to long term leadership rather than short term demand management—unless both parties agree to reduce their independence through discretionary coordination.[24] That is a general result: it holds for any model where inflation and output both depend on both monetary and fiscal policy, and where inflation is targeted to some degree by both players (Hughes Hallett and Viegi 2002). Our results are therefore robust.[25]

8.5.6 Fiscal Sustainability in This Regime

Fiscal leadership, as defined in this model of policymaking, provides for long-run sustainable public finances (as claimed in the U.K. Treasury's analysis). Equation (8.29) shows that $E(y^*) = 0$ and $E(\tau^*) = 0$ under fiscal leadership, whereas $E(y^*) = 0$ and $E(\tau^*) < 0$ under simultaneous decision making (or, for that matter, monetary leadership[26]): see (8.30)–(8.32). Fiscal leadership therefore generates balanced budgets *on average*, both in terms of the level of the deficit and as a proportion of GDP, whereas simultaneous decision making or monetary leadership lead to persistent deficits and hence an accumulating debt burden (absolutely, and as a ratio to GDP). Hence the United Kingdom's sustainability of public finances target is also better served with this leadership regime, than by its natural alternatives.

Interestingly, table 8.2b shows that this is exactly what has happened in practice. The U.K. fiscal surpluses have increased with the debt-to-GDP ratio since 1997, and significantly so.[27] That is entirely consistent with Bohn's test for fiscal sustainability (chapter 2, proposition 1), although a test on a single coefficient in such a relationship is neither necessary nor sufficient on its own. Additional restrictions are needed to ensure that the surplus is actually large enough to compensate for slow growth or high interest rates (Wierts 2007; Hughes Hallett and Lewis 2007); or, in Bohn's formulation, that the error term in this relationship (as well as GDP) remains bounded. The latter complicates the formal statistical tests that need to be applied. So, for the

Table 8.3
Expected losses under fiscal leadership and other strategies

	(1) Full dependence $\delta = 1$ $\lambda^{cb} = \lambda_1^g$	(2) Fiscal leadership $\delta = 0$ $\lambda^{cb} = 0$	(3) Simultaneous moves $\delta = 0$ $\lambda^{cb} = \lambda^{cb*}$	(4) Growth rate equivalents lost %
France	5.78	0.00	0.0125	1.26
Germany	16.14	0.00	0.0079	0.79
Italy	1.28	0.00	0.0116	1.16
Sweden	4.51	0.00	0.0098	0.98
New Zealand	8.40	0.00	0.0104	1.04
United Kingdom	3.37	0.00	0.0113	1.13

Note: The losses reported in column (3) were calculated using $\lambda_1^g = 1$ and $\lambda_2^g = 0.5$ for each of the six countries in the sample.

purposes of this chapter, we rely on the theoretical result that a regime of fiscal leadership, as the United Kingdom appears to have adopted, is sustainable in the long run.

8.5.7 *Empirical Evidence*

Whether or not these results are of practical significance is an empirical matter. In table 8.3 we computed the expected losses under the simultaneous move and government leadership regimes for six countries when fiscal policy and the central bank are optimally constructed. The data we used is from 1998, the year in which the Eurozone was created. The data itself, and its sources, are summarized in the appendix to this chapter.

The countries selected fall into two groups: (1) Eurozone countries (France, Germany, and Italy), and (2) countries with explicit inflation targets (Sweden, New Zealand, and the United Kingdom).

In the first group, monetary policy is conducted at the European level, and fiscal policy is conducted at the national level. Policy interactions in this group can be characterized in terms of a simultaneous move game with target as well as instrument independence. The second group of countries has adopted explicit, and mostly publicly announced, inflation targets. Central banks in these countries have been granted instrument independence but not target independence.

The government either sets, or helps set, the inflation target value. In each case the government has adopted longer-term (supply side) fiscal policies, leaving active demand management to monetary policy. These are clear cases in which there is both fiscal leadership and instrument independence for the central bank.

The results of these calculations are reported in table 8.3. Column (1) shows the losses under a dependent central bank in welfare units, leadership or not. Column (2) reflects the losses that would be incurred under government leadership with an independent central bank that directs monetary policy exclusively toward the achievement of the inflation target (i.e., with $\delta = \lambda^{cb} = 0$). The third column gives the minimum loss associated with a simultaneous decision-making version of the same game.

Evidently, complete dependence in monetary policy is extremely unfavorable although the magnitude of the loss varies considerably from country to country. The losses in column (3) appear to be relatively small compared to those in column (2). However, when these figures are converted into "growth rate equivalents," we find these losses to be significant. A growth rate equivalent is the loss in output growth that would produce the same welfare loss if all other variables remain fixed at their optimized values.[28]

The figures in column (4) show that the losses associated with simultaneous decision making are equivalent to having permanent reductions of around 1 percent in the long-term growth rate of national income. That is, Germany, France, and Italy could have expected to have grown about 1 percent faster (or double their 2003 growth rates) had they had this regime; and Sweden, the United Kingdom and New Zealand by 1 percent slower had they not done so. These are significant changes and are equivalent to two-thirds of the gains that might have been expected from international coordination (Currie, Holtham, and Hughes Hallett 1989), or from the European single currency itself (European Commission 1990).

8.6 Conclusions

1. Fiscal leadership leads to improved outcomes because it implies a degree of coordination and reduced conflicts between institutions, without the central bank having to lose its ability to act independently. This places the outcomes somewhere between the superior but

discretionary policies of complete cooperation; and the noncooperative but inferior policies of complete independence.

2. These results show that the important property for monetary policy is instrument independence. Given that, target independence brings few additional gains and may have the effect of undoing the complementarity between fiscal and monetary policies.

3. The United Kingdom appears, both from its institutional structure and the available empirical evidence, to have adopted this leadership framework since 1997. This is perhaps the main reason for the country's improved performance both in terms of outcomes and in making more effective use of her fiscal and monetary instruments.

4. Although it is hard to get definitive results from statistical tests, the incentive to adopt fiscal leadership is clear from the theoretical results. Confirmation of those results then comes from the outcomes. The leadership with separation model predicts improvements in growth, inflation, or income distribution of the order of 1 percent of GDP. And that is exactly what we have observed since 2000. In addition, the leadership framework requires less precise information on the strategic and institutional parameters than do other strategies.

Appendix: Data Sources for Table 8.3

The data values used in table 8.3 are set out in the table that follows. They come from different sources and represent best practice estimates of the relevant parameters.

The Phillips curve parameter, α, is the inverse of the annualized sacrifice ratios on quarterly data from 1971–1998 by Turner and Seghezza (1999) at the OECD. The values for β and γ, the impact multipliers for fiscal and monetary policy respectively, are the one-year simulated multipliers for those policies in Taylor's multicountry model (Taylor 1993a). The national savings ratios, s, were obtained from OECD data (*Economic Outlook*, various issues). I used 1998 figures since that was the year that EMU started, and the year that new fiscal and monetary regimes took effect in the United Kingdom. I also used 1998 to set θ, the desired level of income inequality. Since θ measures the desired proportion of national income accruing to the rich, it is set at one minus the proportion of fiscal expenditures allocated to social programs in each country. Finally, I set $\lambda_1^g = 1$ and $\lambda_2^g = 0.5$ in each country. The value of φ follows from there.

	α	β	γ	s	θ	φ
France	0.294	0.500	0.570	0.211	0.620	1.072
Germany	0.176	0.533	0.430	0.216	0.583	1.040
Italy	0.625	0.433	0.600	0.214	0.651	1.187
Sweden	0.333	0.489	0.533	0.206	0.504	1.107
NZ	0.244	0.400	0.850	0.124	0.596	1.035
UK	0.385	0.133	0.580	0.180	0.675	0.980

Notes

I am grateful for comments from two referees, Gottfried Haber, and participants at the CESifo-LBI Conference on the Sustainability of Public Debt, and to Petra Geraats, Sean Holly, and others at Cambridge University. The policy response functions in section 8.4 were developed in conjunction with John Lewis of de Nederlandsche Bank, and the model used in section 8.5 is adapted from my work with Diana Weymark at Vanderbilt University. Neither is responsible for my interpretation of events.

1. The U.K. Treasury estimates that the automatic stabilizers will, in normal circumstances, stabilize some 30 percent of the cycle, the remaining 70 percent being left to monetary policy (HM Treasury 2003). The option to undertake discretionary stabilizing interventions is retained "for exceptional circumstances" however. Nevertheless, the need for any such additional interventions is unlikely: first, because of the effectiveness of the forward-looking, symmetric, and activist inflation targeting mechanism adopted at the Bank of England; and, second, because the longer-term expenditure (and tax) plans are deliberately constructed in nominal terms so that they add to the stabilizing power of the automatic stabilizers in more serious booms or slumps.

2. For details on how this leadership vs. stabilization assignment is intended to work, see HM Treasury 2003 and section 8.3. Australia and Sweden operate rather similar regimes. But their arrangements differ in a number of important technical details that affect the degree of coordination that emerges, and hence in the outcomes and strength of commitment to the given path and policies.

3. Stackelberg games, with fiscal policy leading, produce fiscal commitment: i.e., subgame perfection with either strong or weak time consistency (Basar 1989). In that sense, we have "rules rather than discretion." Commitment to the stabilization policies is then assured by the independence of the monetary authority.

4. A common inflation target will take this process further in the case of Great Britain, as I have argued elsewhere (Hughes Hallett 1998). But it is not an essential point once the coordinating elements of leadership are put in place since a tighter target at the central bank will cause its reaction function to shift. The government, as leader, will incorporate that change into its own decision making and then reoptimize to offset it (Hughes Hallett and Weymark 2004a).

5. Dow 1964; see also Radcliffe Report 1959, Plowden Report 1961, Prest 1968, Price 1978, and Hatton and Chrystal 1991.

6. This follows the recommendations in Taylor 2000. However, because of the inevitable trade-off between cyclical stability and budget stability, it is likely to be successful only in markets with sufficiently flexible wages and prices (see Fatas et al. 2003).

7. This summary is taken from the U.K. Treasury's own view (HM Treasury 2003, secs. 2 and 4, pp. 34–38).

8. In this section, page, box, table, and section numbers given without further reference are all taken from HM Treasury 2003.

9. The credibility of fiscal policy, and by extension an independent monetary policy, depends on these steps, and on *symmetric* stabilization. See also Dixit 2001 and Dixit and Lambertini 2003.

10. The model for this appears to be the Australian Charter of Budget Honesty, which has a horizon of four years rather than three for expenditure plans.

11. See Basar and Olsder 1999, Hughes Hallett 1984, and Brandsma and Hughes Hallett 1984.

12. One can argue that policy should be based on fully optimal rules (Svensson 2003), of which (8.1) will be a special case. But it is hard to argue that policymakers actually do optimize when the additional gains from doing so may be small; and when the uncertainties in their information, policy transmissions, or the economy's responses may be quite large. In practice, therefore, the Taylor rule approach is often found to fit central bank behavior better.

13. In principle, k and h may be positive or negative: positive if the policy rule is based on future expected inflation, to head off an anticipated problem, as in the Bank of England, but negative if interest rates are to follow a feedback rule to correct past mistakes or failures.

14. See Taylor 2000, Gali and Perotti 2003, and Turrini and in't Veld 2004 for similar formulations. The European Commission (2002) uses a similar rule but defines $d > 0$ to be a deficit. They therefore expect γ to be negative.

15. Buti, Eijffinger, and Franco 2003. The presence of debt in the U.K. rule indicates that sustainability has been a primary target in the United Kingdom but not in the Eurozone.

16. Barro (1981) argues that government purchases have a contractionary impact on output. Our model, by contrast, treats fiscal policy as important because (1) fiscal policy is widely used to achieve redistributive and public service objectives; (2) governments cannot precommit monetary policy with any credibility if fiscal policy is not precommitted (Dixit and Lambertini 2003); and (3) central banks, and the ECB in particular, worry intensely about the impact of fiscal policy on inflation and financial stability (Dixit 2001).

17. In adopting a linear representation of the output objective, we follow Barro and Gordon (1983). In the monetary delegation literature, the output component in the government's loss function is usually represented as quadratic to reflect an output *stability* objective. In our model, the quadratic income redistribution term allows monetary and fiscal policy to play a stabilization role as well as pick a position on the economy's output-inflation trade-off. For a full derivation of the results in this section, see Hughes Hallett 2005.

18. In other words, target independence must be defined in terms of priorities as well as targets.

19. Because η is a function of δ, (8.21) is quartic in δ. This polynomial has four distinct roots, of which only two are real-valued. Details of the complete solution can be found in Hughes Hallett and Weymark 2002.

20. This does not necessarily imply that the central bank's loss function will be minimized at the same time.

21. See Hughes Hallett and Weymark 2002, 2004a for these results.

22. Note that tax revenues are lower, on average, under the simultaneous move game because $\lambda^{cb} < \lambda_1^g$. Redistribution is positively related to the amount of tax revenue because $(b-\theta)Ey_t^* = 0$, so that τ_t^* determines the amount of income redistribution actually achieved: $E\tau^* = 0$ in (8.29) vs. $E\tau_t^* \leq 0$ in (8.32). The reasons for this result are discussed in Hughes Hallett and Weymark 2004b.

23. See, e.g., Currie, Holtham, and Hughes Hallett 1989, Currie and Levine 1991, and Hughes Hallett 1992, 1998.

24. The key point for our results here is that we require no precommitment beyond leadership, and no punishment beyond electoral results. The former holds because governments have a natural commitment to public services (health, education, defense) and some notion of equity or economic efficiency—all long-term issues. The latter arises from the political competition inherent in a democracy.

25. But this does not say that both players will gain equally. If the priority for inflation targeting is increased after leadership has been granted, then the leader will gain by less. That is important because it explains why, in a world with inflation targeting, granting leadership to a central bank whose tolerance for inflation is already lower, and whose precommitment is already greater, produces no *extra* gains—although that solution may still be better than that in the simultaneous moves game.

26. Hughes Hallett 2007.

27. The Eurozone, by contrast, shows no such relationship at conventional levels of significance.

28. Currie, Holtham, and Hughes Hallett 1989 and Oudiz and Sachs 1984. To obtain these figures, we computed the marginal rates of transformation around each government's indifference curve to find the change in output growth, dy_t, that yields the welfare loss in column (3). Formally, $dy_t = dEL_t^g/[\lambda_2^g\{(b-\theta)y_t - \tau_t\}(b-\theta) - \lambda_1^g]$ using (8.9). The minimum value of dy_t is therefore attained when tax revenues τ_t grow at the same rate as the redistribution target $(b-\theta)y_t$. These are the losses reported in column (4).

References

Barro, R. J. 1981. Output effects of government purchases. *Journal of Political Economy* 89:1086–1121.

Barro, R. J., and D. B. Gordon. 1983. Rules, discretion, and reputation in a model of monetary policy. *Journal of Monetary Economics* 12:101–121.

Basar, T. 1989. Time consistency and robustness of equilibria in non-cooperative dynamic games. In *Dynamic Policy Games in Economics*, ed. F. van der Ploeg and A. de Zeeuw, 9–54. Amsterdam: North-Holland.

Basar, T., and G. Olsder. 1999. *Dynamic Noncooperative Game Theory.* SIAM Classics in Applied Mathematics. Philadelphia: SIAM.

Brandsma, A., and A. Hughes Hallett. 1984. Economic conflict and the solution of dynamic games. *European Economic Review* 26:13–32.

Buti, M., S. Eijffinger, and D. Franco. 2003. Revisiting the stability and growth pact: grand design or internal adjustment? Discussion Paper no. 3692. London: Centre for Economic Policy Research.

Currie, D. A., G. Holtham, and A. Hughes Hallett. 1989. The theory and practice of international economic policy coordination: Does coordination pay? In *Macroeconomic Policies in an Interdependent World*, ed. R. Bryant, D. Currie, J. Frenkel, P. Masson, and R. Portes, 14–46. Washington, DC: International Monetary Fund.

Currie, D., and P. Levine. 1991. The international coordination of monetary policy: A survey. In *Surveys in Monetary Economics*, vol. I, ed. C. Green and D. Llewellyn, 379–417. Oxford: Blackwell.

Dieppe, A., K. Kuster, and P. McAdam. 2004. Optimal monetary policy rules for the Euro Area: An analysis using the Area Wide Model. ECB Working Paper no. 360. European Central Bank, Frankfurt.

Dixit, A. 2001. Games of monetary and fiscal interactions in the EMU. *European Economic Review* 45:589–613.

Dixit, A. K., and L. Lambertini. 2003. Interactions of commitment and discretion in monetary and fiscal issues. *American Economic Review* 93:1522–1542.

Dow, J. C. R. 1964. *The Management of the British Economy 1945–1960.* Cambridge: Cambridge University Press.

European Commission. 1990. *One Market, One Money.* European Economy no. 44. Luxembourg: EU Official Publications.

European Commission. 2002. *Public Finances in EMU*: 2. European Economy: Studies and Reports 4. Brussels: European Commission.

Fatas, A., J. von Hagen, A. Hughes Hallett, R. Strauch, and A. Sibert. 2003. *Stability and Growth in Europe.* CEPR MEI-13. London: Centre for Economic Policy Research.

Gali, J., and R. Perotti. 2003. Fiscal policy and monetary integration in Europe. *Economic Policy* 37:533–571.

Hatton, T. J., and A. Chrystal. 1991. The budget and fiscal policy. In *The British Economy since 1945*, ed. N. Crafts and N. Woodward, 52–88. Oxford: Oxford University Press.

HM Treasury. 2003. *Fiscal Stabilisation and EMU.* HM Stationary Office, Cmnd 799373. Norwich. Available at www.hm-treasury.gov.uk.

Hughes Hallett, A. 1984. Noncooperative strategies for dynamic policy games and the problem of time inconsistency. *Oxford Economic Papers* 36:381–399.

Hughes Hallett, A. 1992. Target zones and international policy coordination. *European Economic Review* 36:893–914.

Hughes Hallett, A. 1998. When do target zones work? *Open Economies Review* 9:115–138.

Hughes Hallett, A. 2005. In praise of fiscal restraint and debt rules: What the Euro zone might do now. CEPR Discussion Paper no. 5043. London: Centre for Economic Policy Research.

Hughes Hallett, A. 2007. Fiscal sustainability and monetary leadership; or why Europe needs a fiscal constitution. Mimeo., School of Public Policy, George Mason University.

Hughes Hallett, A., and J. Lewis. 2007. Debt, deficits, and the accession of the new member-states to the euro. *European Journal of Political Economy* 23:316–337.

Hughes Hallett, A., and N. Viegi. 2002. Inflation targeting as a coordination device. *Open Economies Review* 13:341–362.

Hughes Hallett, A., and D. Weymark. 2004a. Policy games and the optimal design of central banks. In P. Minford, ed., *Money Matters*. London: Edward Elgar.

Hughes Hallett, A., and D. Weymark. 2004b. Independent monetary policies and social equity. *Economics Letters* 85:103–110.

Hughes Hallett, A., and D. Weymark. 2005. Independence before conservatism: Transparency, politics and central bank design. *German Economic Review* 6:1–25.

Hughes Hallett, A., and D. Weymark. 2007. Government leadership and central bank design. *Canadian Journal of Economics* 40:607–627.

Lucas, R. E. 1972. Expectations and the neutrality of money. *Journal of Economic Theory* 4:103–124.

Lucas, R. E. 1973. Some international evidence on output-inflation trade-offs. *American Economic Review* 63:326–334.

McCallum, B. T. 1989. *Monetary Economics: Theory and Policy*. New York: Macmillan.

Oudiz, G., and J. Sachs. 1984. Macroeconomic policy coordination among the industrial economies. *Brookings Papers on Economic Activity* 15:1–64.

Plowden Report. 1961. *Report of Committee in Control of Public Expenditure.* Command 1432. London: HMSO.

Prest, A. R. 1968. Sense and nonsense in budgetary policy. *Economic Journal* 71:1–18.

Price, R. W. R. 1978. Budgetary policy. In *British Economic Policy 1960–74*, ed. F. T. Blackaby, 135–227. Cambridge: Cambridge University Press.

Radcliffe Report. 1959. *Committee on the Working of the Monetary System Report.* Command 827. London: HMSO.

Svensson, L. 2003. What is wrong with Taylor rules? Using judgment in monetary rules through targeting rules. *Journal of Economic Literature* 41:426–477.

Taylor, J. B. 1993a. *Macroeconomic Policy in a World Economy: From Econometric Design to Practical Operation.* New York: W. W. Norton and Company.

Taylor, J. B. 1993b. Discretion vs. policy rules in practice. *Carnegie-Rochester Conference Series on Public Policy* 39:195–214.

Taylor, J. B. 2000. Discretionary fiscal policies. *Journal of Economic Perspectives* 14:1–23.

Turner, Dave, and Elena Seghezza. 1999. Testing for a common OECD Phillips curve. OECD Economics Department Working Paper no. 219.

Turrini, A., and J. in't Veld. 2004. *The Impact of the EU Fiscal Framework on Economic Activity*. Brussels: European Commission, DGII.

Wierts, P. 2007. The sustainability of Euro-Area debt: A reassessment. Discussion Paper no. 134. De Nederlandsche Bank, April.

Woodford, M. 2003. *Interest and Prices: Foundations of the Theory of Monetary Policy*. Princeton: Princeton University Press.

9 On the Effectiveness of Debt Brakes: The Swiss Experience

Lars P. Feld and Gebhard Kirchgässner

9.1 Introduction

Current policy debates on public finances in OECD countries focus on the question of how a sustainable fiscal policy can be obtained. The most pertinent discussion is taking place in the European Union (EU) where the Stability and Growth Pact (SGP), as a follow-up to the fiscal convergence criteria of the Maastricht Treaty, requires EU member states to keep budget deficits below 3 percent of GDP and public debt below 60 percent of GDP. Deviations from this general rule are only allowed for specific circumstances like severe economic downturns or extraordinary events like natural disasters.[1]

Whether this rule makes sense or not has been debated for as long as there have been discussions about the Maastricht Treaty. After all, the precise limits defined by this treaty are quite arbitrary decisions: other criteria like, for example, a maximum deficit of 2.5 or 3.4 percent could have been chosen with similar arguments.[2] On the other hand, the idea that sustainability of public finances implies that the ratios between debt and GDP, and, correspondingly, also between the deficit and GDP, are bounded from above is rather trivial, and it may even be seen as the most natural definition of sustainability, as already implied in the seminal contribution of Domar (1944), even if he did not use the term *sustainability* since it was not introduced into the policy debate until several decades later.

The discussion in the EU is not, however, unique. In the United States, the Gramm-Rudman-Hollings (GRH) act was passed in 1985 in order to reduce federal public debt.[3] In Switzerland a discussion about a "debt brake" for the federal budget was inspired by a strong increase in federal debt during the 1990s. The corresponding amendment to the Swiss Constitution was accepted on December 2, 2001, with an overwhelming majority (and a turnout of 37 percent). At the same time, there are similar rules in several cantons, some of which have been in place for several decades, which are really effective. They are stricter than the new procedure at the federal level, the effectiveness of which has to be proven in the future.

In federal states, however, the prescription of such a limit is not sufficient to guarantee fiscal sustainability, as there is no single actor who even rudimentarily has the potential to restrict the total public deficit. In Germany, Austria, and Spain, for example, the federal government is unable to do so because the regional authorities have a certain fiscal autonomy that allows them to have deficits that cannot be controlled by the federal authorities. This problem became obvious in Germany in the spring of 2002: despite the fact that the federal government had—at least in comparison with its predecessors—reduced the issuance of new debt, the Federal Republic of Germany nearly got a warning from the European Union because the expected deficit for 2002 was 2.7 percent of GDP and, therefore, far from its former stabilization objective and quite close to the Maastricht limit of 3 percent of GDP, which it actually exceeded in the following years. The reason for this was a considerable increase in the deficits of the Bundesländer and the local communities.

Thus, in federal countries, a second-order problem of sustainability arises: namely, how subnational governments with fiscal autonomy can be forced to contribute to the overall fiscal objective of the country. In principle, there are two ways to cope with this problem.

1. A national stability pact might be concluded in analogy to the SGP of the European Union. This is the procedure that was chosen in Germany, but it lacks effectiveness because—so far—no sanctions are available to be applied to those Bundesländer that do not conform to the given rules.[4] Obviously, the smooth functioning of such a pact presupposes at least some possibility for the federal government to intervene in the finances of the lower governmental level whenever their financial decisions violate the prescriptions of the pact.[5]

2. An alternative is institutional rules at the constitutional and/or statutory level that provide incentives for the subnational governments to stick to a sustainable policy. This is the route taken in Switzerland where, since the 1990s, about one-third of the cantons has introduced "debt brakes," namely, rules that force the subnational governments to strictly follow a sustainable policy without any intervention of the national government (or a supreme court). Several U.S. states also have

formal fiscal restraints with characteristics that vary strongly across the states.[6] Obviously, a precondition for the smooth functioning of such rules is that a bailout by the federal government is no realistic possibility on which the lower-level governments can speculate when drawing up their fiscal policy.

It is this second-order problem of fiscal sustainability, of tremendous importance in federal states, that is the topic of this chapter.

In contrast with nearly all other OECD countries, the Swiss and the U.S. fiscal systems have two special features: fiscal federalism, which is organized in a competitive way and gives the lower-level jurisdictions (cantons/states and local communities) the power to tax, and direct popular rights in political decision making, which include fiscal referenda at the subfederal levels. However, large differences persist between the Swiss cantons with respect to the institutional design that even exceed those between U.S. states, thus making Switzerland a unique laboratory where the effects of fiscal institutions can be studied.

Since the 1990s, several empirical studies have considered the effectiveness of the different institutional designs of fiscal systems in the United States and Switzerland. Bohn and Inman (1996), for example, extensively study the impact of balanced budget requirements on the public finances of U.S. states by investigating which specific design is most successful at restraining governments.[7] O'Sullivan, Sexton, and Sheffrin (1995, 1999) analyze how Proposition 13 has affected the fiscal policies of U.S. states and local jurisdictions.[8] The effectiveness of fiscal restraints has also been investigated for Switzerland. Using a panel of the twenty-six Swiss cantons and the years 1986–1997, Feld and Kirchgässner (2001a) show that cantons with such restrictions have significantly lower debts and deficits. Similar results are obtained by Schaltegger (2002) for a different time period.

The cross-country and the U.S. results on the impact of fiscal federalism on public finance are more ambiguous.[9] According to the theoretical arguments of Brennan and Buchanan (1980), fiscal decentralization reduces the ability of governments to exploit tax bases because they have increased exit possibilities in a federal system. While several authors find evidence of this proposed effect of fiscal decentralization on the size of government, others do not. In a recent paper, Feld, Kirchgässner, and Schaltegger (2003) present evidence of the Swiss cantons from 1980 to 1998 showing that fiscal decentralization decreases government revenue mainly because of intense tax competition. Rodden and Wibbels (2002) provide analogous empirical evidence relating to public deficits in fifteen federations between 1978 and 1996 that fiscal decentralization increases the combined central state surplus while grants reduce it.

Finally, there is a large body of evidence on the impact of referenda and initiatives on public finance. Matsusaka (2004) provides a comprehensive discussion on the impact of legislative initiatives on the spending and revenue of U.S. states and local jurisdictions, while Kiewiet and Szakaly (1996) present evidence on the influence of referenda on the guaranteed debt of U.S. states. These U.S. studies show that direct democracy is associated with sounder public finances. The studies on Swiss cantons and local jurisdictions corroborate this conclusion.[10]

Besides discussing the development at the Swiss federal level, the main purpose of this chapter is to consider the effects of the three types of constitutional or statutory clauses—namely, fiscal decentralization, direct popular rights, and formal fiscal restraints—on public deficit and debt in the twenty-six Swiss cantons. In order to find out whether the cantons are shifting deficits to the local communities, we consider not only the deficit of the cantonal budget but also the combined deficit of the cantonal budget and the budgets of the local communities within a canton for the period from 1980 to 1998. In doing so, this analysis deviates in several respects from existing studies that investigate a shorter time period, such as 1986–1998 in Feld and Kirchgässner (2001a, b), for example, or focus on expenditure and revenue but not on deficit and debt,[11] or do not consider all three types of constitutional or statutory clauses.[12] Our main results are that direct democracy leads to significantly lower debt but does not have a significant effect on the budget deficit. The fiscal constraint, on the other hand, significantly reduces budget deficits. Moreover, cantonal debt is lower the higher the share of local expenditure. Taking all these results together, those cantons with "strong" fiscal instruments at least have the institutional prerequisites to conduct a sustainable fiscal policy. They can serve as examples not only for other Swiss cantons but also for other federal countries in order to develop similar fiscal rules.

The chapter is organized as follows: in section 9.2, we describe cantonal institutions (called "debt brakes") that are intended to prevent public debt from getting out of control and especially discuss the St. Gall model, the oldest one. To allow for a more systematic analysis of their effects, we present an econometric model in section 9.3. In section 9.4, we discuss the empirical results. We consider the new debt brake that has been introduced at federal level in section 9.5. In section 9.6, we discuss the problem of overindebtedness at lower governmental levels that might arise in any federal country. It is shown that with well designed institutions, federal states might even be able to follow a sustainable fiscal policy better than unitary states. Alongside fiscal restrictions, fiscal referenda are useful in achieving that.

9.2 The Cantonal Institutions

In 1981, the conference of the cantonal Ministers of Finance edited a *Handbook of Public Budgeting* (vol. 1), presenting a role model law for cantonal budgeting (Konferenz der Kantonalen Finanzdirektoren 1981). According to Article 2, the principle of a balanced budget has to be observed. This is stated more concretely in Article 4, according to which the current budget must be balanced in the medium term, and in Article 18, which requires that accumulated cantonal debt be cut back in the medium term. "Medium term" means within about ten years.[13] Today, such rules can be found in nearly all cantonal constitutions and in the corresponding budget laws. The cantons are obliged to balance their budgets over the business cycle and also to reduce accumulated debt. However, this was not able to preclude cantonal debt from increasing considerably in the last decade, partly because of unfavorable economic developments. There was an average increase of about 106 percent (in real terms), but the development varied widely in different cantons.[14] Figure 9.1 shows the development of cantonal public debt in four selected cantons, St. Gall, Fribourg, Vaud, and Geneva, from 1980 to 2002. While two of them, St. Gall and Fribourg, reveal only modest increases in their debt, cantonal debt increased considerably in Vaud and even dramatically in Geneva, leading to a public debt per capita of CHF 41,791 in 2002, which is 418 percent of the national average.

A specialty of the cantonal constitutions, in contrast to the new Swiss Federal Constitution as well as to the Austrian and German constitutions at all three governmental levels, is the existence of fiscal referenda: if the outlays for a project exceed a certain limit, the citizens have to be asked whether they agree to the spending project. This limit can be different for nonrecurring and for recurring expenditure. With the exception of Vaud, all cantons have such referenda.[15] Because the citizens know that, sooner or later, they must pay for the projects that are carried out by the canton or the local community, it imposes a restraint on projects that are too ambitious.

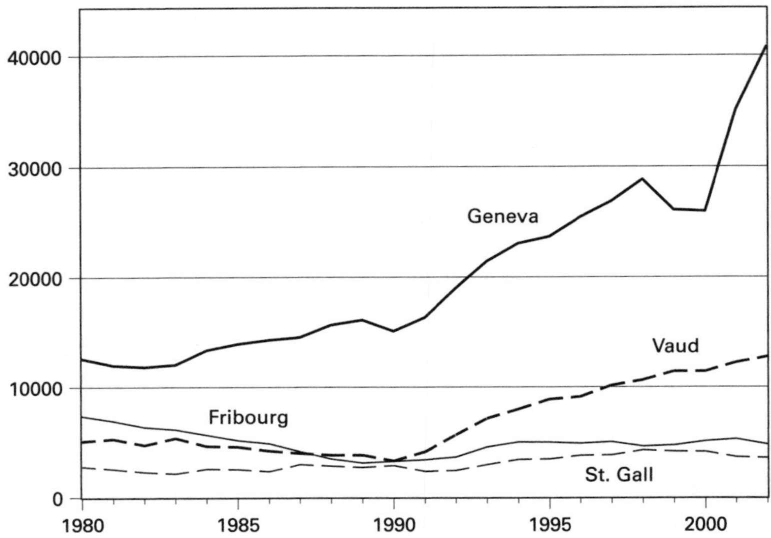

Figure 9.1
Public debt of selected cantons, 1980–2002 (real debt per capita, 2000 = 100)

However, even the existence of fiscal referenda (in addition to regulations for a balanced budget) has been insufficient to prevent public debt from increasing as described earlier. Therefore, within the past ten years, eight cantons have introduced new instruments to limit the deficits: St. Gall (1994), Fribourg (1994), Solothurn (1995), Appenzell Outer Rhodes (1995), Grisons (1998), Lucerne (2001), Berne (2002), and, the last one for the time being, Valais (2002).[16] These regulations are laid down partly in the cantonal constitutions, but mainly in the cantonal budget laws.

The canton of St. Gall may be used as an example or "case study."[17] The rules require that the current budget has to be balanced. The deficit may not be larger than 3 percent of the "simple tax revenue," which at the moment is about 60 percent of total tax revenue.[18] Whenever a deficit is expected, the tax rate has to be adjusted in order to respect this limit. Moreover, if a canton has no accumulated savings, the deficit is transferred to the budget of the year after next. Whenever there is a surplus—for example, because of an economic upswing—this money has to be saved and/or used for additional depreciation. The tax rates cannot be reduced before these savings have accrued to seven times the maximum allowed deficit.

Besides the current budget there is the capital budget, which is used to finance public investment. Investment projects up to CHF 5 million have to be included in the current budget, while projects between CHF 5 and 10 million have to be depreciated within five years and projects higher than 10 million within ten years. The depreciations have to be included in the current budget. Thus, such projects cannot lead to a long-run debt increase. It is possible to raise debt in order to buy shares of firms, for example, of the cantonal banks, but there have to be returns as compensation.

On the spending side, fiscal referenda restrict new spending. They are optional for recurring expenditure of more than CHF 300,000 and for nonrecurring expenditure of more than CHF 3 million and mandatory for recurring expenditure of more than CHF 1.5 million and for nonrecurring expenditure of more than CHF 15 million. In relation to the budget, which was about CHF 3.46 billion in 2002, these limits amount to 0.009 or 0.043 percent respectively for current expenditure and 0.09 or 0.43 percent respectively for nonrecurring expenditure. Compared to the regulations of other cantons, these limits are rather low. In order for an optional referendum to take place, four thousand signatures have to be collected within thirty days. This corresponds to about 1.5 percent of the electorate.[19]

Thus, the citizens have—within the boundaries of the federal constitution—competence with respect to the tasks the canton has to perform and the necessary expenditure. With respect to the revenue side, they decide on all constitutional and statutory rules, especially different taxes and tariff schedules (including the progressivity of direct taxes) but not tax rates. Competence with respect to the latter is with the cantonal parliament that, however, is very much restricted by the regulations described previously. A fundamental (and special) feature of these regulations is the fact that the canton is obliged to accumulate savings (to a certain amount) before tax rates can be reduced. This implies that surpluses are saved in "good" years that can be used to cover (to a certain extent) deficits in the downswing. This institutionalizes anticyclical fiscal policy at the cantonal level, which—contrary to the situation that led to the proposals of Buchanan and Wagner (1977, 1978)—has not led to an increase in public debt.[20]

This combination of direct democratic expenditure restrictions, quasi-automatic revenue adjustment, and the accumulation of savings has proven to be successful. In 2002, cantonal public debt per capita was CHF 3,678 in the canton of St. Gall; only the cantons of Schwyz, Zug, Aargau, and the two cantons of Appenzell had lower cantonal public debt. Even more important, interest payments of CHF 41 million were overcompensated for by returns of CHF 81 million. Thus, the tax burden per capita was reduced by CHF 88.[21] The most important part is the revenue from shares in (semi-)public enterprises, especially in the St. Galler Kantonalbank. One might debate whether it is reasonable today for a government to intervene in private markets in such a way; it is often demanded (and often for good reason) that such enterprises should be privatized. This does not preclude the canton of St. Gall from having net financial assets, however.

It is also useful to compare this situation with the one in 1990, namely, before the long lasting recession of the 1990s, when cantonal debt was CHF 2,524 per capita and thus 56.8 percent of the national average. At that time, only three cantons had lower debt: Zug, Grisons, and Aargau.[22] The counterpart of interest payments of CHF 32.8 million was returns of "only" CHF 30.5 million. Compared with its cantonal income, the debt of the canton of St. Gall rose from 7.6 to 8.5 percent between 1990 and 2001. This statement does, however, have to be qualified, first, because the average cantonal public debt rose from 11.8 to 20.3 percent (in relation to cantonal income) during this period and, second, because the value of its financial assets increased even more during this period. With respect to its finances and compared to the other cantons, the position of St. Gall improved during this period while its relative economic position remained almost the same: cantonal income per capita was 91.4 percent of the Swiss average in 2001 compared to 87.4 percent in 1990, but according to this criterion its rank fell from 14 to 15 of the 26 cantons.[23]

As mentioned earlier, similar rules exist in seven other cantons today. The cantons of Solothurn and Grisons also accumulate savings in order to smooth revenue fluctuations over the business cycle. In Appenzell Outer Rhodes, no deficit is allowed to be budgeted as long as there is an accumulated deficit of more than 5 percent of the cantonal and local tax revenue budgeted for the current year.[24] This rule is intended to force the government to build up reserves in "good times" and to eliminate structural deficits.[25] While the canton of Fribourg also strives for a budgetary balance over the business cycle, the regulation is even stricter with respect to balancing the annual budget: the tax rate has to be increased as soon as the deficit in the proposal for the current budget exceeds 3 percent of total revenue.[26]

As far as they exist, experiences from these cantons have been positive to date. In Fribourg, debt per capita rose from CHF 2,871 to CHF 4,924 between 1990 and 2002, or by only 46 percent (in real terms), which is far below the average of the Swiss cantons at 92 percent. In a similar way, although, at 12 percent, to a lesser extent, the returns on financial investments are larger than interest payments. In Appenzell Outer Rhodes, debt per capita even declined from CHF 3,060 to CHF 2,545 between 1990 and 2002, that is, by 29 percent (in real terms). However, a major reason for this was the sale of the cantonal bank which brought about a considerable reduction in total cantonal debt. In Grisons public debt rose by about 150 percent from CHF 2,306 to CHF 6,996 between 1990 and 1998, when the debt brake was introduced; this large increase was a major incentive to introduce this institution. Subsequently it declined to CHF 5,285, or by 27 percent, in 2002. Finally, in Solothurn, between 1994, the year before the debt brake was introduced, and 2002, debt per capita rose only from CHF 5,826 to CHF 6,255 and, therefore, by only 3 percent altogether. Thus, all those cantons that have had debt brakes for more than five years show a good performance in this respect.

9.3 An Econometric Model

In order to present more than just this casual evidence, we use an econometric model with the budget deficit and cantonal debt as dependent variables.[27] The variables of interest are the institutional variables that represent the constitutional and legal structures of fiscal policy decisions in the Swiss cantons. The first and most important variable is the index of direct democracy as employed by Frey and Stutzer (2000, 2002) in various studies. Most cantons have some form of semi-direct democracy in a parliamentary system with legislators elected according to proportional representation. Only two rural cantons, Appenzell Inner Rhodes and Glarus, make political decisions in cantonal meetings (Landsgemeinde). In addition, the cantons have different institutions of political participation rights.[28] Proposals can be initiated by voters, and new laws passed by the legislature are, to varying degrees, subject to an optional or mandatory popular referendum. Given the results of Peltzman 1992 that voters are fiscally more conservative than their representatives, we can expect fiscal referenda to restrict the spending capabilities of the latter. It should lead to lower spending and revenue and possibly also to lower deficits.

As a second explanatory variable, an index of the statutory fiscal restraints described previously is employed. The more restrictive the statutory fiscal constraints are, the lower budget deficits and debt should be. However, since it takes a considerable time after their introduction for such restraints to exhibit their full impact on debt, it might be that the corresponding coefficient in the debt equation is not significantly different from zero.

The third institutional peculiarity of Switzerland is the strong extent of fiscal autonomy at subfederal level that establishes a system of competitive federalism. To analyze the impact of federalism on cantonal fiscal policy, two different variables are used: decentralization and tax competition.

Decentralization is proxied by the ratio of local expenditure to aggregated state and local expenditure. Tax competition is measured by the inverse of the weighted average of the competing cantons' tax burden in the highest income tax bracket of a million Swiss francs annual taxable income. The competing cantons are all cantons except the one under consideration, weighted by the inverse of the distance.[29] This variable is included to indicate that the lower the average tax burden of the other cantons, the higher the pressure of tax competition on the cantonal and local tax authorities, which should have a dampening effect on government revenue and spending. The impact of tax competition on the budget deficit and public debt is, however, indeterminate.

In order to control for the impact of intergovernmental grants between jurisdictions, the model also contains federal unconditional grants per capita. In contrast to matching grants, unconditional grants enable cantons to allocate the funds according to their own priorities. A higher level of unconditional grants should lead to higher spending as well. In the literature on the flypaper effect, there is much discussion on whether the availability of lump-sum grants increases public spending by more than the amount of these grants.[30] Unconditional grants may also be used to reduce spending from the canton's own public funds such that the increase in spending owing to the grants is less than 100 percent. In addition, a high level of grants is related to a higher extent of bailout by other jurisdictions. This might lead to lower incentives to use the resources economically. Therefore, it may—ceteris paribus—incur higher budget deficits.

We also include a regional dummy variable that reflects language differences among the Swiss cantons and takes the value of one for cantons with a French or Italian-speaking population. A quite common prejudice is that "Latin" cantons and communities have stronger preferences for "public-sector solutions" to social problems and are thus inclined to have more "unsound" public finances—namely, higher spending, higher revenue, and higher deficits. Moreover, the model contains a political variable that follows the arguments of the partisan cycle models that left-wing parties generate unsound public finances. The share of left-wing parties in the government should have a positive impact on the level of public spending, public revenue, and budget deficits.

We additionally include economic, demographic, and political control variables. The economic and demographic variables are those usually employed in models of fiscal policy. The most important of these variables is the disposable income per capita. Generally, higher income is supposed to lead to higher spending and revenue. Higher spending results because citizens increase their demand for public services when their income increases. Higher revenue results because the revenue of the Swiss cantons is mainly derived from progressive personal income taxes. Whether lower or higher deficits occur because of higher income is not easy to determine a priori. On the one hand, higher income may be accompanied by a lower level of public deficits for liquidity reasons. On the other hand, subfederal jurisdictions with higher incomes may have to contribute larger amounts to fiscal equalization systems and thus have an incentive to increase public deficits in order to reduce these contributions. In this case, higher income might be associated with higher deficits.

Since the number of inhabitants can play a crucial role on the level of public expenditure, a population variable has to be included in the equation as well. However, the expected sign of this variable is ambiguous. On the one hand, more inhabitants will pay for public goods. Due to economies of scale in consumption, this reduces cost per capita and should lead to lower public expenditure. On the other hand, some public goods might only be provided in agglomerations because of indivisibilities and economies of scale in provision. In this case, the overall level of public expenditure for the agglomeration might increase and—ceteris paribus—budget deficits might also rise. In order to disentangle both effects, the share of the urban population is additionally included in the model. Moreover, we control for the demographic structure of a canton by using the shares of the population older than sixty-five and younger than twenty. Both variables may be interpreted as indicating the demand of these two particular population groups for public spending as well as for their ability to generate public revenue. Finally, a dummy variable for the canton of Appenzell Outer Rhodes in 1996 is included. In this year, cantonal revenue of that canton lay about 50 percent above its "normal" value, because it sold its "own" Cantonal Bank to the Union Bank of Switzerland (UBS), creating large additional revenue.[31]

In earlier estimations, we also included a variable for the number of parties in the government and the unemployment rate. Since these variables did not, however, prove to be significant and did not have a relevant impact on the estimated coefficients of our variables of interest either, we deleted these variables from the estimation equations in order to increase the degrees of freedom.

When estimating models for government expenditure, revenue and debt, logarithmic transformations are usually employed. This is not, however, possible for the deficit equation. Thus, for these equations we measure the dependent variable in real Swiss francs per capita, while we employ the usual logarithmic formulation[32] for the debt equation.

Thus, for our empirical analysis we end up with the following model:

$$\begin{aligned} y = {} & \alpha_0 + \alpha_1 Dem + \alpha_2 Constr + \alpha_3 Fed + \alpha_4 Taxcomp + \alpha_5 grants \\ & + \alpha_6 Ideol + \alpha_7 inc + \alpha_8 pop + \alpha_9 Urban + \alpha_{10} Latin + \alpha_{11} Old \\ & + \alpha_{12} Young + \alpha_{13} DAR96 + \varepsilon, \end{aligned} \tag{9.1}$$

where the dependent variable y stands for the following variables (all in per capita): the cantonal deficit, the cantonal and local deficits together and the logarithm of cantonal debt. The explanatory variables are

Dem index of direct democracy,

Constr statutory fiscal constraints, which takes on values between zero for the cantons with no statutory fiscal restraint and three for those with the strongest,

Fed share of local spending from the sum of cantonal and local spending,

Taxcomp inverse of the weighted average of the competing cantons' tax burden in the highest income tax bracket of CHF 1 million annual taxable income (logarithms in the debt equation),

grants federal unconditional grants per capita (logarithms in the debt equation),

Ideol	ideological position of the cantonal government,
inc	disposable income per capita (logarithms in the debt equation),
pop	population (logarithms in the debt equation),
Urban	share of urban population,
Latin	dummy variable = 1, for cantons with a French or Italian-speaking population,
Young	share of population younger than 20,
Old	share of population older than 65,
DAR96	dummy variable = 1, for the canton of Appenzell Outer Rhodes in 1996,
ε	stochastic term.

The analysis uses annual data for the twenty-six cantons from 1980 to 1998 deflated to the year 2000. The empirical analysis is performed using a pooled cross-section time-series model. We follow Feld and Kirchgässner (2001a), who argue that despite the panel structure of the data, the inclusion of fixed effects in the cross-section domain is inappropriate because the institutional variables vary only very little or even remain constant over time in most cantons. Accordingly, cantonal intercepts do not make sense as the captured impact on fiscal outcomes is either solely driven by the time variation or in the case of time-invariant variables, fixed effects are likely to hide the effect of institutional variables and render them insignificant. Cantonal dummies are, however, used as instruments in order to cope with the possible endogeneity of the decentralization variable. Moreover, year dummies are included to circumvent time dependency and the standard errors are corrected by a GMM method (Newey-West). The deficit equations are formulated in absolute terms (CHF per capita), while the debt equation is estimated in logarithms.

9.4 Empirical Results

The results are given in table 9.1.[33] Our model explains nearly half the variance in the deficit equations and nearly two thirds of the variance in the debt equation. As far as the two deficit equations are concerned, neither the index for direct democracy nor fiscal decentralization has a significant impact on the budget deficit. The signs indicate that direct democracy and fiscal decentralization might have a negative impact

Table 9.1
Cantonal deficits and debts per capita, 1980–1998

Dependent variable	Cantonal deficit	Cantonal and local deficit	Log of cantonal debt
Constant	−1726.722(*)	−2961.395*	20.478***
	(1.94)	(2.53)	(5.20)
Direct democracy	−49.489	−23.493	−0.123*
	(0.82)	(0.82)	(2.05)
Fiscal constraints	−106.768***	−109.545***	−0.048
	(3.67)	(2.96)	(1.18)
Fiscal decentralization	−299.387	24.694	−1.433***
	(0.85)	(0.06)	(3.93)
(Log of) tax competition	617.461	726.284	−0.267(*)
	(1.41)	(1.41)	(1.83)
(Log of) unconditional grants	−0.756**	−0.928**	−0.395**
	(2.82)	(2.72)	(2.92)
Ideology of the government	69.039	110.891	0.109
	(0.43)	(0.56)	(0.52)
(Log of) disposable income	0.012*	0.014*	−0.587(*)
	(2.13)	(2.02)	(1.86)
(Log of) population	0.067	0.100	−0.230***
	(0.52)	(0.63)	(3.77)
Urbanization	499.292*	591.414*	1.597***
	(2.23)	(2.25)	(6.05)
Dummy for French and Italian	−313.814*	−528.718**	0.269
	(2.05)	(2.75)	(1.41)
Share of young population	52.883*	80.145**	−0.038
	(2.46)	(3.01)	(1.53)
Share of old population	37.062*	63.159***	−0.042(*)
	(2.57)	(3.59)	(1.96)
Dummy for Appenzell Outer Rhodes in 1996	−3065.430***	−3038.398***	−0.273**
	(25.78)	(22.33)	(2.68)
$\bar{R}^2$	0.489	0.478	0.633
SER	348.798	433.530	0.310
JB	205.347***	82.908***	22.871***

Note: The numbers in parentheses are the absolute values of the estimated t-statistics, based on the Newey-West autocorrelation-consistent standard errors. ***, **, *, or (*) show that the estimated parameter is significantly different from zero at the 0.1, 1, 5, or 10 percent level, respectively. SER is the standard error of the regression and JB the value of the Jarque-Bera test for normality of the residuals.

on the cantonal deficit, but the t-statistics are far from significant. On the other hand, fiscal constraints have a highly significant dampening effect on the cantonal deficit. Moreover, the fact that the two coefficients in the two deficit equations are nearly identical indicates that the deficit is not shifted to the local communities: there is no relevant impact on the local deficits. Tax competition among the cantons seems to increase the cantonal deficit, but the estimated coefficients are not significantly different from zero either. Moreover, as with fiscal constraints, tax competition at cantonal level does not seem to have any impact on local deficits. A left-wing orientation of the cantonal government increases public expenditure (as expected), but this effect is not significant either. Contrary to what is usually considered to be a result of cultural differences, deficits are significantly lower in those cantons where French or Italian is the dominant language. This does not only hold for the cantonal budget deficits but also for the sum of the local ones. Finally, the amount of unconditional grants reduces deficits considerably: an additional franc of grants reduces cantonal deficits by about 75 cents and the sum of all deficits together by more than 90 cents.

These results might be objected to on the grounds that, according to the Jarque-Bera test, the estimated residuals are not at all normally distributed. This might impair the validity of the results. Owing to the large number of observations, this should not be that much of a problem. However, to consider this argument, we reestimated the model excluding some outliers. Then, the null hypothesis that the estimated residuals are normally distributed can no longer be rejected even at the 10 percent significance level, while the results show only minor changes.[34]

One might argue that there is an endogeneity problem: cantons whose populations are more effective at demanding balanced budgets adopt the corresponding fiscal rules. Thus, the "true" factor influencing fiscal balance is the preferences of the citizens. This might be the case, but it does not impair our estimates. If the citizens are convinced that such rules are appropriate institutions for reaching fiscal sustainability and if they impose them for this reason, these institutions still matter. This holds all the more for those cantons that introduced the debt breaks during our observation period. It is obvious that they were introduced because the citizens wanted to balance the budget and believed in the effectiveness of these institutions. However, statistical causality (and the consistency of the estimates) does not depend on whether the preferences are the final reasons why these institutions were introduced. Whether this is the case, namely, whether the institutions are endogenous in this respect, could only be tested if we had independent measures of the preferences. The only variable that is available in this respect is the language variable. Introducing it does not render the estimated coefficients of the fiscal rules insignificant. Thus, these rules might have an effect regardless of the preferences of the citizens.

The important question is, however, whether these impacts are not only statistically significant but also economically important. To address the economic significance, we calculated the difference in cantonal and local deficits and debts between those cantons where the corresponding variables take on their maximum value in our sample and those cantons where they have their minimum.[35]

The results are given in table 9.2. It reveals that unconditional grants, fiscal constraints, and the culture (language) of the population have strong, dampening effects on cantonal deficits that are quantitatively well above the average deficit with a maximum effect of more than 5 percent or about 3 percent, respectively, of total expenditure.[36] Direct democracy and tax competition also seem to have a considerable impact, but bear in mind that their estimated coefficients are not significantly different from zero. Finally, in addition to being not statistically significant, neither fiscal decentralization nor the ideology of the government seems to have quantitatively relevant impacts on the cantonal deficit.

The results are somewhat different for the debt equation. Direct democracy and fiscal decentralization have a significant negative impact, whereas the impact of fiscal constraints is negative (as expected) but not significant. These results also hold if we exclude the outliers in order to get normally distributed residuals. As discussed in Schaltegger and Feld 2004, the differences between direct and representative democracies in public debt result from stronger restrictions on logrolling and fiscal commons problems in direct democracies. At first glance, differences between the debt and deficit equations are astonishing because public debt is nothing more than temporally aggregated deficit. Thus, while the deficit equations rather capture the short-run effects, the debt equation captures the long-run effects of these institutions on the sustainability of public finances. But this implies that those institutional variables that are almost constant over time, such as the extent of direct democratic rights as well as of fiscal decentralization,

Table 9.2
Quantitative impacts of the explanatory variables

Explanatory variables	Cantonal deficit	Cantonal and local deficit	Cantonal debt
Direct democracy	−199 CHF (1.88)	−95 CHF (0.89)	−3,131 CHF (49.55)
Fiscal constraints	−320 CHF (3.03)	−329 CHF (3.11)	−907 CHF (14.34)
Fiscal decentralization	−93 CHF (0.88)	8 CHF (0.07)	−2,871 CHF (45.42)
Tax competition	168 CHF (1.87)	198 CHF (1.87)	−2,206 CHF (34.91)
Unconditional grants	−593 CHF (5.60)	−728 CHF (9.60)	−3,167 CHF (50.10)
Ideology of the government	69 CHF (0.65)	111 CHF (1.05)	691 CHF (10.98)
French- and Italian-speaking population	−314 CHF (2.97)	−529 CHF (5.00)	1,725 CHF (26.90)
Mean (standard deviation) of the dependent variable	156 CHF (488 CHF)	237 CHF (600 CHF)	6,411 CHF (4,533 CHF)

Note: For public debt, the numbers in parentheses are in percent of the mean. In the case of budget deficits, it is in percent of expenditure. The amount in Swiss francs is in prices of the year 2000.

might exhibit their impact more in the debt equation, while those that have a high variation might do so in the deficit equations. The latter certainly holds for the impact of fiscal constraints because in some cantons they have only been introduced quite recently and, therefore, cannot yet show their (long-run) impact on public debt.

The level of unconditional grants reduces not only the deficit but also public debt to a considerable extent. For this variable, there is no difference in the signs and significances of the different equations. But the same does not hold for the impact of tax competition or the language of the population, where we even get different signs. Again, a possible (but, of course, rather tentative) explanation might stress the difference between long-run and short-run effects. A strengthening in tax competition might increase the current deficit at the moment, but in the long run it might also provide incentives for a sounder fiscal policy and might therefore lead to lower public debt in the end. With respect to the culture of a canton, French-speaking cantons might have had a looser fiscal policy in the past, leading to larger debt burdens, but are now being forced to limit the deficit more strictly. Of course, further analyses are necessary to support such conclusions.

The maximal quantitative impacts are shown in table 9.2, and again they are quite considerable.[37] A comparison of the two most extreme cantons in this respect, Geneva and Obwald, shows that direct democracy has led to a reduction in public debt by about CHF 3,000.[38] This is nearly 50 percent of the average debt. Fiscal decentralization has a similar impact, but this is somewhat trivial as cantonal debt should—ceteris paribus—be smaller if the canton is more decentralized and therefore has fewer tasks to perform and less need for revenue and expenditure. Because no data for the sum of cantonal and local debts in a canton are available, we cannot say whether there is an additional effect from fiscal decentralization (besides this shifting).

Though its coefficient is not statistically significantly different from zero when all observations are included, the culture of a canton also seems to have a considerable impact: non-German-speaking cantons have—ceteris paribus—a debt that is about CHF 1,700 higher. This result is reinforced by excluding the outliers: not only does the estimated coefficient increase such that the effect accounts for about CHF 2,000, but it is also almost significant at the 5 percent level. This is somewhat astonishing because—contrary to general belief—cantonal public debt in the German speaking cantons is about CHF 1,600 higher than in "Latin" Switzerland.

Finally, unconditional grants also have a quantitatively significant impact, which amounts to about 20 percent of average public debt. The effects of the other explanatory variables are not only statistically insignificant, but are also quantitatively less important.

These results are in line with previous results mentioned in section 9.1 and support the political conjecture of the usefulness of fiscal restraints to obtain sound public finances. They also corroborate the findings of Freitag and Vatter (2004) on the impact of fiscal referenda and fiscal decentralization as well as those of Schaltegger and Feld (2004) on the impact of fiscal referenda and fiscal restraints on deficits and debt. They are also in line with U.S. evidence as well as with international evidence reported by Rodden and Wibbels (2002). However, in contrast to the United States, the effective fiscal restraints in Switzerland are at the statutory level only while, for example, Bohn and Inman (1996), in their study of the United States, conclude that constraints grounded in a state's constitution are more effective than constraints based on statutory provisions. Most Swiss cantons have constitutional provisions for balanced budgets, but those that additionally have fiscal restraints at the statutory level have sounder public finances.

9.5 The Debt Brake at the Federal Level

How does the new "debt brake" at the federal level compare to the statutory fiscal restraints at the cantonal level? If we disregard some exceptions at the cantonal and local levels, the problem of limiting public debt is much more serious today at the federal level than at lower governmental levels. As figure 9.2 shows, total public debt increased quite a lot during the 1990s, but the main increase was due to the rise in federal debt. It increased from CHF 38.5 billion in 1990 to CHF 122.9 billion in 2002, which is a real increase of 173 percent, compared to an increase of 105 percent at the cantonal level and only 14 percent at the local level.[39] Moreover, although it has been discussed in the national parliament, no law on fiscal referenda at federal level has been introduced to date. Except when a new law is necessary, Swiss citizens generally do not have the possibility to reject planned expenditure.[40] On the other hand, people vote not only on the tax

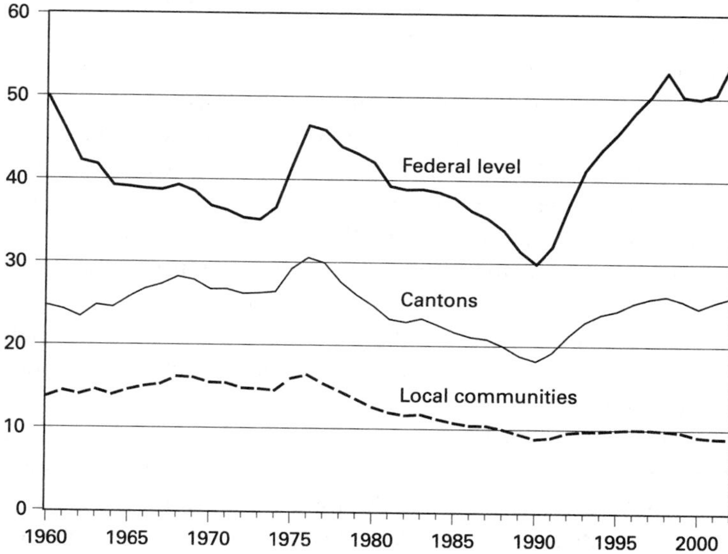

Figure 9.2
Development of Swiss public debt, 1980–2002 (in percent in relation to GDP)

structure but also on the maximum rates. As far as the latter are fixed in the federal constitution, since increases in the tax rates (e.g., for value-added tax and for direct federal [income] tax) are subject to a mandatory referendum and in addition to the majority of voters, the majority of cantons have to agree as well.

This has two consequences: First, citizens can deny parliament additional revenue without necessarily having an influence on spending. This holds in particular if expenditures that are determined by statute develop "dynamically" and the revenue does not keep pace with them. Such a situation exists today, for example, with respect to the mandatory first pillar of the Swiss old-age pension system that is financed by a pay-as-you-go (PAYG) system. Second, it is much more difficult and takes more time to adapt the revenue to changing situations. These two effects led to considerable deficits in the 1990s and—as a consequence—to the strong increase in federal debt mentioned earlier.[41]

One possibility to change this situation would be to introduce fiscal referenda at the federal level as well. This idea was part of the proposal of the Bundesrat (1995) for a reform of direct popular rights.[42] However, parliament did not follow the government in this respect and refused to adopt a federal fiscal referendum. Quite recently, the situation has changed and the Swiss parliament seems to be willing to discuss this issue now.[43] Thus, while not available so far, such referenda might be introduced within the next few years.

After several, hardly successful attempts to get back to fiscal discipline,[44] the actual crisis at the end of the 1990s was solved by a corporatist procedure, the "budgetary objective 2001," which was decided at a "roundtable" and accepted by the people on June 7, 1998. Its objective was to limit the federal deficit to CHF 5 billion in 1999, to CHF 2.5 billion in 2000, and to less than 2 percent of the federal revenue from 2001 onward. Because of a surprisingly strong economic recovery and some other special reasons, this objective was easily met in 2000 when the federal budget had a surplus of CHF 3.8 billion. However, since 2001 we have faced considerable budget deficits again.

As experiences from other countries also show, such a corporatist procedure seems to be a feasible (and sometimes well-suited) instrument to cope with current crises. In the long run it cannot, however, substitute appropriate institutions. As the cantonal solution of citizens determining expenditure on the one hand and revenue being automatically adjusted on the other cannot be realized at the federal level (at least at the moment) and because the introduction of an "expenditure brake" in 1995 did not prove to be efficient,[45] only the reverse solution remains possible: the revenues are (as up to now) decided by the people and parliament has to be forced to adjust public expenditure to the revenue.

This is the approach of the "debt brake," which was accepted by the people on December 2, 2001, and which—in a somewhat simplified manner—operates as follows:[46] expenditures have to be adjusted to revenue, which is, however, smoothed over the business cycle. In calculating smoothed revenue, extraordinary revenue is not considered; it has to be used to pay back debt. "Normal" surpluses and deficits are accounted in a separate account and they have to be balanced over several years. Deficits that exceed 6 percent of the expenditure of the preceding year have to be balanced within the next three years. Extraordinary expenditure (which is not included in these calculations) can be decided on by the majority of the members in both chambers of the federal parliament.

To make the necessary expenditure cuts, the federal government can decide on additional savings, as long as legal entitlements are not violated. Moreover, it has to propose changes to laws to parliament in order to make additional cuts possible.

There are two points that are remarkable in this concept:

1. The philosophy behind it is to limit public revenue and to adjust expenditure to revenue.[47] It is also possible to adjust revenue by increasing taxes, thus changing the projections that are relevant for expenditure planning, but because this generally demands changes to laws and/or to the constitution, such increases are difficult to carry through (and only in a process that takes some time). This voluntarily designed asymmetry is in accordance with international experience that shows that effective stabilization of public finances was reached in some cases by cutting expenditure and not by increasing revenue.[48] It negates, however, the positive experience in the Swiss cantons described earlier where the reverse causal direction has proven to be successful.

2. There is no really strong pressure to balance the budget. On the one hand, there is the possibility of extraordinary expenditure. On the other hand, the possibilities of the government to cut expenditure are rather limited. Parliament is still free to pass laws with financial consequences and it does not have to agree to the changes to laws that are proposed by the government either.[49] To this extent, these

regulations are much weaker than the corresponding ones in the cantons.

The original idea was to apply the debt break for the first time in 2003, namely, for the 2004 budget. However, the financial situation of the Swiss Federation deteriorated considerably following the referendum on the debt brake in 2001 and a "new" structural deficit was detected in 2003. In order to give the government and parliament three more years to cope with this deficit, a temporary solution was decided by parliament in 2003 that shifted the full effectiveness of the debt break to the year 2007. At the moment, considerable efforts are being undertaken to make this possible. Nevertheless, we will have to wait another few years to see whether this debt brake really is well suited to stabilizing (and in the long run also to reducing) public debt. The willingness with which center-right coalitions in the lower chamber of the Swiss national parliament were ready to reduce taxes and center-left coalitions were ready to decide on new expenditure during the period of a surplus at the turn of the century, both of which increased expected future deficits, justifies at least some skepticism.

9.6 The Bailout Problem

What, however, happens, if the lower-, cantonal-, or local-level jurisdictions do not follow a sustainable fiscal policy but instead violate fiscal discipline and raise excessive debt? How far can they hope that there will be a bailout by the upper, federal, or cantonal level, or, to put it differently, how credible is the statement that such a bailout will not take place? For many citizens it is difficult to believe that a member state (canton) or a local community can actually go bankrupt. Moreover, Switzerland (as in all other countries, too) does not have explicit bankruptcy rules or laws for such situations.

The Swiss Federal Constitution provides the cantons with a sufficient financial basis; they have, in particular, tax autonomy with respect to (personal as well as corporate) income and property taxes. Thus, there is no reason why the federal government would have to intervene if a canton got into financial difficulties. After all, the cantons can increase tax revenue should this be necessary. Actually, there has not yet been a situation in which the federal government was asked to intervene to support a canton financially or in which the federal government intervened on its own initiative. This does not preclude that the possibilities to raise tax revenue and—in addition—that the expectations about what they have to contribute to national tasks are quite different in the different cantons. However, the problems that arise from this situation have to be solved with the fiscal equalization system that—right now—is being newly designed; on November 28, 2004, the people accepted the new system, which will be effective from 2007 onward.[50] A reasonable solution to this problem should prevent a division of the country into rich and poor communities but at the same time sustain the incentives that the cantons have to take care of their own tax base. If this objective can (at least approximately) be met by the fiscal equalization system, there is no reason why the cantons should not take on their own fiscal responsibility. According to their preferences, they will have different debt burdens and their different indebtedness will, as is actually the case in Switzerland, be reflected in different ratings on the capital market.

The picture is somewhat different at the level of local communities. In principle, they also have a sufficient tax base to perform their tasks. If a local community is highly indebted and actually goes bankrupt, as was the case in the community of Leukerbad, first of all the private banks (and those individuals who hold the corresponding bonds) have to depreciate their loans, at least partially. On the other hand, it is the duty of the canton to monitor the situation. In the case of Leukerbad, the banks blamed the canton of Valais for having violated this duty and took it to court. However, the Supreme Court in Lausanne decided that Valais was not responsible.[51] Thus, there was no bailout.

In reality, however, at least if a financial crisis is foreseeable, cantons intervene long before attempts to reach a settlement are necessary. If, for example, the financial situation of a local community in the canton of St. Gall deteriorates strongly and therefore has to be included in the cantonal fiscal equalization system, it partly loses its sovereignty. This allows the canton to prevent the local community from going bankrupt by simply pooling resources. Because, on the other hand, the local communities have a strong interest in their sovereignty, they try to avoid such a situation as far as possible.

Of course, it can never be totally excluded that such a situation might occur in a federal country where a lower level community pursues an "irresponsible" fiscal policy and hopes for a bailout by the upper-level community. The Swiss example shows, however, that with appropriate institutional rules, the bailout problem can be solved in a federal country in a satisfactory way; it does not have to lead to irresponsible behavior by the lower level communities. Possible objections that a federal country should not be able to conduct a sustainable fiscal policy for this reason are, therefore, unfounded.

9.7 Summary and Concluding Remarks

In this chapter, institutions have been described that are designed to reach sustainability of public finances at the different levels of a federal state. Besides the debt brake introduced in 2001 at the federal level, the St. Gall model has been presented as an example at cantonal level. Using an econometric model, it is shown that the institutions that exist in some cantons are quite successful. At the federal level we still have to wait before we can evaluate the results. Finally, we describe how the problem of a possible bailout of cantons and local communities is solved in Switzerland. It is shown that even this problem can be handled in a federal state by choosing appropriate institutions.

An important precondition for using such instruments is that the member states and local communities possess their own tax authority, namely, that they have their own broad tax base and sufficient leeway in determining the tax rates. A second precondition is direct popular rights with respect to the budgetary process. Because these preconditions are not realized to the same extent in other countries, the Swiss results presented here cannot be directly transferred to other federal countries like Germany and Austria, for example. This does not, however, speak against the institutions that have proven to be effective in Switzerland, but rather implies that in other countries reforms should be conducted that lead in this direction.

As, in addition, political decisions are made closer to the citizens (even in purely representative systems), the civic sense of responsibility can be more effective in federal states as compared to unitary ones. Thus, contrary to what one might assume a priori, a federal constitution can—ceteris paribus—be helpful in conducting a sustainable fiscal policy rather than impeding it.

Appendix

Source of data:

- cantonal and local public deficits per capita
- cantonal debt per capita

Source: Swiss Federal Finance Administration.

- disposable income per capita
- cantonal population
- share of population younger than twenty

• share of population older than sixty-five

• share of urban population, that is, of people living in local communities with more than ten thousand inhabitants

Source: Swiss Federal Statistical Office.

• federal unconditional grants per capita

• tax burden in the highest income tax bracket of CHF 1 million annual taxable income, weighted with the inverse of the distances between the cantons' capitals

Source: Our own calculations on the basis of data from the Swiss Federal Finance Administration.

• ideological position of the cantonal government

Source: Our own calculations on the basis of data from the Swiss Federal Statistical Office.

• index of direct democracy

Source: Our own calculation of an index proposed by Frey and Stutzer (2000), using additional data from Trechsel and Serdült 1999.

• index of constitutional constraints

Source: Our own calculations, based on Stauffer 2001.

All monetary data have been deflated using the implicit GDP deflator on the basis of 2000 = 100.

Table 9A.1 provides summary description of data.

Table 9A.1
Descriptive statistics of the explanatory variables

Variables	Mean	Standard deviation	Theoretical range	Empirical range
Fiscal decentralization[a]	0.331	0.109	0–1	0.152–0.462
Direct democracy	4.285	1.224	1–6	1.627–5.653
Fiscal constraints	0.298	0.820	0–3	0.000–3.000
Tax competition	0.237	0.079	0–1	0.101–0.373
Unconditional grants	458.004	182.544	0–...	307.13–1,091.37
Ideology of the government	−0.100	0.185	−1–1	−0.600–0.400

Note: The empirical range is calculated for the average values of the cantons over the total observation period, with the exception of the ideology of the government. For this variable the empirical range is calculated for the most left-wing and the most right-wing government.

[a] The canton of Basel City is excluded from the empirical range because its cantonal budget is nearly identical with the local budget.

Table 9A.2 offers additional regression results.

Table 9A.2
Cantonal deficits and debts per capita, 1980–1998

Dependent variable	Cantonal deficit	Cantonal and local deficit	Log of cantonal debt
Constant	−1623.805*	−3052.820**	19.833***
	(2.18)	(2.97)	(5.58)
Direct democracy	−42.381	−17.195	−0.126*
	(0.93)	(0.26)	(2.23)
Fiscal constraints	−97.665***	−106.330***	−0.58
	(4.24)	(3.05)	(1.48)
Fiscal decentralization	−324.413	−0.324	−1.729***
	(1.25)	(1.25)	(6.13)
(Log of) tax competition	746.060*	605.947	−0.261(*)
	(2.17)	(1.26)	(1.94)
(Log of) unconditional grants	−0.535**	−0.789*	0.300**
	(2.78)	(2.56)	(2.75)
Ideology of the government	25.656	33.630	0.084
	(0.20)	(0.19)	(0.44)
(Log of) disposable income	0.008(*)	0.012*	−0.580*
	(1.84)	(1.96)	(2.07)
(Log of) population	0.105	0.144	−0.206***
	(1.01)	(0.95)	(3.62)
Urbanization	400.974*	563.710*	1.383***
	(2.47)	(2.50)	(5.96)
Dummy for French and Italian	−248.905*	−498.359**	0.327(*)
	(2.03)	(2.97)	(1.96)
Share of young population	40.477*	79.520**	−0.037
	(2.45)	(3.29)	(1.64)
Share of old population	41.504**	63.986***	−0.039*
	(3.39)	(3.86)	(2.05)
Dummy for Appenzell Outer Rhodes in 1996	−3110.939***	−3034.673***	−0.271**
	(31.88)	(23.97)	(2.94)
$\bar{R}^2$	0.533	0.504	0.685
Number of observations	476	487	482
SER	272.582	390.030	0.277
JB	3.909	4.471	4.177

Note: The numbers in parentheses are the absolute values of the estimated t-statistics, based on the Newey-West autocorrelation-consistent standard errors. ***, **, *, or (*) show that the estimated parameter is significantly different from zero at the 0.1, 1, 5, or 10 percent level, respectively. SER is the standard error of the regression and JB the value of the Jarque-Bera test for normality of the residuals.

Notes

1. For the current discussion of this pact see, e.g., Buti, Eijffinger, and Franco 2003.

2. For an early critique, see, e.g., De Grauwe 1995, 1996.

3. See, e.g., Gramlich 1990.

4. For the German discussion see, e.g., Wissenschaftlicher Beirat beim Bundesministerium der Finanzen 2003.

5. In 2002, the Swiss State Secretariat for Economic Affairs presented similar considerations. See also Ammann 2002.

6. See, e.g., Schaltegger 2002 for a survey.

7. Poterba 1997, Kirchgässner 2002, and Schaltegger 2002 provide surveys about the effects of constitutional and/or statutory rules that are intended to reduce expenditure and/or deficits.

8. Kirchgässner (2002) summarizes the subsequent U.S. studies about the impact of Proposition 13 on the quality of public goods and services, in particular the quality of public education.

9. See Kirchgässner 2002 as well as Feld and Kirchgässner 2004.

10. See Feld and Kirchgässner 1999, 2001a, b and Feld and Matsusaka 2003.

11. This is the case, e.g., for Schaltegger 2001, Feld, Kirchgässner, and Schaltegger 2003, and Feld and Matsusaka 2003.

12. Feld and Kirchgässner (2001) as well as Schaltegger and Feld (2004) leave out fiscal decentralization; Vatter and Freitag (2002) as well as Freitag, Vatter, and Müller (2003) leave out fiscal restraints; Schaltegger (2002) leaves out fiscal federalism; and Feld and Matsusaka (2003) leave out fiscal decentralization and fiscal restraints.

13. See also Stauffer 2001, pp. 83ff., for more extensive information.

14. Source of data: Eidgenössische Finanzverwaltung, *18 Öffentliche Finanzen der Schweiz*, 1990 (52) and Eidgenössische Finanzverwaltung, *18 Öffentliche Finanzen der Schweiz*, 2002, p. 74.

15. See also the overview in Lutz and Strohman 1988, p. 151.

16. In St. Gall they actually codified a practice which had already been in place for over sixty years, or in Fribourg for twenty-four years. For a detailed description of the different regulations, see Stauffer 2001, pp. 85ff., as well as Verwaltungsrat des Kantons Basel-Stadt 2002. Attempts to introduce similar regulations are currently underway in various other cantons as well. Whether they will be successful or not is an open question. Not all such attempts have been successful in the past. In the canton of Vaud, for example, such a proposal was rejected in 1998. See also Stauffer 2001.

17. See Article 82 of the cantonal constitutions and especially Articles 61 and 64 of the "Staatsverwaltungsgesetz." A detailed description of these institutions in the canton of St. Gall is given in Schönenberger 1995. See also Stauffer 2001, pp. 86–87.

18. The "simple tax revenue" is the basis for the income and property tax revenue; actual revenue is given by the simple tax revenue times a multiplier in the sense of a surcharge (called "tax foot"), which is currently 115 percent.

19. See also Trechsel and Serdült 1999, pp. 330–331.

20. This is also interesting for another reason. Usually, it is assumed that anticyclical fiscal policy can only be conducted successfully at federal level; the medium and lower levels are supposed to conduct a procyclical policy. As a classical reference, see: "It remains to note that responsibility for stabilization policy has to be at the national (central) level. Lower levels of government cannot successfully carry on stabilization policy on their own for a number of reasons. This is obviously the case for the unitary state, where fiscal decentralization is limited to the provision of local public goods. But it also holds for the federation" (Musgrave and Musgrave 1984, 515).

21. Source of data: Eidgenössische Finanzverwaltung, *18 Öffentliche Finanzen der Schweiz* 2002, p. 74.

22. Source of data: Eidgenössische Finanzverwaltung, *18 Öffentliche Finanzen der Schweiz* 1990, p. 52.

23. Source of data: *Statistisches Jahrbuch der Schweiz* 2004, p. 244, as well as the sources mentioned in nn. 21 and 22. Usually, debt is related to GDP. However, for the Swiss cantons only national income (NNP) figures are officially available.

24. Article 9, Finanzhaushaltsgesetz des Kantons Appenzell Ausserrhoden of April 30, 1995.

25. See also Buschor, Vallender, and Stauffer 1993 (12ff.).

26. Article 38 (3), Gesetz vom 25. November 1994 über den Finanzhaushalt des Staates, Kanton Freiburg. This rule goes back to the Finanzhaushaltsgesetz des Kantons Freiburg of 1960; this law had similar regulations in Article 5. As in St. Gall, the law introduced in 1994 did not create a really new situation. See also Stauffer 2001, p. 93.

27. The model we use is quite common in the study of fiscal policy: it corresponds, e.g., to the deficit and debt models of Roubini and Sachs 1989.

28. See also Trechsel and Serdült 1999.

29. See Feld and Reulier 2002 for a discussion of empirical studies.

30. See Feld and Schaltegger 2005.

31. Because these variables might have an impact on cantonal public finances, we have to include them in order to obtain unbiased estimates for the coefficients of the other variables. However, we restrict the discussion of our results to the interesting institutional and political variables.

32. We obtain quite similar results if we alternatively use the ratio of the deficit to public expenditure or the logarithm of the share of public expenditure and revenue as dependent variables.

33. The estimations were performed with EViews, Version 4.1.

34. We did the same with similar results for the debt equation. The results of these additional regressions are given in the appendix.

35. Descriptive statistics of the political and institutional data are given in the appendix.

36. When comparing the (maximal) quantitative impact of the different variables, the fact that the deficit variables are highly non-normal should be taken into account. However, excluding the obvious outlier of Appenzell Outer Rhodes in 1996, we get a skewness of

0.928 and a kurtosis of 7.731 for the cantonal deficits. This leads to a Jarque-Bera statistic of 531.537. For the sum of all deficits, the deviation from normality is somewhat lower but still very considerable: with a skewness of 0.271 and a kurtosis of 5.539, we get a Jarque-Bera statistic of 138.761. This is still greatly above any conventional significance level.

37. Due to the logarithmic functional form, we calculated percentage changes and applied these to the mean of the debt variable.

38. However, when making this comparison, as in the case of the deficit equations, the even more extreme non-normality of the debt variable should be taken into account: with a skewness of 2.732 and a kurtosis of 10.776 we get a Jarque-Bera statistic of 1858.874.

39. Calculated according to the figures in *Statistisches Jahrbuch der Schweiz* 2004, p. 821.

40. If, for some expenditure, a new legal basis is necessary, the citizens can vote against this law in a referendum. On this basis the Swiss people voted twice on the New Alpine Railway Axis (NEAT), on September 27, 1992 (Bundesbeschluss über den Bau der schweizerischen Eisenbahn-Alpentransversale [Alpentransit-Beschluss]) and on November 29, 1998 (Bundesbeschluss vom 20. März 1998 über Bau und Finanzierung von Infrastrukturvorhaben des öffentlichen Verkehrs). Moreover, it is possible to start a constitutional initiative to prevent some expenditure. This was done (without success) in June 1993, for example, when, by starting the initiative "Switzerland without new military aircraft," some citizens tried to prevent such new aircraft being bought. Compared to fiscal referenda, the constitutional initiative is, however, not a well designed instrument to attain such objectives and the chances that it gets the necessary majority of the people and the cantons are generally rather small.

41. It should also be noted that the responsibilities of the federal and the subfederal jurisdictions differ to a certain extent. While federal jurisdiction has the main responsibilities for income redistribution, traffic, and defense, the cantons and local jurisdictions—besides additional income redistribution—provide public infrastructure to a larger extent. Thus, the share of the redistributive budget is larger at federal than at cantonal and local levels.

42. See also Kirchgässner, Feld, and Savioz 1999, pp. 45–46.

43. Fiscal referenda do not seem to be very popular with governments and parliamentarians generally because they intervene with the budgetary sovereignty of parliament. This is also argued in Germany. Contending that this would endanger the solidity of public finances, which is—according to the available empirical evidence—not at all convincing, fiscal referenda are explicitly excluded from the (rather limited) popular rights which are guaranteed by the constitutions of the German Bundesländer. They were also explicitly excluded in the Weimar Republic at the federal level. It seems as if parliaments do not want to lose the budgetary sovereignty that they bullied from the kings and princes in favor of the people.

44. Besides the introduction of value added tax and the increase in its rate by 0.3 percentage points in 1993, the proposal for an "expenditure break" was accepted on March 12, 1995.

45. In analogy to fiscal referenda, not only a simple majority but a majority of all members is demanded in both chambers of the Swiss parliament for new recurring expenditure of more than CHF 2 million and for new nonrecurring expenditure of more than

CHF 20 million. But this higher hurdle for new expenditure did not prevent the strong increase in public debt in the following years.

46. For more details, see the legal documents: Bundesbeschluss über eine Schuldenbremse vom 22. Juni 2001 (BBl 2000, p. 4653) as well as Änderung des Bundesgesetzes über den eidgenössischen Finanzhaushalt vom 22. Juni 2001 (BBl 2000, pp. 4728–4729, Entwurf). See also Eidgenössisches Finanzdepartement 2001 as well as Bundesrat 2000 and 2001a, b.

47. This was one of the main reasons why the Social Democrats opposed this regulation. See also, e.g., H. Fässler, Bremst die Schuldenbremse!, *Neue Zürcher Zeitung* no. 265, November 14, 2001, p. 15.

48. See, e.g., Alesina and Perotti 1995.

49. Contrary to the Federal Republic of Germany, e.g., in Switzerland there is no constitutional court that could be appealed to if parliament passes a law that violates the constitution. In this respect, there is neither an abstract nor a concrete norm control.

50. See also Bundesrat 2001b, Frey and Schaltegger 2001, and Schaltegger and Frey 2003.

51. Decisions 2C.1/2001, 2C.4/1999, 2C.4/2000 and 2C.5/1999 of July 3, 2003. See Blankart and Kleiber 2004.

References

Alesina, A., and R. Perotti. 1995. Fiscal expansions and adjustments in OECD Countries. *Economic Policy* 21:205–248.

Ammann, Y. 2002. Quelques réflexions à propos des règles de politique budgétaire. Staatssekretariat für Wirtschaft, Wirtschaftspolitische Grundlagen (WP). Discussion paper no. 13, May.

Blankart, Ch. B., and A. Kleiber. 2004. Wer soll für die Schulden von Gebietskörperschaften haften? In *Perspektiven der Wirtschaftspolitik*, ed. C. A. Schaltegger and S. C. Schaltegger, 137–150. Zurich: vdf.

Bohn, H., and R. P. Inman. 1996. Balanced-budget rules and public deficits: Evidence from the U.S. states. *Carnegie-Rochester Conference Series on Public Policy* 45:13–76.

Brennan, G., and J. M. Buchanan. 1980. *The Power to Tax: Analytical Foundations of a Fiscal Constitution*. Cambridge: Cambridge University Press.

Buchanan, J. M., and R. E. Wagner. 1977. *Democracy in Deficit: The Political Legacy of Lord Keynes*. New York: Academic Press.

Buchanan, J. M., and R. E. Wagner. 1978. The political biases of Keynesian economics. In *Fiscal Responsibility in Constitutional Democracy*, ed. J. M. Buchanan and R. E. Wagner, 79–100. Leiden/Boston: Martinus Nijhoff.

Bundesrat. 1995. *Reform der Bundesverfassung: Verfassungsentwurf*. Bern.

Bundesrat. 2000. Botschaft zur Schuldenbremse vom 5. July. BBl 2000-1318:4653–4726.

Bundesrat. 2001a. Zusatzbericht zur Botschaft zur Schuldenbremse vom 10. January. BBl 2001-0022:2387–2420.

Bundesrat. 2001b. Botschaft zur Neugestaltung des Finanzausgleichs und der Aufgaben zwischen Bund und Kantonen (NFA) vom 14. November. BBl 2001-01.074:2291–2581.

Buschor, E., K. Vallender, and T. Stauffer. 1993. Kommentierter Entwurf für ein Finanzhaushaltsgesetz des Kantons Appenzell Ausserrhoden, ausgearbeitet für die Finanzdirektion des Kantons Appenzell Ausserrhoden. Institut für Finanzwirtschaft und Finanzrecht an der Hochschule St. Gallen.

Buti, M., S. Eijffinger, and D. Franco. 2003. Revisiting the Stability and Growth Pact: Grand design or internal adjustment? *European Economy Economic Papers* 180.

De Grauwe, P. 1995. Alternative strategies towards monetary union. *European Economic Review* 39:483–491.

De Grauwe, P. 1996. Monetary union and convergence economics. *European Economic Review* 40:1091–1101.

Domar, E. D. 1944. The burden of the debt and the national income. *American Economic Review* 34:798–827.

Eidgenössisches Finanzdepartement. 2001. *Die Schuldenbremse: Dokumentation*. Bern, 2. Auflage, September 2001. Available at http://www.efd.admin.ch.

Feld, L. P., and G. Kirchgässner. 1999. Public debt and budgetary procedures: Top down or bottom up? Some evidence from Swiss municipalities. In *Fiscal Institutions and Fiscal Performance*, ed. J. Poterba and J. von Hagen, 151–179. Chicago: Chicago University Press.

Feld, L. P., and G. Kirchgässner. 2001a. The political economy of direct legislation: Direct democracy and local decision making. *Economic Policy* 33:329–367.

Feld, L. P., and G. Kirchgässner. 2001b. Does direct democracy reduce public debt? Evidence from Swiss municipalities. *Public Choice* 109:347–370.

Feld, L. P., G. Kirchgässner, and C. A. Schaltegger. 2003. Decentralized taxation and the size of government: Evidence from Swiss state and local governments. CESifo Working Paper no. 1087, December.

Feld, L. P., and G. Kirchgässner. 2004. Sustainable fiscal policy in a federal system: Switzerland as an example. Working Paper no. 2004-09, July. University of St. Gall, Department of Economics.

Feld, L. P., and J. G. Matsusaka. 2003. Budget referendums and government spending: Evidence from Swiss cantons. *Journal of Public Economics* 87:2703–2724.

Feld, L. P., and E. Reulier. 2002. Strategic tax competition in Switzerland: Evidence from a panel of the Swiss cantons. Unpublished manuscript, University of St. Gall.

Feld, L. P., and C. A. Schaltegger. 2005. Voters as hard budget constraints: On the determination of intergovernmental grants. *Public Choice* 123:147–169.

Freitag, M., and A. Vatter. 2004. Föderalismus und staatliche Verschuldung. Ein makroquantitativer Vergleich. *Österreichische Zeitschrift für Politikwissenschaft* 33:175–190.

Freitag, M., A. Vatter, and C. Müller. 2003. Bremse oder Gaspedal? Eine empirische Untersuchung zur Wirkung der direkten Demokratie auf den Steuerstaat. *Politische Vierteljahresschrift* 44:348–369.

Frey, B. S., and A. Stutzer. 2000. Happiness, economy and institutions. *Economic Journal* 110:918–938.

Frey, B. S., and A. Stutzer. 2002. *Happiness and Economics*. Princeton: Princeton University Press.

Frey, R. L., and C. A. Schaltegger. 2001. Ziel- und Wirkungsanalyse des Neuen Finanzausgleichs: Bericht zu Handen der Eidgenössischen Finanzverwaltung (EFV) und der Konferenz der Kantonsregierungen (KdK). WWZ, University of Basel, May.

Gramlich, E. M. 1990. U.S. federal budget deficits and Gramm-Rudman-Hollings. *American Economic Review* 80 (2): 75–80.

Kiewiet, D. R., and K. Szakaly. 1996. Constitutional limitations on borrowing: An analysis of state bonded indebtedness. *Journal of Law, Economics and Organization* 12:62–97.

Kirchgässner, G. 2002. The effects of fiscal institutions on public finance: A survey of the empirical evidence. In *Political Economy and Public Finance: The Role of Political Economy in the Theory and Practice of Public Economics*, ed. S. L. Winer and H. Shibata, 145–177. Cheltenham, UK: Edward Elgar.

Kirchgässner, G., L. P. Feld, and M. R. Savioz. 1999. *Die direkte Demokratie: Modern, erfolgreich, entwicklungs- und exportfähig*. Basel: Helbing und Lichtenhahn/Vahlen.

Konferenz der Kantonalen Finanzdirektoren. 1981. *Handbuch des Rechnungswesens der öffentlichen Haushalte*, vol. 1. Berne.

Lutz, G., and D. Strohmann. 1998. *Wahl- und Abstimmungsrecht in den Kantonen*. Berne: Haupt.

Matsusaka, J. G. 2004. *For the Many or the Few: How the Initiative Process Changes American Government*. Chicago: University of Chicago Press.

Musgrave, R. A., and P. B. Musgrave. 1984. *Public Finance in Theory and Practice*. 4th ed. New York: McGraw-Hill.

O'Sullivan, A., T. A. Sexton, and St. M. Sheffrin. 1995. *Property Taxes and Tax Revolts: The Legacy of Proposition 13*. Cambridge: Cambridge University Press.

O'Sullivan, A., T. A. Sexton, and St. M. Sheffrin. 1999. Proposition 13: Unintended effects and feasible reforms. *National Tax Journal* 52:99–111.

Peltzman, S. 1992. Voters as fiscal conservatives. *Quarterly Journal of Economics* 107:327–361.

Poterba, J. M. 1997. Do budget rules work? In *Fiscal Policy: Lessons from Economic Research*, ed. A. J. Auerbach, 53–86. Cambridge, MA: MIT Press.

Rodden, J., and E. Wibbels. 2002. Beyond the fiction of federalism: macroeconomic management in multitiered systems. *World Politics* 54:494–531.

Roubini, N., and J. D. Sachs. 1989. Political and economic determinants of budget deficits in the industrial democracies. *European Economic Review* 33:903–938.

Schaltegger, C. A. 2001. The effects of federalism and democracy on the size of government: Evidence from Swiss sub-national jurisdictions. *ifo Studien* 47:145–162.

Schaltegger, C. A. 2002. Budgetregeln und ihre Wirkung auf die öffentlichen Haushalte: Empirische Ergebnisse aus den US-Bundesstaaten und den Schweizer Kantonen. *Schmollers Jahrbuch* 122:369–413.

Schaltegger, C. A., and L. P. Feld. 2004. Do large cabinets favor large governments? Evidence from sub-federal jurisdictions. Mimeo., Philipps-University of Marburg.

Schaltegger, C. A., and R. L. Frey. 2003. Finanzausgleich und Föderalismus: Zur Neugestaltung der föderalen Finanzbeziehungen am Beispiel der Schweiz. *Perspektiven der Wirtschaftspolitik* 4:239–258.

Schönenberger, P. 1995. Institutionelle Massnahmen zur Verschuldungsbegrenzung im Kanton St. Gallen. Manuscript, Dornach, March.

Stauffer, Th. 2001. *Instrumente des Haushaltsausgleichs: Ökonomische Analyse und Rechtliche Umsetzung*. Basel: Helbing und Lichtenhahn.

State Secretariat for Economic Affairs. 2002. Überlegungen zu einer Budgetregel auch in den Kantonen. *Konjunkturtendenzen* 2:27–31.

Trechsel, A., and U. Serdült. 1999. *Kaleidoskop Volksrechte: Die Institutionen der direkten Demokratie in den schweizerischen Kantonen 1970–1996*. Basel: Helbing und Lichtenhahn.

Vatter, A., and M. Freitag. 2002. Die Janusköpfigkeit von Verhandlungsdemokratien: Zur Wirkung von Konkordanz, direkter Demokratie und dezentraler Entscheidungsstrukturen auf den öffentlichen Sektor der Schweizer Kantone. *Swiss Political Science Review* 8:53–80.

Verwaltungsrat des Kantons Basel-Stadt. 2002. 2. Zwischenbericht der Verfassungskommission Finanzverfassung: Einführung einer Schuldenbremse. Basel, 5. March 2002 (B/Nr. 503).

Wissenschaftlicher Beirat beim Bundesministerium der Finanzen. 2003. *Verbesserungsvorschläge für die Umsetzung des Deutschen Stabilitätspaktes*. Bonn: Stollfuss Verlag.

Contributors

Torben M. Andersen
University of Aarhus

Henning Bohn
University of California Santa Barbara and CESifo

Marco Buti
European Commission, Brussels

Olaf de Groot
University of Groningen

Jakob de Haan
University of Groningen and CESifo

Sylvester Eijffinger
CentER Tilburg University, RSM Erasmus University, CEPR and CESifo

Lars P. Feld
University of Heidelberg

Daniele Franco
Banca d'Italia

Emma Galli
Università di Roma "La Sapienza"

Gottfried Haber
University of Klagenfurt

Svend E. Hougaard Jensen
CEBR, Copenhagen Business School

Andrew Hughes Hallett
George Mason University

Gebhard Kirchgässner
University of St. Gall, CESifo, and Leopoldina

Reinhard Neck
University of Klagenfurt and CESifo

Fabio Padovano
Università Roma Tre

Lars Haagen Pedersen
Danish Rational Economic Agents Model

Jan-Egbert Sturm
Swiss Federal Institute of Technology (ETH) Zurich and CESifo

Index